INNERLAND

INNERLAND

A Guide into the Heart
of the Gospel

EBERHARD ARNOLD

THE PLOUGH PUBLISHING HOUSE

© 1999 by The Plough Publishing House
of The Bruderhof Foundation
Farmington PA 15437 USA
Robertsbridge East Sussex TN32 5DR UK
All Rights Reserved

Translated from *Innenland: Ein Wegweiser in die
Seele der Bibel* (Buchverlag des Almbruderhof e. V., 1936)

First English edition: 1975
Second Edition (paperback): 1999

Cover photograph: © Paul Clancy

A catalog record for this book is available from the British Library.

Library of Congress Cataloging-in-Publication Data

Arnold, Eberhard, 1883–1935.
   [Innenland. English]
   Innerland : a guide into the heart of the Gospel / Eberhard
Arnold. -- 2nd ed.
     p. cm.
   ISBN 0-87486-978-1 (pbk.)
   1. Spiritual life--Bruderhof Communities 2. Bruderhof Communities
-Doctrines. I. Title II. Title: Inner land.
BX8129.B65A72413 1999
248--dc21

99-13145
CIP

Printed in the USA

CONTENTS

PREFACE

I t is hard to exaggerate the significance of *Innerland,* either for Eberhard Arnold or his readers. The author's magnum opus, it absorbed his energies off and on for most of his adult life – from World War I, when he published the first chapter under the title *War: A Call to Inwardness,* to 1935, the last year of his life. The fruit of this long labor of love was not only a book, but a wellspring of remarkable depth.

Packed in metal boxes and buried at night for safekeeping from the Nazis, who raided the author's study a year before his death (and again a year after it), *Innerland* was not openly critical of Hitler's regime; nevertheless it attacked the spirits that animated German society: its murderous strains of racism and bigotry, its heady nationalistic fervor, its mindless mass hysteria, and its vulgar materialism. In this sense *Innerland* stands as starkly opposed to the zeitgeist of our own day as to that of the author's.

At a glance, the focus of *Innerland* seems to be the cultivation of the spiritual life as an end in itself. Nothing could be more misleading. In fact, to Eberhard Arnold the very thought of encouraging the sort of selfish solitude whereby people seek their own private peace by shutting out the noise and rush of public life around them is anathema. Thus he writes in the section "The Inner Life:"

> These are times of distress. We cannot retreat, willfully blind to the overwhelming urgency of the tasks pressing on society. We

cannot look for inner detachment in an inner and outer isolation…The only justification for withdrawing into the inner self to escape today's confusing, hectic whirl would be that fruitfulness is enriched by it. It is a question of gaining within, through unity with eternal powers, a strength of character ready to be tested in the stream of the world.

Innerland, then, calls us not to passivity, but to action. It invites us to discover the abundance of a life lived for God. It opens our eyes to the possibilities of that "inner land of the invisible where our spirit can find the roots of its strength and thus enable us to press on to the mastery of life we are called to by God." Only there, says Eberhard Arnold, can our life be placed under the illuminating light of the eternal and seen for what it is. Only there will we find the clarity of vision we need to win the daily battle that is life, and the inner anchor without which we will lose our moorings.

The Editors
March 1999

INTRODUCTION

The object of this book is to make an appeal in the midst of today's political, social, and economic upheaval. It is an appeal for decision in the area of faith and beliefs, directed to the hearts of all those who do not want to forget or lose God and his ultimate kingdom. This book attempts to point out that God's approaching judgment is aimed at our hearts, that the living Christ wants to move our innermost being through his quickening spirit. Through this spirit, who moves and stimulates everything, we are meant to gain, from within, a life that outwardly demonstrates justice, peace, and joy in the Holy Spirit, as a way of life shaped by God's active love.

In contrast to the path generally trodden today – one that tries to reach the inner life from the outside – this way must shine outward from within. Our spirit, received by the first man as God's breath, must first of all be at home in our innermost being; our spirit must find the living roots of its strength there before it can press on to the periphery of life. Yet its calling – to gain mastery over all external things – has been to a large extent lost in the world of today. We have lost rulership over the earth and the just use of its wealth and resources because, through deep inner revolt, our spirit has been estranged from the breath of God and his love.

This book, then, should indicate a way into the inner land of the invisible; it should bear witness to the way of God and of the Spirit – to the way of love. Fichte says:

Blessed for me the hour when I decided to think about my destiny. All my questions are answered; I know what it is possible
for me to know; and I have no worries about what I cannot
know. I am satisfied; there is perfect agreement and clarity in
my spirit, for which a glorious new existence begins. What the
whole of my destiny will be, I do not know: what I am to be
and will become is beyond my comprehension. Part of this destiny is hidden from me, visible to one alone, the Father of spirits, to whom it is entrusted. I only know that it is secure, and
that it is eternal and glorious, as he himself is. But that part
which is entrusted to me, I know thoroughly, and it is the root
of all the rest of my knowledge.*

In recognizing this destiny, which the Father of spirits alone
sees quite clear and open before him, Fichte came progressively closer to the Bible. For him it was the book of those
witnesses who were filled with the spirit of all good spirits,
the book in which God's spirit has found the deepest and
purest expression.

I *nnerland* is meant as a guide into the heart of the gospel.
The heart of the gospel is more than its letters. Even with
the Bible, literal interpretation leads to spiritual death, to inner
untruthfulness. Only the spirit that fills the words of the Bible
can lead us to its heart in spiritual freedom, and through that,
on to the holy bond of a divine calling. The path this calling is
to take starts in the human soul. Yet not for a moment must
this calling draw the soul away from God's history in the
whole of humankind, away from his calling in the world outside. What is said in the Bible about the stirring of life in the
soul, about the workings of the soul, and about its goal is to be
interpreted and clearly presented in a concentrated form here.

*Johann Gottlieb Fichte, 1762–1814.

With this, the book's task and its limitations could be considered well enough described. And yet *Innerland* is not meant to serve some purely abstract purpose. Rather, as with the prophets and apostles of the Bible, its real task is to take hold of life vigorously and master it – not by means of theoretical discussion, but through something much more important: through witnessing to an inner energy that finds practical expression in work that is vital and has visible results.

At this point we cannot speak simply about the outward effects of this work, about the community life that arises out of it and the public responsibility involved. First of all, we have to speak about what is individual and personal – precisely this land of our inner being. Then it will become clear that a soul filled with the spirit of love cannot get stuck in individualism (which is the starting point), let alone in the private sphere of subjectivism. This soul, impressed by events in God's history, will gain power in its innermost depths from the Holy Spirit to intervene in history, making God's kingdom a reality.

For this, however, the deepest feeling, thought, and will of the soul has to be enlightened and clarified. The conviction basic to this book is this proverb: "As a man thinks in his heart, so he is." Our attention should not be arrested by the dreary mixture of those outward habits, relationships, and subserviencies with which the life of an unfree soul exhausts itself. What is not clarified cannot lead us to God's kingdom either in inward or outward events. Only the pure spirit of God can do this. He does it through the true human nature to which our innermost destiny calls us, hidden or buried though it often is. It is with this final nature, the nature of the spirit created by God, that we must encounter God's spirit calling us to his kingdom.

> My earthly deeds flow away in the stream of time, perceptions and feelings change, and not one can I hold on to. The scene I set up so easily for myself vanishes, and the stream always bears me on its steady wave toward new things. As often as I turn my gaze back into my inner self, though, I am immediately in the kingdom of eternity; I look upon the work of the Spirit, which no world can change and no time destroy, which itself creates world and time first of all.*

If Schleiermacher's words imply that the depths of God and the depths of the soul are one and the same depth – or that men are part, breath, and motion of God's spirit – I do not share his view. Even the outward events of world history point to God's kingdom; and in any case our inner being is never to be placed on a level with God or seen as a part of God. We are convinced that there is a way to get rid of this conception, which is given new emphasis nowadays and leads in the end to making the soul into the creator of God or into a nascent Christ.

There is, however, only one way. It must be taken seriously that our highest calling is to have personally, in our inmost heart, a common will with the inmost heart of God. When God enters my innermost being, life comes to me, the all-embracing life of God as the life that has become mine, the life that now I myself may live and must live. The approach of God's kingdom in his mighty, world-embracing history is bound up with the penetration of his spirit into my heart. Consequently my life is so completely transformed from within to without that, as it goes in the direc-

---

*Friedrich Schleiermacher, 1768–1834.

tion of the coming kingdom of the last times, it comes nearer and nearer to it in outward form.

Pascal therefore was right in saying, "Knowledge of our true nature, knowledge of our real happiness and true virtue, as well as knowledge of true religion, are inseparably bound together."* When we had not yet broken community with God, God himself was to be found on all the paths of the soul's inner land. And at that time He was to be encountered in the garden of creation. It was meant to be preserved and built up by the hand and spirit of man and woman for God's kingdom, yes, penetrated in all its parts, named, and mastered as well. Today, the deeper the way leads us into the hiddenmost recesses of the inner land, the more we are bound to come across the recollection of God and the longing to renew our bond of life with him. It is in these innermost regions that God enters into the soul and wants to win over and penetrate our whole life. The book of nature, of visible creation, remains our task just as much as the book of history and of end-history – these gifts laid before our eyes and given to us by God. Through them we can recognize him even though they often seem still sealed with seven seals. Yet nature and its origin, history and the end of history, eternity and infinity, the beyond and the future, the kingdom of God – all these should light up for us not only in an outer way but just as much, and even more, in an inner way.

From all this, it follows clearly that this book has nothing to do with discussions on psychology and least of all on experimental psychology, which deals with the physical senses. The efforts made by researchers need to be mentioned only

*Blaise Pascal, 1623–1662.

where the new psychology of religion and modern psycho-analysis touch on the deepest areas of the life of the soul. In spite of all recent work, the hidden ways into the inner land of our being remain so similar in the most dissimilar people and times, and so hard to describe, that part of the task of this guide must be to recall those precious old tablets set up hundreds and thousands of years ago on Mount Sinai.

Every deep experience must lead to deep self-examination. Then, from within, we will be equal to the onslaught of unaccustomed events. War, for instance, is a challenge to inwardness in the sense of self-examination because the developments that lead up to war lead us further and further away from the roots of true strength. The increasing prosperity of any country and all the work that is achieved are significant outer blessings for which we cannot be thankful enough. But they lose their value entirely and turn immediately into a ruinous curse as soon as they begin, like a top-heavy load, to crush the inner life. With precipitous speed, we are being deprived of the inner blessing of our human calling by the outer blessing of our rapid development. Our public life has lost its human character; and inwardness has been damaged as a result of the rush and hurry of all the work there is to do on the one hand, and on the other hand by the luxury, excess, and feverishly accelerated pleasure-snatching that has become part of life.

The distress of our times can help us forward only if we remember our divine calling, only if instead of haste and excitement we learn to seek the roots of strength again: an inwardness founded in God. God has already awakened spiritual movements that have wanted to turn away from what is false in our corrupt civilization and seek a more genuine life, which was to be more truthful, more inspired, more inward, human, brotherly, and communal. The intoxication of a superficial existence, however, has led us again from one injustice to another, from one soulless action to another, from one spiritual murder to another, from death to death.

Without a deep inner uplift at the heart of the people, we will not have the staying power to cope with the effects of all this. Without an examination of our hearts in the light of God's kingdom, we will continue to fall prey to new errors, expecting society to be lifted up by a human kingdom devoid of God's spirit.

Jesus saw into a time when the earth was to experience the horrors of universal war and bloody revolts, severe privations and plagues. In this connection, he predicted that love would grow cold and lawlessness and injustice would increase. The truth of this prediction has been seen in those who wage war and prepare for it. The disturbances of our time now let disorder, lovelessness, and injustice of all kinds increase. All the consequences of war – even if they seem only outward events – will develop into the most terrible judgment ever to fall on humankind. All inwardness will be destroyed if our love to God grows cold with icy fear for our individual or collective existence, our so-called security. All inwardness will perish if we no longer love God, if the glowing love to brothers and sisters, as well as the radiant energy of love to our enemies, is drowned because of boundless sin and the struggle for material advantage – so coldly calculating

yet so madly passionate at the same time. Further, it will be
the end of all inwardness if greed for power and the resulting
violence gain the upper hand once more; they are born of
hate and severed from the depth of the soul and the spirit of
God at work in it. They seek only external things, exhausting themselves in superficialities. And if there is such destruction of inwardness it means destruction altogether.

In the same context in which Jesus spoke about war among
all nations and kingdoms, about lawlessness, and about love
growing cold, we hear from him about enduring to the end,
about a movement truly born of God, about mission, and
about the working of the Spirit throughout the world. In
hard times like these, nothing but a thorough and deep-going revival of our inner life, a great and full awakening to
God and his all-determining rulership, can bring the gospel
to the whole world – the joyful news that Christ alone matters. For that to happen, however, the life of a missionary
church must be given: a life that is in keeping with the kingdom of God from its core to the last detail of its outer form,
as peace, unity, and community and as love and joy in the
Holy Spirit.

This hour of world history is a challenge to inwardness. It
represents a call to be at work in the world; it implies tasks
that are literally boundless. Therefore it is high time that we
gather ourselves for serious thought, going deeper and deeper,
in order to gain clarity about our inner life. We have to know
the foundations and laws of inwardness. Then we will also
gain more and more clarity for the whole shaping of life – in
what divine order, under what rulership of Christ, and under what decrees of the Holy Spirit we are to set about this

shaping of life, and how to carry it out. Most of all, it is important that we experience the power of God in our inner being, because only then are we capable of standing firm and holding out in the storms to come. Only when our inner life is anchored in God can we gain the strength to take up the enormous tasks of the future with the courage of faith. When unity and clarity bring order in our innermost being, then, and only then, can our life attain the warming and radiating power of the light on the lampstand. Then, representing the unity and freedom of the city on the hill, it will become a light for the whole world.

Eberhard Arnold

THE INNER LIFE

In the first decades of this century, the will to power has asserted itself in the most diverse forms. It has ensnared everyone in the bustle of outer activity, making them devote all their energy to increase material possessions. More and more, the will to live our own life as a nation or as individuals has laid claim on our whole being, just for the upkeep and improvement of our material existence; it has not provided us with any inner foundation. On the other hand, a will for the innermost life and for the all-commanding power of the kingdom of love and justice – a will for God – forces us into an inner detachment. In this detachment, the solitariness of the soul with God should become a community of two, and then, with his church, a community of many.

This is why Eckhart (who in many ways knew the inner life as few others have done) said: "Nowhere is there perfect peace save in the detached heart. Therefore God would rather be there than in any other being or in any other virtue."* Yet this saying is true only when detachment is a separation from the unfruitful and dead works of darkness, when it leads to the living building-up of the city of light. In this city of light, the nature of the kingdom of God will be revealed to everyone. It will be seen as unity, shown in all the diligence and courage of the loving works of community.

Wherever God is, his kingdom – the final kingdom – draws near. He is the God of peace, whose presence brings

*Johannes Eckhart, c. 1260–1327.

freedom from all inner restlessness, all dividedness of heart, and every hostile impulse. However, Eckhart forgets all too easily that the living God is action just as much as peace. His peace is indeed the deepest unity of heart, the harmonious accord of the great diversity of all the gifts and powers of the soul. But on this foundation he brings into being as the goal of his creation an outer unity of all action, a unity that rejoices in every object of love, brings justice into operation for all, and builds a material world that makes peace a reality on every front through the Holy Spirit.

God wants to bestow an indestructible harmony upon our inner life: harmony that shows itself in mighty melodies of love. The energy born of inner gathering empowers. When hearts are gathered, people are gathered. Their industrious work shows that the kingdom of God is justice, peace, and joy in the Holy Spirit.

Today we must emphasize it once more: our capacity for work is sure to become exhausted and mechanical – our strength will be sapped at the core – if no deepening is given to the inner life. As soon as inner stillness and quiet are lost, the holy springs of the inner world that bring life-giving water to our spiritual life are bound to fail at the very source. Like people dying of thirst, the overburdened long for their inner life to be strengthened and quickened. They feel how miserably they will die otherwise.

Inner strength comes from the source. In tranquil silence it lets God himself speak and act. Instead of letting the believer sink in death, it lets him rise again to a life that flows outward in streams of creative spirit, without losing itself in externals. This strength, this "active stillness," leads the believer to work for the world in such a way that he does not become "worldly," yet never becomes inactive.

These are times of distress. We cannot retreat, willfully blind to the overwhelming urgency of the tasks pressing on society. We cannot look for inner detachment in an inner and outer isolation, as Eckhart's easily misunderstood sayings seem to imply. We are thankful that the highly mechanized nature of world economics today does not allow this pious selfishness anymore. It gives us more protection from self-deception than we had in earlier times. But the lack of vital and effective action shows us when our striving after detachment has not penetrated to the inmost springs of creative power. Where this power is at work, there is a detachment which is a thorough letting-go of self and therefore a freedom for the hardest work; this gathers believing people into the most living kind of community. Their love to all now presses forward out of all isolation to the ends of the earth. Yet they will never be able to give up the common gathering at the focal point of strength.

To the conscientious soul, the only justification for withdrawing into the inner self to escape today's confusing, hectic whirl would be that fruitfulness is enriched by it. It is a question of gaining within, through unity with eternal powers, a strength of character ready to be tested in the stream of the world. That alone can cope with the demands of this age.

Not flight but gathering for attack is the watchword. We must never withdraw from the rushing stream of present-day life into a selfish life. That would make love grow cold in the face of need and the countless paths of guilt connected with it. Our detachment, turned into coldness of heart, would then reach such a height of injustice that it would exceed the injustice of the world. Unless we share the distress and guilt of the world, we fall prey to untruthfulness and lifelessness, to eternal and temporal death. And those prepared to share only the inner need of their fellows, and not their outer need as well, fully and completely, cut life into halves. Then they lose the inner half of life, the very part they are supposed to gain or hold on to. Jesus Christ is forgotten, who took on outer just as much as inner need: in his eyes the two are inseparably one.

It is possible to share lovingly and militantly in the life of our times. But we can do this only when we respond with every fiber of our being to the work demanded, when in every drop of our heart's blood we feel the distress, want to share in suffering it, and so actively overcome it. It is in quietness that we find the way to give this help.

Jean Paul* describes a raging tempest in which the surface of the water is broken up in jagged and foaming confusion. Yet the sun still shines on it, and turbulent clouds do not hide it. With all the seething activity in which we are obliged to live and carry on our work, the mirror of our feelings cannot help becoming stormy and agitated. Yet our hearts know of a heaven with a sun which in radiant quiet preserves an untouched and inviolable strength. This heaven is the rising sun of God's approaching reign. Jesus Christ, the morning star of the future, not only proclaimed it to us – he also brought it close to us all in his life and death, in his word and deed. The following words of Fichte will be understood by

*Jean Paul (pseudonym for Jean Paul Friedrich Richter), 1763–1825

anyone who sees this heaven: "Do you wish to see God face to face as he himself is? Do not look for him beyond the clouds; you can find him everywhere, wherever you are." The kingdom of God draws near over all the earth. God is near wherever a complete reversal of all things is looked for – the reversal that brings his rule with it. His kingdom has no territorial boundaries.

We are not Christians (in the only sense in which it is possible to be Christians – the inner sense that affects all outward things as well) until we have experienced in our own hearts the following decisive words about the presence of Christ. Righteousness based on faith says: Do not ask in your heart, "Who will ascend into heaven?" (that is, to bring Christ down) or "Who will descend into the abyss?" (that is, to bring Christ up from the dead). Instead it knows: The word is near you, on your lips and in your heart (Rom. 10:6–8). The word comes into our hearts because it has come into the world. The eternal word became temporal flesh; God's son became the Son of Man. Every time that you act sincerely, believe wholeheartedly, and confess openly, the word will again become body and flesh in your mouth, in your heart, in the work of the believing church, in the loving, active community – its organism. It is through the Holy Spirit that this comes about, just as it did when the Son came for the first time.

In order to penetrate our lives, the word goes to our inmost hearts again and again. The kingdom has no time boundaries. No eye can see light apart from itself, only in itself. Light comes from outside, and its rays illuminate the inside. God's morning star and his rising sun draw near to us from the other world. When we believe this fact – when this news reaches our inmost life – the morning star has arisen in our hearts. We are filled with light because Jesus, the light of the world, has reached us from afar. So it gives light to everyone who comes into this world. Seeing takes place only when the eye receives light-rays in its own deepest depths. To quote Fichte again: "Therefore you cannot grasp God apart from yourself. In order to know him, he himself must let the rays of his spirit pierce deep into the depths of your heart to stamp his image there." In Jesus, the image of God has appeared so clearly and so undeniably that from now on it is from him that we receive a calling in our hearts. The image of God that Jesus brings to us is love: love that wants unity. We are called to be images of God, and through this calling his spirit wants to rule all people and all things, forming them into one united whole. The kingdom has no subjective boundaries.

As soon as the light is no longer eclipsed by all the busyness of our ego obstinately pushing its way to the fore, we see God directly before our inmost heart. God shows himself to us as the beaming sun that alone can bring abiding life. He brings in the new day, which as his day brings judgment on the dark life of self. He seeks to bring everyone into redeeming light and unite them under his rulership.

We find the focal point of our inner life in God, the central sun of our existence, because in him we recognize the central fire of all creation, of history, and of the history of the last things. Without him, collectedness of spirit in the depths of our soul will be cast to the winds again and again. Only through becoming one with God in the depths of our being will it become possible.

A battle can be won only when the field marshal and his staff keep completely calm in the midst of all the turmoil. Each one of us, too, is able to cope with the demands of today's need and distress only by finding an inner collectedness in God. And we shall find this only when lightning from the kingdom of God has struck and lit up the whole horizon.

There is no life that does not have a center. The earth without its glowing center would be as dead as the moon; the inner core contains the life-strength of the fruit; a flower's beautiful petals shield the organs of fertilization – in the same way there can be only one center for all life-energy: the hidden and the inner. The power of God's kingdom lies hidden in its innermost core, in the heart of God. It comes to light in Jesus, the hidden focus of all history.

Jesus reveals this power at the very heart of faith to the simple and to children. It remains hidden from the wise and clever because only the childlike heart is able to grasp the plan of love. The only way our soul can know God and be known by him is for us to become one in our own inner depths with the center of all worlds and all life in them. The inmost core decides between life and death.

Therefore, the most dangerous sickening does not halt at externals. It proceeds to attack the innermost core with decay and destruction. In fact, if the core of our being were to be untouched by sickness, life could not really be affected by it. We are sick, and we do fall prey to death, because we are estranged from the fire at the core of all life, the core of all that takes place. In this state of sickness we understand nothing of God's judgment in his history. Through this sickening, our inner eye is blinded so that it cannot see the kingdom of God. Every weakening of inwardness strikes at the source of our life-power. Every strengthening of our outward existence that is won at the expense of inwardness squanders our vital strength and endangers our inner existence. Only wealth of life gathered in the innermost depths makes us capable of that quality of generosity that finds its happiness in giving.

The innermost core of God's kingdom is the pure life that surrenders and sacrifices everything in love. In the same way, it is in the innermost core of our life that the love of the sacrificed Christ kindles the rich fire of renunciation, letting go and surrendering everything given us in the way of personal abilities and possessions. Every impoverishment and sickening of our inner being means a loss of warmth and depth. It shows up plainly in all our efforts and activities. Every healing of the inner life leads to loving sacrifice, that is, to purer and more vigorous action.

Jesus has wielded the sword of speech more powerfully than any other against the danger of religion (as an inward treasure) becoming a merely outward form. No one has stressed more than he did the vital importance of the actual state of our inner life. Because he is the heart of God, he brought the kingdom of God. This kingdom seeks to gain authority over everything, touching hearts and changing everything, starting with the heart. That is why he seeks the inner life. We know from him that even the most untruthful, even those farthest from God, have an inner being.

God seeks with all the means of judgment and love to move each heart: he wants the approach of his day, the effect of his love, to bring each one to look in his or her own heart and turn around. In this way, everything will be changed –

overthrown and set up new. And he sees our hearts as they are. All purifying or whitewashing of externals is in vain. "Inwardly you are full of hypocrisy and lawlessness." "Inwardly they are full of greed and self-indulgence, full of dead men's bones and all kinds of rottenness" (Matt. 25–28). Jesus hates the outward appearance of piety and holiness when the heart dishonestly boasts of spiritual values it does not possess, sinking further and further away from God. He himself said the most serious thing that can be said about this: "This people draws near to me with their mouth and honors me with their lips, but their hearts are far removed from me. But they serve me in vain because they teach teachings that are nothing but the commandments of men" (Matt. 15:8–9).

As a result of all the bloodshed in our century and its consequent chaos and confusion, we should feel that God wants to use the heavy burden of our times to make us examine ourselves. Again it is all important that it is not with our mouths only that we promise to change and not with our lips only that we honor the Ruler to whom alone all power is given. The will of the heart must be turned into deed if it is serious and sincere. Sincerity is decisive. Through the judgment of his earnest love, God wants to bring about a real transformation in all who are ready for it – a change of heart, a change in actual inner condition, and with that a change in our whole attitude to life.

And what glimpses into the dark recesses of our hearts have war and its savagery given us! Fear for existence, greedy possessiveness, nationalistic fervor, and revolutionary passions – all these are stirred up by war and continue to work on and on. Our times have once more revealed the state of our inner life, filled with everything but God. Yet he alone fulfills our destiny. And we still deceive ourselves.

People speak of dedication and sacrifice of life – devotion unto death for the sake of brothers, friends, comrades, the homeland, freedom, or justice. What they mean by all this is killing and plundering all those they look upon as enemies of what is so precious to them. Just this is what makes Jesus give such a strong warning about those who come in sheep's clothing: "Inwardly they are ravening wolves!" Their hearts are set on plunder and destruction because the essence of sin – unbroken self-seeking – rules in them as much as ever in spite of all Christian disguises and all quasi-prophetic banners of justice. The gruesome violence that fills people's inner being exposes the condition of any war-torn nation in an appalling way – also the subsequent opportunities for power politics. Truly, our condition today appears just as in the words of the psalm on which the Letter to the Romans throws so serious a light: "Their heart is destruction," destruction that we prepare for ourselves and others.

Like the fate of countries devastated by war, our inner being today can be compared to a deep mountain ravine: dark shadows of judgment are spread over it. Only withered trunks and bony roots betray to a discerning eye the fact that death did not always rule here. The water that used to be the life of this valley has been blocked. Stones and boulders fill the ravine and seem to have buried every hope.

The deeper and more truthfully we see into the actual condition of our inner life, the more hopeless and desperate our fate seems. What amazement must have filled the Samaritan woman when the infallible mouth of the Messiah declared that her buried inner life was to be completely renewed and filled forever with fresh strength and rich content! There is a life-giving water that today too transforms the darkest abyss or the most awful desolation into a place of joy and surging life. It is the spirit of him who said: "The water I shall give him will become in him a spring of water welling up to eternal life." From this deepest of all springs even the uttermost devastation that has come upon lands and peoples shall be transformed everywhere into a region and people filled with far-reaching peace, a place where the powers of God's future world shall be poured out through the Holy Spirit.

God does not want our inner self to remain bleak and desolate – a dark abyss. He is able to change the storms of his judgment, which threaten the terrified soul, into the sunshine of undeserved love. He wants to bring peace and clarity to the heart where until now disruption and darkness have reigned. God's day of judgment threatens to smash conquered and unconquered nations alike; yes, the entire mammonistic world economy. But once we renounce the kingdom of mammon and murder and lying and impurity in order to belong from then on to the kingdom of God, his day of judgment, the day of the Lord, will become the day of salvation.

God knows of the inner fight: how it goes on with deep pain in the hidden recesses of the heart. He knows that the conscience lives there, bringing its witness again and again to the heart's awareness. He knows the hidden thoughts, how they accuse and excuse each other. He knows how many wrestle in vain with inner ties that bind them to what is base. He knows with what lying power false demonic ideals and idols try to assert themselves. He knows that the ravening beast of prey confuses the conscience in the guise of an angel of light and so-called liberation.

The inward person delights in God's law and so would gladly live according to it. At the same time, along with the demands made by God's justice, other claims stir them – the claims of their own lives and nations, or of the oppressed classes. They would like to be free for God's justice in both the inner life and the outer circumstances. And they cannot. The spirit draws them toward the heavenly city of God's church and God's kingdom. But they are bound by the heavy weight of the iron-fisted autonomy of those other things – bound to the earthly cities of human community and human sovereignty and their bloody interests. God knows that all nations, all people, live in this inner struggle. For God has written the book of the law on the hearts of even the remotest nations. He alone, and whoever is in unity with him in the all-discerning spirit, can judge and discern the hidden depths in people. The Father sees into what is hidden. He delights in the truth that is within the heart. He wants to teach us to know the truth in the hidden depths, in the innermost recesses of the heart. And only God's pure truth in his perfect love, as it took shape in Jesus and his first church, has the power to set us free. Everything else is lying and deceit.

The fate of so many countries today brings to mind a re-markable story about a remote, parched valley whose impoverished inhabitants vaguely remembered a time when it had been different and better. Once upon a time, a life-giving mountain stream had flowed there and brought wealth and happiness to the valley. But guilt, in which all who lived there had a share, had ruined everything; the great mountains began to move. Huge boulders plunged into the valley. It seemed as though absolutely everything was about to be buried under the debris. Neither buildings nor rows of houses were any protection. Then the hurtling masses of rock stopped. They halted in front of the houses. But the river was blocked. The life that had flourished seemed destroyed forever. Poverty and distress began their rule. Even memories of the past began to fade slowly away.

But a son of the valley grew up, despised by the others. He was moved by the fate of his people. Day and night he thought about delivering them, ready to attempt it. He knew about the stream and where it was blocked. He accomplished the colossal task, moving the mountainous weight of rocks; but as he moved the last boulder, letting the water flow once more into the valley, he, the savior of his people, was buried under it. Yet he rose to life again, this man who had risked his life for their sake. He ruled forevermore over his people, who had had everything given back to them.

It is Jesus who has moved the boulder of our mountainously heavy guilt so that the river of life can flow unhindered into our inner being. As lord over our innermost being, Jesus brings riches and happiness to our inner life. And just as he healed the bodies of the sick and possessed, also now in this relentless catastrophe of world history he wants to set free the buried bodies and ruined workplaces and make a new life possible in his land. Our hearts cannot be set free from the deadening pressure of hidden sin until his liberating action, given as his gift, gains room in our innermost being.

And when this experience has become ours, it is essential for us to allow him to take command and have more and more authority.

When his kingdom comes to us in this way, we live from within according to the spiritual laws of this kingdom, also in our work and in the communal order of our life. Even the outer shape of our life will be in accord with the kingdom of God as his prophets portrayed it. When his word rules in us, when his nature unfolds in us, it is wealth of life undreamed of. It floods the parched depths of our inner being and pours out into the world outside as living, active love. The cloud of judgment that threatens everything is replaced by the super-abundant light of revelation. This light shows the living way. Then the church of faith and love today has the possibility of judging and ordering all details of life, the innermost as well as the outermost, according to the justice, peace, and joy of his kingdom.

Jesus' light reveals the somber darkness of life without him – all its causes and consequences. In so many people in so many places, guilt causes the river of life to be blocked. They forget the life that he alone can bring. Because they seek vitality from other sources, it is inevitable that everything becomes blocked and buried. Then God must let chaos loose over them in a divine attempt to awaken them through radical intervention. But it turns out as the Revelation of John foretold about the last times: "And those that remained, who were not killed by these plagues, still did not repent of the work of their hands. Neither did they repent of their manifold murders. Indeed, they blasphemed God in heaven instead of repenting of their deeds."

Untold numbers contiue to turn from the way of Jesus.
They seek out the way of idols so that they can continue to
worship mammon all the more zealously – mammon, the
murderer from the beginning, the father of lies, the prince of
impure spirits. They endeavor to make themselves strong
through nationalism, racism, and imperialism instead of at
long last looking for the one pure spring.

Through collapse on all sides, we are directed more earnestly than ever before to the one who took upon himself
our poverty and distress to make us pure and strong in his
spirit. Every person should be able to recognize at least at
one time or another that no human, self-made effort can
bring peace and life to the earth. Only the sovereign reign of
God can do this. In the midst of our serious situation today,
God himself wants to be the savior and helper in our inner
life, also in every other area of our life. There is only one gospel for all creation, one and the same gospel for everyone, for
every class of people, and for every tribe and nation. Those
who represent a different gospel for themselves, their class,
or their nation bring a curse with them.

The reality of God is proved – it is he who renews and
strengthens our hearts. Without him it cannot happen. The
unity of Jesus with the Father is the living reality of his divine sonship. It is the same as the unity of God and Christ
with the Holy Spirit. This unity shows itself in our innermost life. For there his spirit works the powerful religious
and moral transformation that we could never attain without him. He is unity in himself and in us. Therefore his spirit
can represent and spread only unity and peace, also in outer
life. He knows of only one way and one leadership. Jesus

Christ, who is lord and spirit, goes no roundabout way and knows no separate mediator.

God gives himself in the certainty of direct contact. In him alone the heart's need for security finds the firm ground of the here and now, for which it must long continually. The presence of Christ is a wonderful gift of God. In it we receive perfect unity with God in love and faith. Through this experience, however, the stark difference between his purity and our guilt dawns on us just as powerfully. We stand in the midst of disunity between people, classes, and nations, while he is and remains one. It is in this oneness that we become aware of the abysmal difference that separates our nature from his.

The writings of the apostles call this experience the illumination of our hearts by God. It brings the brightness of his glory into our inner being. God shines in Christ and in his countenance. Illuminated by the presence of God, the hidden recesses of the heart are revealed, so that we have to cast ourselves down and worship him. What overpowers us is the fact that the light of his incomprehensibly glorious nature makes us feel all the more deeply the darkness of our own being. If we accept the life of Jesus with his unmistakable words and deeds, if we accept them unadulterated and without any devious interpretations, our entire life, private and public, will be revealed as utterly opposed and hostile to him.

Only in Jesus can our inner being find happiness and inmost satisfaction: nothing else corresponds to what our innermost being is and should be, in the light of its origin. Only when our life is hidden with Christ in God do we experience our real, unique destiny, which without him has to remain buried in the dark. This destiny is to be God's image: to be led by his spirit in everything through love's creative power. The more we experience his wealth of life, the more we long with all our heart to grow in this inner experience and this creative shaping of life. For the experience of God's gifts and the knowledge of his divine rulership over everything can never reach a conclusion in this life. It needs to be renewed every day.

The great agitation in the world of today makes it more and more urgent to gain inner strength in those quiet encounters with Christ that make it possible for us to remain under his rule and authority. Situated as we are in the midst of a world that is so terribly unpeaceful, we need constant nourishment for our inner life. It is important to look upward and outward beyond confining externals, even in direct contrast to the outward form they take today. Instead of following the weak and alien spirits of hatred and violence, of lying, impure, and greedy possessiveness, we must learn to follow the one spirit who alone is stronger than all other spirits. Only the strongest power of inner resistance can prevent our inner life from being buried by what is happening around us now on the earth.

Without a rebirth in our hearts, we will glean from fluctuating world events either a false meaning – based perhaps only on material considerations or on emotional or racial ties – or no meaning at all.

The course of history is interpreted falsely by very many in the interests of their own nation, for example, or their own society. For most people, though, it never has any meaning at all. There is only one possible way of bringing this confusion to an end: the whole person, for the whole of life, must undergo a complete about-face toward the kingdom of God.

Rebirth is the only name we can give to such a radical change with its childlike trust in God's intervention and firm, manly expectation of it – the complete opposite of our former life. Only through such a complete change – by undergoing judgment – can we see in all that happens the approach and intervention of God's rule. We can never see the kingdom of God or have any part in it without a rebirth of heart, breaking down the whole structure of our life and then making a completely new start. Only a new beginning that proceeds from the very bottom – only a rebirth that goes back to the very beginning – is able to prepare us for the kingdom of God. We need a new foundation for our entire personal life.

It is only through the spirit who embraces all the powers of the future kingdom of God that this can happen. Only the spirit of the kingdom of God can put a seal on the passport. Without this passport to God's kingdom, which confirms that we already live in the Spirit *now,* the door into the kingdom remains shut.

But just as a tiny newborn baby is far from being able to cope with life on its own, so the rebirth brought about by the Holy Spirit is only a beginning; we will still need to be nourished and strengthened. In our weakness, however, this is possible only as a slow process of being made fit for God's kingdom and his righteousness. Even after rebirth has given us the first glimpse into the kingdom of God, our hearts may still remain subject to old inhibitions and restrictions.

This weakness has been called "the flesh" by Paul, that methodical thinker of early Christian times. He explicitly said of himself that his flesh had no peace, not only because of struggles from without but just as much because of fears from within.

What is incomplete in our existence gives us as believers a powerful incentive to deepen our inner lives. It is of the utmost importance, therefore, that in these extremely serious and menacing days we grow clearer about the state of our inner life. We cannot let our emotional nature deceive our hearts in these agitated times. Even when it has been touched by the Holy Spirit, our excitable inner nature remains weak. Our hearts are flooded as the blood circulates; our emotional life flows in this bloodstream and is often determined for as long as we live by its urges and feelings.

If our blood is gripped and swept along by the excitement in those around us, we will fall prey to it. We are not able to put up a true resistance born of the Spirit. The distress of our own class or our own nation has a particularly strong effect on us. Mass suggestion as utilized by great national movements appeals to blood ties and class solidarity. It often works on us so decisively that we utterly forget the call to the kingdom of God and his spirit, or we completely falsify it. Even if we continue to profess him, emotional ties and fear for survival drive the Spirit from us. In order to face all fears, and still more, in order to resist the impure and bloody "raptures" of fanaticism, our consciences need steady healing. This healing can be given solely through the all-holy and completely true spirit of Jesus Christ. He unites all good in himself. His objectivity is sober and clear.

No experience, however agitating, and no shock, however violent or bitter, must be allowed to sweep past without the rule of Christ in us gaining ground in our hearts and in our whole lives. The aim of his rule is to fill our inner life with an objective clarity so that no force of circumstance can shatter it. His word and his spirit want to work in us uninterruptedly as his instruments in order to make us strong in every battle, capable of the hardest work. The blessing of all good shall conduct us so firmly and clearly on the way of Jesus Christ – the way that leads straight ahead – that neither successes nor failures in the world can make us swerve into false ways.

We have to follow the same way as Jesus; we must follow it just as he did. Then no seductive call will divert us from this mission, which he left to us as his mission. In just the same way as the Father sent him into the world, he sends us: in just the same way, with the same stand in life, completely free from adulteration by other elements! Only in this way will our life be fruitful. He wants all our gifts to come to life and unfold in order to equip us for the new tasks of the changing world situation.

The rulership of Christ means strength for the inner life through inner gathering and consecration. Through this, alone, also strength for an outer life with a living influence in the right work or occupation.

To become strong in our inner being can mean only one thing: that Christ lives in our hearts through faith because we are being grounded and rooted in love. We need Christ all the time in our inner being, the Christ who was crucified for us, the Christ who is alive for us. He invades us with his fullness, with all the fullness of God, which wants to pour itself over all spheres of our activity as the supreme authority of love.

God is love. Only he who remains in love remains in God and God in him (John 1:4–16). God's rulership is the kingdom of love. Love is his justice. Because his kingdom knows no frontiers, his Messiah-king has put the love of God to friend and foe into our hearts. It is poured into our hearts through the Holy Spirit. Whoever betrays this by shutting out love to their opponents or to enemies of their class or nation drives away the Holy Spirit. They deliver up their hearts to deceptive spirits. Love wants to flood our private as well as our public life and rule in such a way that there can be no rival authority. Paul prays for this for everyone because it is the true – the only – strengthening for our inner being. In our inner life we need an experience of Christ that transcends all knowledge. This means that as king of the final kingdom he rules over our lives already here and now in exactly the same way as he will in his final kingdom.

We need people who pray – people who, like Paul, bend their knees and lift hands unstained with blood or any kind of impurity so that through the spirit of God in them, others may be strengthened in their inmost being – strengthened in their whole attitude to life. We need to be reminded daily that our inner selves must be renewed from day to day even if the outer self, the body, perishes in hunger, distress, and misery or is carried off and destroyed by persecution and death for the sake of truth. If we want to keep a clear, firm course instead of inwardly suffering shipwreck in the storm of public opinion and the towering waves of chaos, then our hidden inner being needs daily the quiet haven of communion with God.

THE HEART

World war and crisis bring deep affliction. They test our endurance to its very limits, bringing in their train the loss of national wealth and the disruption of whole economies, unemployment and impoverishment, mutual hostility, and untold ills that shatter public confidence. Even the most indifferent must feel that whether they will pass the test or not depends on what their hearts are able to bear. Those who had nothing but a smile for demands made by the inner life then feel how important it is that their hearts are firm. They realize that their ability to stand strong depends on the heart's capacity to keep hold of good energies, while warding off destructive ones. They see that they need stout hearts if they are to be able to bear the consequences of upheaval and distress without permanent injury.

Suffering is an appeal to our hearts. It forces us to be on the watch for ways of finding necessary strength and courage. For the heart affects the whole person. Being the inmost core, it means more than anything else, not only for the spirit, but just as much for the body. Even physical capacity depends on strength of heart. No feeling, thought, or motion of the will is without influence on the body. Ovid recognized this even in his ancient times: "Even in the human body, the heart counts more than the hand; the strength that gives life to the body is in the heart."

Life radiates from the heart. It preserves the center of its strength in this innermost core. The outer shell perishes.

The heart decides between life and death. It is so closely linked with the soul and so attuned to the life of the spirit that, like the soul, it has everlasting life.

People who are guided by superficialities cannot stand up to any hard trial: their concept of what wealth and strength of life can fill the heart is too feeble. The most important things in life are lost to them. Only events that have a powerful outer effect give them some idea of what power the inner life can have.

The wide mouth of a mighty river once showed a great explorer what riches must lie hidden in the interior beyond the newly discovered coast. This coast could not possibly be mistaken any longer for the edge of a small island. It promised to lead to the heart of a continent – and no one could remain indifferent to that! The sun that shone above it might have been familiar; so were the clouds gathering over it. But no longer could the discoverer be satisfied with a mere shoreline – a beach strewn with shells and wreckage and pounded monotonously by the sea of the world. No, the explorer could not rest until the secrets of the interior lay visible before his eyes.

By the stream of light radiating from the seven lampstands of John's Revelation, the whole world will recognize the secret land of light, the as yet undiscovered part of God's kingdom that is given to the church of Jesus Christ. The city of God – the city on the hill – must be made visible far and wide so that all seeking people may be stirred in their longing to know the center of its inner life, the secret of its free citizenship and its church-like unity. Over all the earth, people will ask about the citizenship of the kingdom of God, about his embassy here and now, and about the future order it represents. And they will recognize one thing above all – that they must become one with the heart of this church, this city of God, before they can enter its gates.

World history shows us: neither foreign rule nor home rule will come to any good unless the heart of a country is won. All wealth lies hidden within. Whoever does not learn to understand the heart of God in Jesus Christ, whoever will not begin to journey through all the outlying regions of God's world rule to the very center in order to become one with the ultimate will of God's heart, whoever does not seek the holy of holies, will never understand that God wants only one thing. He will never understand that in spite of the fact that in history God has appointed a bloody, diplomatic world government anchored in the right to property, God wants only one thing in the end: love without violence, freedom from all possessions and property rights, simple truthfulness and brotherly justice, community of all people without self-interest and property – that is, the kingdom and the church.

Whoever is estranged from the heart of God will be just as perplexed when confronted by the mystery of the human heart. For that is where the likeness of God shall be revealed. Such people will never be able to grasp:

> The greatest wonder in all creation,
> Of time and space the masterpiece:
> The human heart with its elation,
> The heart with all its ecstasies.

The Bible, which speaks of the heart in such a rich and profound way, is of all books the only one that can satisfy the inner life and fill the heart. If it is not seen superficially according to its letter but deeply in its heart and soul, it witnesses everywhere to the heart as the innermost mystery. It even goes so far as using the Hebrew expressions for "heart" and for "that which is within" as synonyms. In the Bible the heart is the antithesis of superficiality and pretense. What penetrates to the inmost depths does not simply stay on the surface.

What comes from the inmost depths is the noblest and sincerest of all. If our heart is corrupt, nothing we touch remains incorrupt. But the outer life resists the inner life and strives against it. There is seldom harmony between them.

A pure, creative spirit expresses what is within very clearly and intelligibly by outward and visible signs. An impure and untruthful spirit, on the other hand, misuses the outward expression to falsify the true state of affairs. Then the outward appearance is there only to hide what is within, as public economy and politics reveal so painfully in war and in peace.

We in our days have had to look on with horror while spirits who have fallen prey to hate and hostility, of whatever party or nation, have practiced the most hateful misuse of the spoken, written, and printed word. They all, every one of them, practice it to this day, dishonestly exaggerating and inventing failures and mistakes in the enemy's camp, and, just as much, exaggerating and inventing advantages and elements of truth in the home camp. Every honest person must be warned of the daily flood of printed matter: *Cave canem!* Here you will get barked at and bitten; there is no sense, no understanding, and no insight here because there is no justice. Pass by! Words desecrate the truth! Here the heart is cloaked in lies.

The scriptures call the heart the part hidden in the inner being. The thought is even intensified by terms like the "inmost" heart and the "depths" of the heart. The secrets of the heart are known to the scriptures. In the scriptures, anyone is marked as unhappy who has to hide in an armor of lies and dishonesty in order to appear different from what he or she truly is. Whoever gets entangled in hypocrisy and deceit cannot open up and pour out his or her heart even before God – the very one who wants to make the heart glad because he loves it and wants to give it truth and genuineness.

Ultimately, however, our innermost being cannot be hidden – we must do what is in our heart. And even if we do not want to admit it, our deeds will finally reveal whether our hearts are right or wrong.

War and postwar times have brought surprises for many of us: they should be stamped on our hearts as unforgettable warnings. We must not be indifferent to the abysses that have yawned in front of us: impure and unbridled passions, boundless lies and deceptions, the unrestrained fury of murder and looting, the loveless triumph of ruthless profiteering, the renewed increase of social injustice and oppressions, and the deception of class hatred and racism! All that, and still more, breaks out with the most fearsome violence in war and in the revolutions and violent repression that often follow it, with inflation and with heated political opinions. The shock of these things must be engraved unforgettably on our memory. The dreadful nucleus of these events is something we have to recognize even when it tries to hide behind the glittering armor of the most idealistic words and goals. Not the program but the deed discloses what powers drive the heart on and control it.

All we do is bound to be powerless and evil if the heart is parched and diseased, burdened and faint, or worst of all, if it is hostile, filled with the impure fires and poisonous smoke of blind hate. Only an inner life that is recollected and that lives in the strength of concentrated peace, only a harmonious heart that does not disintegrate in quarrels and strife, can give proof of strength to act. For only good works are constructive. Everything else is destructive. We can see outward effects, but God tests and knows the inner recesses of the heart. He wants to lead our hearts away from murderous demolition to the living work of building up. He alone knows how to guide them, just as we guide streams of running water to one place or another in our gardens. God wants to let all hearts flow together into one great garden, into the kingdom of his unity, love, and justice, where all do what is good because their hearts move them to it and the Spirit leads them and urges them on.

The Bible makes the heart responsible for bringing something new to us. As the Bible sees it, everything of significance is decided in the inner recesses of the heart. From the heart flow not only the streams of blood that fill our veins – no, also the pure winds and waters of the Spirit. That can be seen in the contrasting statements about the heart in prophetic and apostolic writings: what defiles the heart is not what enters it from without but what comes from within, from the inner being. It is false to maintain that our nature can be influenced by food taken in by the body or by hygiene or gymnastics. This is in distinct opposition to the word and life of Jesus. It leads to this thoughtless and deceptive saying: "A man is what he eats," set up in opposition to the truth of Jesus. Those who believe this have had to realize only too often that the defilement of our inner being lies deeper than in eating and drinking. The true food, the food of the spirit, remains decisive, though to be sure the abuse of eating and drinking through luxurious living can also burden the heart.

In truth it is quite the other way round: a luxurious and voluptuous life has its origin in the heart. What we do, we are. There are deeper signs of this than diets and rules of hygiene. As long as we think first and foremost of our health and our own well-being, we remain unredeemed, with a sick and self-seeking heart. Because we love our life, we lose it. Only when we give it up, do we find it.

What comes to light out of the heart is of vital significance. Every sort of idolatry will inevitably be exposed. The words uttered by the mouth (outward speech) come from the overflowing of the heart (the inner being). What we speak about, we are — that is, of course, provided we are speaking from our hearts. Nevertheless, the sincerity or insincerity of our words cannot be hidden in the long run. A watchful spirit, clearly discerning the spirits, hears the tones of the heart and sees the lights of the soul. All empty talk is useless, however lofty the words. What use is all outward service to God if our inner being, our heart, stays at a distance? Only what we do for the Lord with all our heart has any value. What point is there in letting our feet take paths and steps if our hearts do not go along too? All that is done and carried out in imagined strength remains a mere nothing if the living heart does not beat and pulse in it. As long as our heart stays quick and alive, even the weakest, those incapable of productive work, can have the strongest influence. The heart is the inner core that does not rest even when the outer person is inactive. God does not look at outward appearance but at the heart.

Strength and weakness lie in our innermost being. Although our inner attitude can be hidden or disguised on the outside, it nevertheless makes all the difference to our character. Only what passes through one heart to another has any value or strength, because it comes from the heart. Whoever has experienced how complete or almost complete strangers open their innermost hearts to one another will feel again and again the genuine heartbeat in each true word and turn away from empty words in which the heart does not speak.

The living church receives its unity and unanimity from the continual outpouring of the Spirit. It is there that the harmony of all hearts reaches its climax, for there all have become one heart and one soul. And this they will be over and over again, every time they believe in the Holy Spirit.

Whoever wants to forgive with the mouth only or preach with the lips can only disappoint us. "A preacher must have a heart on fire before preaching." With these words Francis of Assisi revealed the secret of his fruitful life. "For anything that is to move hearts must come straight from the heart." That is what Phorkyras demands in Goethe's *Faust*.

The heart is rich in strength. What a wealth and diversity of lively emotions are embedded in the heart! Many people associate the heart only with feelings. And indeed, language does not go far wrong when it speaks so often of the emotional life as the heart's affair. The best and deepest feelings are seated in our innermost being, but just as much our most wicked and harmful ones.

All true joy comes from the heart and fills it with jubilant exultation or quiet happiness. All genuinely good deeds touch the heart. Every joyful hope has its life in the heart. The refreshing of the spirit, and not only that but also the refreshing of body and soul, is a gift for the inner life, for the heart. For the heart is grateful for every consolation that offers bread and not stones. The heart really does have to fight against fear and unrest, pain and sadness.

Our times have shown us all too clearly that the heart does not burn with love and joy only. All too often it plunges into the consuming fires of discontent and hate. We must be surprised to the point of being horrified how for one reason after another passion causes the heart to flare up in rage and distress! What a catastrophe it would be for the heart if it were to exhaust all its wealth on its conflicting feelings! And how deluding these storms are even though they are often only big enough to fill a teacup! Strong impressions produce shaking emotions. Miserable lusts cramp the heart. Deep emotion alternates with very petty feelings. It can happen that unclarified, unconscious, and subconscious feelings lead to something good. But often they veil urges that are dangerously apathetic and can lead the heart to destruction.

It is not true that the heart can only feel. No, the heart as the inner core is more than feeling: it is intention and will. It is the seat of all deep thoughts, which have meaning only if they move our inner being. "Great thoughts come from the heart." Everything that is great seeks the living core. The heart is not only inner feeling: it is also inner thought. There is a speaking and talking going on in the heart that tries to bring inner clarity to all its thinking. Reason is not alien to the heart. To be sure, there are some unreasonable hearts who by their errors show nothing but folly. But what the sensible and understanding heart thinks out is wisdom. It understands how to know and recognize the best counsel. Just in the inconceivably heavy things that war and its historical consequences bring upon us all, just in the incalculable and unfathomable tasks that confront us, the heart needs the greatest and deepest thoughts. These God alone can give.

There are indeed thoughts that will always be alien to the heart. There are indeed hearts that hate thinking. But without a certain rich and deep fusion of thoughts there is no fruitful inner life. The whole wealth of life intended for the heart is available to it only when the heart is ready to open itself to the deepest thinking and reflection. It is in the nature of the heart to think and reflect.

"Your heart is you yourself. Blessed are you if understanding always dwells in your heart." Only the consecrated thoughts of a dedicated life lead to this deep understanding. True understanding is given solely in the thoughts of God, which turn his will into the holy "thou shalt."

The effect that thoughts have on the heart's feelings provides a certain criterion of their value, though not always an infallible one. As Ruskin expressed it: "Literature, art, science – they are all fruitless and worse than fruitless if they do not enable us to be glad, and glad of heart at that." A heart that is truly alive passes a kind of higher judgment about those intellectual ideas that cannot fit into our life at the moment, and perhaps never will. "Like a sun, the heart goes through our thoughts and on its way extinguishes one constellation after another!" Jean Paul saw his inner life before

him in this picture. All knowledge related only to the thinking brain is dead, including mere intellectual knowledge of
biblical things. Such knowledge brings life into deadly danger unless the heart takes a stand and unless it is so moved
and alive that it is capable of making a choice between light
and darkness, bright and dark rays, evil stars and good stars.
Only thoughts that have glowing warmth and strength penetrate a pure heart and stream out from it again. Mirza-
Schaffy's search for a completely integrated inwardness comes
to expression when he proclaims:

> Head without heart breeds bad blood;
> Heart without head is still no good.
> For joy and blessing to last forever,
> Heart and head must go together.*

This cooperation of two instruments demands an inner energy to hold together what so often threatens to disintegrate.
No heart is without energy. Yes, the heart is will. God's
heart – being love – is the will to gather, the will for his
kingdom. The heart of Jesus wants to gather everything that
is to be united in his church: in the same way, the human
heart that is healed in him is the clarified will to gather and
unite. If our inner being is not to let the precious wealth of
truly great thoughts go rushing by, we must have a heart
with a will that is active and glowing, able to accept words of
truth and hold on to them firmly, just as Mary did. A will
made weak by brooding and a nature ruled by feelings have
never yet been capable of anything great. Faith received the
word of the Holy Spirit into the heart. This is the only way
the word can penetrate our life.

*Mirza-Schaffy (pseudonym for Friedrich von Bodenstedt), 1819–1892.

The ultimate nature of the heart is in fact its inner urge, and its yet deeper will. This will is able to comprehend all that is said and to transform it into dynamic life values. All intentions and wishes have their root in the heart. There is not only desire in the heart: deeper than that lie its intentions and resolutions. With its will, the heart holds on to the objects of its love and devotion. It is the inner disposition, the deeper direction of will, that makes the character of the heart what it is. Where our treasure is – the treasure that fills our inner life – there is our heart also.

"There is something in every character that will not let itself be broken, that forms its backbone."* This backbone that is inwardly so firm and stable is the moral, loving, and uniting will. Without a decided will there is no character. Character is moral order. It is all the elements of the heart, ordered according to the laws of divine and human morality, according to the will to unity, and therefore in the active spirit of pure and warm love. The backbone of this order is the will. As will, the heart is the school of character. True, it needs the stream of the world in order to grow strong. The will has to prove itself in work that is a product of active love by helping to build up a life consistent with the unity it aims at. It is steeled for this task in the hard struggle against all the powers opposed to unity. But if our will is not rooted in our inmost being, in our heart, we will be swept downward with the stream.

If it is true that character depends on personality, then personality has its life and strength in the inner will. Only in the inmost recesses of the heart do we become truly free. It is

*Georg Christoph Lichtenberg, 1742–1799.

only there that we take a decisive attitude, one that means either moral stability or spineless instability. It is the direction the inner attitude takes that makes the personality. As long as this direction seeks nothing but itself, it will lead the personality astray. Personality is "the greatest happiness of earth's children" only when the will no longer seeks itself but comes into action and sets to work for what is greatest of all – God's unity in his kingdom and his church.

In the end, only deeds reveal the inner attitude of the heart. Only those actions that require the concentration of all the heart's energies can be called deeds. The true deed unites all genuine powers of each individual, bringing togetherness and community to all: the kingdom of God among us is the concentration of all powers in united deed. Only when we do not seek our own advantage but that of another are our deeds in keeping with the powers of God's spirit at work in us: when in our deeds we sacrifice our own life so that community life may be established in unity, purity, truth, and righteousness.

The greatest deed of the strongest heart was accomplished by Jesus. When he died on the cross, his resolute determination accomplished it. Here an energy of the will found nowhere else – a fire of love, a steadfastness in carrying out God's perfect will – is revealed. Christ's struggle in Gethsemane and his cry of God-forsakenness on the cross give a significant glimpse into what willpower was necessary for the heart of the Son of Man not to be broken by the anguish of his pain. Yet his love remained strong and unbroken till the end. In the very torment of death, the divine life in this heart was marked by a will to unity, consummation of the work of unification, trust in the Father, prayer for his en-

emies, concern for a criminal, tender care for his own, and
the commending of his spirit into the hands of the Father.

Just before that, Jesus' High-Priestly Prayer, as the profoundest speaking of any heart, had proclaimed unity to be
the essence of his will. "May they all be one as thou, Father,
art in me and I in thee, so that in this – their being one –
the world may know and believe that thou hast sent me!"
The farewell words of Jesus – those words with such an inex-
haustible wealth of thought, spoken to those who were his
disciples in community and missionary work – also revealed
the spirit of this relationship of unity. This spirit, the Holy
Spirit, was revealed to be the living representative of Jesus
Christ, the advocate of his kingdom and his church, the
power that thoroughly overwhelms in the conviction that
the love that comes from unity is the truth. The spirit of
truth is the one who calls to mind every word that Jesus said,
including his last words, which prophesy the approaching
kingdom of divine unity. It is the quickening breath of life
who communicates the content and form of the future kingdom for us today. Last but not least, the significant symbol-
ism of the Last Supper proclaims the death of Jesus as
atonement and liberation; it proclaims his death as the living
creation of the new body of Christ, which shall bring the
whole of life into perfect unity.

All this shows, in a profound wealth of feeling and will,
the invincible power of God's thoughts in Jesus Christ, the
power to accomplish this deed, the most dynamic deed that
ever a heart accomplished. As a revelation of God, this deed
of Jesus demonstrates the concentration of all powers on the
one goal that is their task. And this goal is nothing more or
less than peace, reconciliation, and unity!

The heart is the inner character. In Jesus it is so firm and clear that by sacrificing his life he accomplishes the greatest deed of liberation, uniting, and gathering that can ever be imagined. In Jesus, the accomplished deed reveals his inner perfection. In all of us, the nature of our deeds reveals our heart. Deeds reveal the character of the heart. If the heart is not clear and undivided – "single," as Jesus puts it – then it is weak, flabby, and indolent, incapable of accepting God's will, of making important decisions, or of taking strong action. That is the reason why Jesus attached the greatest significance to singleness of heart, simplicity, unity, solidarity, and decisiveness. Purity of heart is nothing else than absolute integrity, which can overcome desires that enervate and divide. Determined single-heartedness is what the heart needs in order to be receptive, truthful and upright, confident and brave, firm and strong.

Yet the spirit of Jesus is seldom accepted. The strength of character that comes from him is seldom achieved. Weakness and dividedness of heart are to blame. How often the heart tries to overcome its own cowardice and faintheartedness through cold pride! The divisive callousness of pride is a weakness that destroys everything, making the inner self numb and stubborn, yet torn and disrupted too. The self-will that splits and divides itself has an arrogance that is the enemy of the love of God.

The heart tries in vain to close itself to the knowledge that it is too weak, too rotten and wicked, too disunited, too divided, and too hostile to help itself. For all its blindness to its own nature, and against its own will, time after time the heart has to uncover pride and arrogance, wickedness and cunning, ruthlessness and deceit, as the self-will and self-interest that continually divide it. Debasement of the heart can go so far in rigid obstinacy that all pretense comes to an end: God is tempted and cursed until darkness fills the heart's inmost recesses.

The heart, however, longs for the opposite – for a development of the inner life that leads to honest self-recognition, single-hearted simplicity, and unfeigned humility. In this spirit of modesty, the consciousness of one's own smallness unites with the divine call to true greatness. Such a development, brought about by God, requires a penetrating insight into everything that is base in one's own heart, an insight that in fact means a revolution in the heart. No one has an innocent heart when faced with this radical revolution.

Consciousness of guilt and unfulfilled longing for God, however, may not only soften the heart but positively tear it apart and crush it. Many people have shattering things to say about the consuming fire of this longing of the heart. Many call it the deepest thing in themselves, the thing they want to gain a glimpse into:

> In my heart there burns an eternal lamp,
> quiet and steady;
> only once in a while it flares up high,
> rises to a flame,
> to a blazing fire
> raging and consuming and destroying –
> then I summon all my energy,
> only one wish have I then,
> only one hope,
> only one thought –
> and the eternal flame flickers and smokes
> for a long, long time

until it is appeased and becomes quiet:
my eternal longing!*

The blazing flame of longing is certainly there, but it will have to flicker, restless and unappeased and impure, until the heart submits to the inner influence of the sharp, clarifying word and cutting wind of the spirit of God. Then the smoky blaze can give way to the perfect light of the "Christ in us." Nevertheless, because the heart is as weak as it is obstinate and only too used to its own divided and disrupted state, it will not surrender lightly. It tries by every possible means to defend itself. It tries passionately to cling to self-chosen, human ideals meant to bolster its self-will and hostile self-assertion – either alone or in community with equally selfish kindred hearts. But it is all in vain, even though the heart can cover up or postpone the decisive battle for a long time.

All attempts to lift the heart up in human, emotional enthusiasm for some god other than the Father of Jesus Christ are made in vain. In spite of every effort, all that the natural state of the human heart reveals is how far it has fallen away from God. Today more than ever this is unintentionally revealed by many movements. Inflamed hearts give rise to movements that use hatred, injustice, and godlessness to pursue the goal of unity and social justice – but in vain. Other movements pay homage (supposedly patriotic but in reality hostile and restricted) to a deity opposed to the living God – a deity alien to Christ and inimical to him.

The veil has to fall away. It darkens the heart and restricts it to itself or to groups bound together by blood ties or a common lot. Nothing must hinder the outlook toward

*Michael Grabowsky, 1805–1863.

God. God, the Father of Jesus Christ, can be seen only by looking with a resolute and unfaltering heart toward the perfect unity of his kingdom, a unity free from all arbitrary boundaries, its one goal an all-embracing justice – the result of the divine joy of perfect love to friend and foe. This free outlook presupposes and demands a complete liberation of the heart from every false emotional tie, yes, a complete change of heart, the new birth brought about by the Holy Spirit.

The heart must not be allowed to remain as it is. It must experience the healing transformation that frees it from all rank and impure growth, all egotistical isolation. If it wants to be really free, the heart must be circumcised – pruned – and the weedy growth of self-will and self-glorification around it must be thinned out and cast away.

The Odes of Solomon, an early Christian collection of hymns from the second century, witness in a profound way to this circumcision of the heart:

My heart was circumcised and its flower appeared.
Grace sprang up in it,
And brought forth fruit for the Lord.
For the Most High cut me by his Holy Spirit
And opened my reins toward him.
He filled me in his love
And his circumcision became my salvation –
I hastened on the way of his peace,
On the way of truth.
From beginning to end
I received his knowledge.
I was firmly established on the rock of truth,
Where he himself set me up.
The Lord renewed me with his raiment

And created me by his light.
From above he refreshed me with immortality
So I became like a land
That blossoms and rejoices in its fruit.
Like the sun upon the face of the earth,
The Lord gave light to mine eyes,
And my face received the dew;
My breath delighted in the precious odors of the Lord.
He led me into his paradise,
Where the pleasure of the Lord abounds.
I threw myself before the Lord
For the sake of his glory, and I said:
"Blessed are they that are planted in thy land,
That have a place in thy paradise,
That grow like the growth of thy trees
And have stepped from darkness into light!
Behold, all thy workers are fair
And do good works.
From unkindness they turn to the strength of thy love.
They cast off the bitterness of the trees
When they were planted in thy land.
For there is much room in thy paradise,
And there is nothing that is useless therein,
But everything is filled with thy fruits!"

Therefore Fichte said: "As long as we want to be something for our own sake, our true nature and our true life cannot develop in us, and for this very reason we also remain cut off from blessedness." Fichte sees all selfishly isolated existence quite rightly as nonexistence, deadly restriction, cut off from the only true existence. It is only in blessed community with the divine being that the greatest inner freedom can exist, replacing the unhappiness of sensual self-love and the insensitivity of moralistic legalism. Circumscribed self-love and heartless legalism are the enemies of the gospel of unity and freedom. The true freedom of a heart ruled by God does away with superficial legalism. An inner urge that comes from perfect love replaces it: the impulse of the Holy Spirit, leading to the divine order of a common life in complete community. Here all isolation and all arbitrary limitations are thoroughly overcome. Through the unity of the Holy Spirit, the church and the kingdom are proved to be the only true existence, the only true life. For it is God's love that reveals itself in the unity of his church and his kingdom.

This experience of God is a decisive enrichment of the inner life. Without it, even the most gifted heart starves inwardly. The inner acceptance of the divine means rebirth for a dead heart, so that it then becomes a new, different heart. It cannot be a good and upright heart until it has experienced a complete turning, a wholehearted conversion that leads away from false narrowness within its own self to true breadth, to the experience of God, who is greater than our hearts. The heart needs to be redeemed from its stubborn self-life. Only in community with the perfect life can it be restored to health. The perfect life is love. The omnipotent breadth and depth of God's greatness is revealed as love. In Christ and his spirit, a complete uniting (as the church and the kingdom) is brought so near to us by love that together we are able to go this way of love.

On the path of faith, the heart is led away from the inner resistance it puts up against perfect love, and closer and closer to openhearted, voluntary obedience. The obedience that springs from faith opens up to the heart of

God and to the heart of his kingdom. It is only through experiencing the free gift of God's love that the human heart
can be purified of its stubbornness and despair. Only unfeigned love from the purest spheres can oust those hostile
elements that are the opposite of love: self-will, wrapped up
in itself, and impure passion of all kinds that destroys root
and branch its own life-energy as well as that of its victims.

The gift that comes from the purifying and liberating love
of the Most High is grace. In this one short word, the Bible
encompasses the wealth of God's heart, which wants to give
itself to us in love. It is in grace that God draws near to us.
The hardship of our times and the abundance of tasks it
brings show us how forlorn we are in the world, and how
helpless, without God. In judgment, grace becomes the
deepest need of our hearts. It is only through the free, communal gift of the Holy Spirit to his church that the hardship
of our times becomes an invigorating mineral bath, immers-
ing us in the salty strength of the future kingdom of God.
Then, in complete community, we can carry out here and
now the tasks of justice. The greater the need and distress,
the nearer draws the kingdom of God.

The nature of grace is made clear in the bitter fate of the
one who was crucified, in the way he sacrificed himself completely to the greatest of all tasks. When the heart experiences the freeing power of his death, scripture calls it being
sprinkled with the blood of the redeemer. The heart, taking
firm hold of unity with Christ through his death, puts the
whole of life into militant action against the powers that put
Jesus to death. Consequently, this baptism of blood means
not only being ready to die for him, but something even
more immediate – being prepared time and again to risk life

itself in the fight against powers that oppose the kingdom of God. For us there is no other basis for true peace of heart than this fight to the bitter end. Right to the point of death by martyrdom, the strength for this fight comes from unity with Christ in his death, from the direct nearness of God's heart. Only the cross brings perfect trust in God. Here, in the sharpest judgment of his wrath over all that is evil, God reveals loving grace to all as his innermost nature.

Through his spirit, God himself lives in a heart united in this way with the cross. His love is poured out in it. In the midst of murderous opponents of peace and justice, a heart filled like this remains joyful in love, in a love that includes all enemies. To this joy and this love the martyrs of both early Christianity and the radical Reformation have testified a thousandfold. This fundamental strengthening of character, proven at that time in death, lets the heart unfold all its powers-to-be with the zeal of inner fire in order that in life as in death they may make an impact on the whole world.

The reason Christ died for all was so that those who live may no longer live for themselves but for him who died and rose again for their sakes (2 Cor. 5:15). That the whole of life up to the very brink of death is meant here – life with all its capabilities and activities – is shown by the other word of the same apostle of Jesus Christ. According to this word, the same people who have just previously let themselves be used in the service of unrighteousness from now on give themselves to God in the service of righteousness (Rom. 6:13, 19). For this is the only way the work of the Holy Spirit can and will be continually built up anew as it once was in Jerusalem, no matter how often Jerusalem is destroyed and no matter how often his church is violently driven apart.

Yet this wealth of power and effective action up to the very threshold of death cannot be won unless complete inner concentration and perfect accord prevail in the heart, as in the primitive church. We know from the history of war that the strongest political power is nothing but a helpless mass of people if a united will is lacking or has been lost. Such was the case with Germany in World War I. Such was the experience of cities and countries in times of siege. And so, too, the Protestant princes and cities were once "wonderfully favored by circumstances" for the Smalkaldic War: never, since the time of the emperors of Hohenstaufen and the Salian emperors, had the tribes of North and South Germany united in such a compact mass against the crown. At that time too, a war council torn by conflicting interests was to blame for the inevitable catastrophe of defeat.

Consequently, only when the heart refuses to let opposing interests split it apart can even the richest powers and gifts be a help and blessing to it. If the heart wants to win the victories of a faith that has courage unto death, it needs the wholehearted decisiveness of a unified will. We cannot serve two masters at once. We cannot pursue two ideals. We cannot seek two goals in two directions. The kingdom of God, as the final kingdom, does not tolerate in any heart any other kingdom besides itself. The way of Jesus is the only way that knows no byways, no wrong ways, and no devious ways. However many roads may lead to Rome or anywhere else – there is only one kingdom, there is only one way: the complete uniting of all believers in all the activity that goes on in the heart and in life as a whole. Through the decisive outpouring of the Holy Spirit, all believers became so much one heart and one soul that they proved the uniting of all their powers, not only in the word of the apostles and in prayer, but also in the breaking of bread and in community – in full community of goods too.

Only when there is an integrated will – one that is decided for God and united with all similar wills – can the heart profess to seek God and his kingdom. He will reveal himself powerfully only through those who have turned an undivided heart toward him. An undivided heart does not tolerate a divided life. Only he is truly with God who surrenders to him as his king with all his thoughts and feelings, all his powers, gifts, and goods in order to live truly for God – an integrated character with an integrated life. The whole heart has to be converted before it is possible to follow him. Where the whole heart is turned toward him, it means that a life that is undivided (with all the powers of the spirit and all the wealth and capacities of soul and body) devotes every area of its existence to his rulership and to the church. That includes professional and vocational activity with all the skills involved in it; it includes all worldly belongings and all temporal possessions.

Unless we stand firmly with God, we cannot carry out our service to him; only when we love him heart and soul can we do his will in everything. Not one of us can do this in our own strength. If we are going to give all our strength and goods, we need strength from the Holy Spirit. It does not proceed from us. It is given to us in the word of the apostles, the community of prayer, and the breaking of bread. Whoever knows what it is to pray from a simple, undivided heart becomes grateful to God for his works and words and finds his happiness in worshiping the greatness of God and doing his will. Nothing will be impossible to one who prays this kind of prayer, the prayer that listens to God with heart and soul. Such prayer gives the inner life the boundless wealth of the truth of God. It leads the heart to the knowledge that truth is unshakable because it is the very essence of life. It has the power to accomplish everything. The impossible becomes possible. Unity is given a place in a torn world. Community in the fullest sense is created and built up, making the unity of God's spirit shine out in truth and deed as the church, the city on the hill.

If we want to wage the spiritual wars of Jehovah and win the land for him, we must acclaim him with our whole heart! When his will rules in our heart, he will give our inner being a wealth of experience and action that it can attain only under his rulership. When our heart is ruled by Jesus Christ as our master, then and only then will we be equipped and qualified for the great tasks that will inevitably confront us in the difficulties of these times and the hardships of the future. These tasks are nothing less than a call to the kingdom of God and the tasks of his church.

SOUL AND SPIRIT

The question of life and death is bound to concern us more than ever before: war has brought death to so many who were in the prime of life. Crime against life has increased atrociously, also crime against unborn children. The question of life and soul is one that people have wrestled with throughout the ages, but the present time is so serious that it should make everything else fall into the background. Then we can concentrate fully on what soul, spirit, and life mean to us.

Is it not an astonishing fact that death overcomes life? Children cannot understand death. Least of all can they see how it is possible to kill people in the service of a higher cause. But even apart from this, to children the thought that human life can one day come to an end is always unreal – contrary to the truth. The unnaturalness of dying is too remote from the simplicity of their affirmation of life. For the same reason, the heathen of old with their zest for life believed in the immortality of the soul. Goethe, too, who was very much akin to them, said "Those who have no hope for a life beyond are dead to this life as well." Life itself witnesses to its own invincible power. Hope is the hallmark of all living things.

As long as we want to deny that life is eternal, everything that belongs to life remains cloaked in tormenting riddles. Eternity remains the deepest longing of the human spirit. When we know that we are immortal, everything we experi-

ence is great and understandable; when we see ourselves as
mortal, it all becomes dark and futile. If there is no other future and no other world (which is bound to be victorious because it is the better world), then the injustice that prevails
makes nonsense of human existence by giving final victory
to "the worst of all possible worlds."

In the inner and outer circumstances of life, every living
person can learn to recognize this other world. Fichte has
declared that we only need to rise to the consciousness of a
pure, moral character to find out who we ourselves are, to
find out that this globe with all its glories, this sun and the
thousands of thousands of suns that surround it, this whole
immense universe at the mere thought of which our sentient
soul quakes and trembles – that all this is nothing but a dim
reflection in mortal eyes of our own eternal existence, hidden within us, to be unfolded throughout all eternity.

And the other way round, this is the truth given to people
since primeval times: our so very small world can be nothing
else than a likeness – bungled, it is true, but nevertheless recognizable – of a bigger, truer, and more genuine world without limits of time and space. Our small world belongs to this
bigger one. It must correspond to it once again. For all of us,
as Kant has said, there is the moral code within us and the
starry heavens above us to bring home a living intimation of
this fact of eternity.*

Our life has its roots in eternity. Its nature presumes im-
perishability. In space, the human spirit goes far
beyond all comprehensible limits. And similarly, the absoluteness of the moral demands it makes knows no limit. The

*Immanuel Kant, 1724–1804.

most certain of all certainties known by our spirit is this: that the ray of truth, the power of life, and the demand of the holy "thou shalt" keeps on coming to us from a living world that lies beyond all space and nevertheless embraces all space. With this energy that comes from absolute authority, the human spirit follows the stream of time long before the beginning and far beyond the end, going outside all boundaries. This is the spirit's most crying need: the origin of all things before the beginning of time and the goal of the future at the end of time.

The thirsting soul pants for its original fountainhead and for its estuary ahead. Once awakened to consciousness of its true self and its divine destiny, it sees in death an enemy of life – an unnatural enemy that fights against the very nature of things. And it sees the same in everything else that tries to sully and destroy the clarity and purity of the eternal.

Everything in our present time and in our earthly space that opposes the soul's holy "thou must" and "thou shalt" must and shall be overcome (as the soul ultimately believes it will be) by the kingdom of God at the end of all ages and beyond all earthly things. The "heavenly kingdom" of the other world intervenes in temporal and earthly life as the power of the future world. It wants to transform life here and now according to the image of what is beyond and to come. This happens as soon as and as long as the soul lets faith rule in it, whenever and wherever that may be.

This other life, which is already possible here and now, means freedom for the soul. But there will never be any such soaring of a free soul as long as an atmosphere antagonistic to life robs it of its breath, obscuring its view into the eternal and everlasting.

The freedom and power of a believing soul goes so far that it expects – with the prophetic spirit – a holy transformation to justice and unity. It expects this also for every detail of material existence in space and time. It is in the hope of the kingdom of God that the soul discovers its life. To the soul, the end of all the ways of God is unity in a tangible and visible form. For that reason, the Bible traces the death of the body back to the fact that sin as separation – as division and isolation – has brought a fatal breach into the living cohesion of creation. To the soul, evil is a power hostile to life, one that carries with it the danger of eternal death by separation from God and people from each other. Sin is crime against life and love. That was the reason why the first son born to those human beings who separated themselves from God inevitably became his brother's murderer.

Nevertheless, the ancient scriptures of truth maintain that it is impossible to extinguish the life that God has given out of his own nature. From generation to generation, physical death comes to everyone as a consequence of separation from God. The body does indeed die when the soul leaves it. The body that is left behind without the soul must fall to dust. Death can never deny that its nature is to separate by division and disintegration. This it has proved since the very beginning through man's separation from God. Yet death is not annihilation.

The writings of both the Old Testament and the New Testament speak again and again about the souls of the dead. Every living soul has a capacity for future life. All vital movements of humankind look to the future. Whenever the soul comes to new life in the Spirit, it waits for God's future. And even if the soul cannot believe wholeheartedly in the coming kingdom, faith tries to salvage this or that small fragment of the world-to-come and then clings to it all the more passionately. If people are not yet ready to fight and die for the final kingdom of love and justice, they cling to a communistic state of the future or to a nationalist government of patriotic and racial alliance. And in the same way, a remnant of faith in immortality and the other world emerges again and again, even in the most unbelieving, and this they can never lose entirely. Something in our being is meant to continue as an active force forever. Our divine home calls us homeward. The spirit wants to return to God, in whom it has its origin. And though God himself is not yet recognized, there is at least an attempt to represent a little of his infinite significance even when it is done by idolatry.

Today we have every reason to recall the faith in eternity and infinity that characterized the early Christians. If we want truth and seek it regardless of the unfounded prejudices of our time, we must and will recognize that here among the early Christians a glimpse into ultimate reality is given. In the face of this reality, no living soul can maintain its opposition. For here the soul is face to face with the life-giving spirit of Jesus Christ. Whoever believes in Jesus will live even through death. And the day is coming when they will awake and arise to a perfect life in an immortal body.

The spirits of the just who have departed this life are at rest in the living God. They wait for the day of his future. The character of this perfect life in the kingdom of God is shown by the parable of the wedding and its joyful uniting, by the comparison with the meal of fellowship, and by the establishment of the thrones (Rev. 20:4); it is a life ruled by a love and a justice that bring about complete unity. In this kingdom, at the end of all things, the one Holy Spirit will master and pervade everything. What constitutes life now is man's soul (that is, the life) in the blood (Lev. 17:11, 14), but then it will be his spirit. Instead of ruling over the soul's human body, the spirit will rule over a spiritual body.

In the kingdom, the Holy Spirit takes the place of the coursing blood. The Spirit does away with fluctuating emotional ties and puts in their place a unity kept constantly alive, a unity that is just as active as it is perfectly clear. In such a body of unity, those who are at all times united in God and serve him under his rulership live in a radically different way from those who are far away from their master and are thus headed toward ruin, body and soul. Because these last have rejected the unity of life, they themselves have chosen death and separation. But even this second death cannot mean annihilation: even this death must show that its nature is separation and division. No more dreadful fate for a living soul can be imagined than to be cast out for all eternity from the life that is in God.

To be excluded forever from the center of life is eternal death. Hell is nothing but the continuation of the lives of those who live for themselves. Their whole existence consists in the worm of decomposition and decay, the worm that does not die, the burning and consuming fire that is not quenched, and the judgment that means dissolution and separation. Simply because he had kept his riches to himself, the rich man – outside whose door the beggar Lazarus lay – met this eternal death. Ignoring the need of others, he had enjoyed his riches as his rightful possession. All he had neglected to do was to give up his goods to become one with the poor.

Only the one who sells everything and gives it to the poor can gain treasure in heaven – life in God. Jesus challenges everyone who is rich to this absolutely necessary action. That is the only way to join the itinerant, property-free community of Jesus, the unity of those who follow him. Humanly speaking, to go this way is and always will seem quite impossible for those who own house and land. But with God all things are possible. History proves it. Wealth is death because it isolates the heart from need and distress and so isolates it from love. But God can give life even to the richest by calling them out of death. He can free anyone by leading him or her to the love that surrenders everything in perfect trust.

How does it happen that God with his unlimited life takes hold of our limited existence and fills it? We must be perfectly clear about the answer to this question and all its consequences. God is life. Only in him do we live, move, and have our being. Physical life throughout nature, like all life, has its origin and being in God alone. God does not disown his creation. He will lead it through fire to a new day. But the souls of people owe their decidedly unique life in a very special way to a direct communication from God. It is from God that we have the breath of life. He is the Father of spirits: just as he created the hosts of heaven with his breath, so on earth we received spirit from him.

Life is not limited to the blood that courses through our veins. The blowing breath of God, breathed into us as spirit, is deeper. It is this spirit that takes up our calling in life. It is this spirit that has to determine the life of the human soul. The blood must not be allowed to rule – it has to serve.

Otherwise it ruins the spirit. The breath we have from God is spirit and soul. For this spirit that was breathed into our soul is the soul's unique life, its deepest life.

What distinguishes the soul and gives it a direction is the spirit. Here lies the boundary between humankind and beast. Animals too have blood and a soul. What they lack is spirit, which is more than reason and understanding. To shed the blood of animals is a responsible business, but anyone who sees the sacrifice of slaughtered animals as similar to killing people, acknowledging only a relative difference between the two – a difference of degree – has misunderstand the spirit God has given to us, and us alone, of all terrestrial beings. We have been placed above animals. Our spirit is meant to rule over the animals. However, we can do so only under one condition, and we can accept the ultimate sacrifice from them – the sacrifice of their blood – only under this one condition: that our life is given to the tasks of the spirit and that, as images of God, we conquer the earth for God's kingdom. But whoever kills people lays violent hands on the countenance of God, committing a sacrilege against the task of the spirit, for the spirit wants to bring everyone together in unity. For no one is without spirit. When people cooperate with every breath of God's spirit, it becomes impossible for them to fight with murderous intent and kill each other. We are given to each other to become united in life, because human spirit belongs to human spirit. The spirit of God unites one human spirit to another by ruling over them.

The spirit is meant from now on to rule as the higher power over all lower powers of the soul and unite them under its dominion. Aristotle knew this even in his time. It is simply impossible for a mere product of the soul's lower faculties to be the distinguishing feature of the human soul. The spirit cannot deny its origin. Therefore to be ruled by the blood or to allow base or superficial things to satisfy us completely is unworthy of our calling. Everything that betrays and destroys community in the spirit must be seen as base. Therefore we see as bestial – and worse than bestial – every debasement that takes place through the unbridled urges of the soul in the blood. More than any madness, it tramples our true identity in the dust.

The human spirit has the very greatest of destinies: God and his kingdom. Like the satanic spirit Lucifer, however, this spirit with such a high destiny has turned away from the highest and precisely for this reason has become a rich breeding ground for the antigod principle. Separated from God, we seek ourselves and our own kingdom. From now on we profess what is high and noble but without the rule and unity of God. We strive for our own exaltation without giving recognition to God's deeds. We live for human self-redemption, without honoring and accepting the deed of Jesus Christ and his redemption. For the people of our own race and blood and our own class, we are even ready to sacrifice human life, rejecting God's kingdom and God's people.

It should be plain to everyone that all these ideals of the human spirit that are separated from God have come to nothing. They have come to nothing in their concept of world peace without Christ. They have come to nothing in their efforts toward justice and freedom without his kingdom and his church. They have come to nothing in their illusion of an international unity without unity in the spirit of truth. Prosperity in a people united by race is founded on property and selfish advantage. In just the same way, the worldwide economic unity of high finance has been built up on the material prosperity of individuals and their mutual advantage. Even the proletarian Internationale has used its solidarity much more for material advantage in the present, for a fraction of the underprivileged (even if it is a large fraction), than for the greater justice of a future that could embrace everyone.

Now when in the face of all this, the policy of isolation makes nations try to close the frontiers of the earth in an effort to establish their economic self-sufficiency, they deny that the earth belongs to God. They deny that God's will is to be the God of all people and that the will of his kingdom is to unite all nations in mutual service and make the products of their work the common property of all. It is impossible, though, for humankind to become an integrated world society, a world community of the Spirit, unless it allows God's spirit to reprove it, judge it, and rule it. God's rule, however, means that people no longer seek their own advantage or privileges anymore, and that self-preservation is nowhere placed above the Spirit's cause – that of unity.

Right up to the present day, there is no political element of worldwide importance that follows this way of God's world-rulership. Consequently, every great movement with a hope for justice has inevitably met defeat again and again. In just the same way, every kind of national self-redemption has come to grief – and will repeatedly come to grief – because, in setting up an idolatry that is supposed to bring recovery to the world, it rejects and even spurns the very nature of divine liberation and healing. As long as the rulership of God and his kingdom are left in the background, efforts toward human progress of any kind will inevitably break down over and over again. All human efforts toward salvation are doomed to fail because, deluded as they are, they presume to lead to the heights – not with God, but with the power of idols. Faith in the masses, faith in blood, faith in any power other than the spirit of God, will be annihilated in the fire of the future. All kinds of false beliefs break down under the horrors of war, but annihilation in the fire of the future will be still more thorough.

However, what remains indestructible in all the waves of battle that surge around us is our spirit – the first thing to surrender to God's will. Here and there in all parties, the inner depths of the spirit are already beginning to open up. Man's spirit is awakening. Its will is aroused. It is still blinded by confusion and unclarity. It is still benighted by separation from God. But the hour is near when our spirits far and wide will be gripped and called by God.

The fact that the soul is pulled in two directions is the cause of all the confusion that hinders this call. Through the spirit the soul is drawn to God on the one side, and through the blood it is bound to what is physical and material on the other side. In this dilemma, it remains dangerously exposed to unspiritual movements that continually attack it and try to sever it from the spirit of God.

The physical and material is not the real enemy of the soul. It is merely the area that the soul has to bring under control as its task. The real enemy of life is the corruption of soul that thwarts all efforts to accomplish this task. It is only since the soul has become degenerate that it has come under the oppressive power of the physical and material. From the beginning, it has been an accepted fact that body and soul pervade each other, but originally it was the spirit that was meant to rule over body and soul. Through repressing the spirit, the diseased soul has brought things to such a pass that the spiritual life nowadays is enslaved to physical conditions.

From the turbulence around us today we can see much more clearly than we might in more settled times: no movement that arises from a human spirit can ever boast of having freedom and independence on account of its own efforts.

Today we are bound to peculiarities of race and nation, dependent on economic situations and on privileges – or lack of them – for our standard and mode of life. We are influenced by powers of suggestion that originate with other people and movements. Not least of all, we are swayed by psycho-physical circumstances and by other powers at whose mercy we are often held – entities that are hostile to the Spirit. All this is in itself proof that only God and his spirit can bring freedom.

Any other freedom is a lie. There is only one way for the individual consciousness to become free from human servitude, for the nations and the masses to become free from enslavement – through the community of human spirits with God's spirit! Without this direct oneness with the whole, the individual soul remains enslaved, impoverished, confined, and limited.

The same happens to the collective soul of a family, a nation, a class, or any other social grouping. It leads deeper and deeper into ruin through the constant escalation of mutual hostility. Ultimately, complete and true liberation will be given to us only when we allow God's unity to break in and take over.

The human soul is a subordinate unit of consciousness. In spite of all ungodly association with kindred lives, it remains lonely and thwarted until it is bound to the superordinate unity of God. Fechner catches a glimpse of this highest unity of consciousness in the way people seek the truly eternal and unchangeable – the divine one who is always true to himself, who wants to be at work in us with rich variety and infinite diversity.* Without God's spirit we are changeable, inconsistent, and unstable – unbalanced and out of proportion and torn and hostile within ourselves and among ourselves. Therefore it must be an experience of absolute unity and, at the same time, absolute disparity that unites the consciousness of the soul with God.

With such an experience, eternity is born in us, and we have to consecrate our life with complete dedication. This experience becomes new every day – a continual process of renewal. As often as we lay hold of life in God, our new beginnings, deeds, and actions are stamped with the seal of eternity. Eternity penetrates time. The spirit of creation seeks out the life of the earth. Being filled with what God's eternal will decrees can never result in alienation from life. On the contrary, the spirit of life can lead only to an unfolding of powers in all the diversity of life's relationships. In our families and in our professional lives, in our work and in our whole sphere of activity, in society and in community, the creative spirit wants to shape life into a productive unity.

As Jacobi put it:

The spirit that aspires to God
Must lift itself from dust.

*Gustav Theodor Fechner, 1801–1887.

But if on earth it does not truly live,
Neither will it live in heaven.*

Whoever is gripped by God's spirit turns to his creation with all the interest that comes from God's love. Life has one goal: God's kingdom shall come to rule over all people on earth, and his will shall be done in our world just as it is in the kingdom of heaven; his name shall be honored in active recognition of his nature, and his holiness shall never be desecrated by any unholy action anywhere – rather, faith shall bring forth a love that makes God's nature recognizable through deeds.

It is through being ruled more and more by God's spirit, and in no other way, that the spirit of humankind can draw nearer to this high and final goal. Only the spirit that is ruled by God is able to see into the depths of revelation. Revealed truth was given on the basis of the prophetic word in Jesus Christ and in his apostolic church. God's spirit wants to lead the human spirit into this truth in such a way that lives become filled and determined by it.

The word of God pierces until it divides soul and spirit. Then we recognize without a shadow of doubt the unspiritual sensuality of the unredeemed life of the soul. The spirit, which thirsts for freedom, comes face to face with God's spirit. If in our inmost being, the spirit (as the breath of God) does not stand out quite sharply and clearly in contrast to the soul (as the impure stream of our blood), we remain in the torpor of spiritual death. Those emotional people who allow the unpurified life of the soul to rule them are unable to receive the divine spirit. There is no sharper

*Friedrich Heinrich Jacobi, 1743–1819.

contrast to the consistent wisdom that comes from God than the worldly wisdom of the soul, which inevitably becomes entangled in untruthfulness when it tries to bring some semblance of harmony to its contradictory aims.

The way the world situation develops during war and the aftermath of war should make it clear to the blindest of the blind that the natural life of the soul is diametrically opposed to the life that comes from God. People believe that they have all the life they need in the evolution of humankind, in patriotic efforts, or in the struggle of their class for justice, just as if they did not need God. They presume to lay claim to things that are God's alone. They even want to decide over the life and death of people and nations. They forget that it is the Lord who kills and makes alive. They scorn the fact that God is life. Yet he alone is Lord over life and death. Whoever honors him in Christ cannot kill or judge any soul. People lose all feeling for the fact that life lies in his hand – that his decree alone has the right to determine the destiny of the soul. They lose all fear of him who can destroy body and soul. They stand before his judgment without awe. They lose all reverence for God.

We know that if the sun were extinguished it would mean instantaneous death for all life on our planet. We admit that an old riverbed will not have running water anymore once the stream has been diverted. It is clear to everyone that even the best water becomes a miserable slough if it has lost connection with its source. Yet we try to silence our conscience when it cries out that every instance of irreverence deals our soul a mortal blow. We try to forget that every sin – every violation of life – brings death to the soul: it means destruction.

Unspiritual desires and the lies that go with them, hostility and the lust to kill, mammon and possessions – they all
hamper life and soul. For these are the forces that constitute
the power inimical to life – that power that has separated itself from God. The spirit is bound up with the life of the
soul: it cannot be pure if the soul does not live in God's purity, and every time the soul touches the rottenness of impurity and allows itself to be contaminated, it is not living in
God's purity. The spirit is then tainted along with the soul
and therefore is incapable of redeeming it. The spirit lives in
the soul. Everything that goes on in the soul influences the
spirit and all the movements of the spirit.

We should not imagine that the spiritual life can work in-
dependently of the world of body and soul as if it were in
splendid isolation on an island, untouched by all that the soul
experiences on the mainland. The entire atmosphere coming
from us influences our thinking. No vibration of the soul
leaves our spirit unaffected. During the second half of the
nineteenth century, the brain was thought to rule from an au-
tocratic throne over the life of the spirit. Recent research has
dethroned it. The brain does not determine the soul's character or attitude as a whole with all its most important impressions, feelings, and emotions. A sick soul can have a brain that
is completely intact. The soul can be healthy even when the
brain is diseased.

The Old Testament is right in implying that the heart, the
organ of circulation and all the structures belonging to it,
and especially the various strains of blood itself, determine
the character of the soul – the spiritual personality of a man
(Deut. 30:14–20; Prov. 15:13). Blood and heart can disperse
melancholy of soul and depression of spirit and provide the

necessary constitution and frame of mind for the highest
achievements – even abstract intellectual ones. Granted, the
brain is a vital organ for the cognitive work of comprehending, thinking, and remembering, yet it is simply one of
many tools in the life of the soul and the spirit. It is only one
of its workshops or transmitting stations, which in a special
way reflects the life of the soul and the life of the spirit; it is
their place of action.

We must not confuse the spirit with brainwork in general
or with its more specialized intellectual functions. The human spirit represents much more the "practical reason" of
the holy "thou shalt," which, according to Kant, makes its
incontestable demands with the firmness of "thou canst because thou shalt." The spirit is not to be found in any specific place in the body. The bearer of the entire soul is the
whole body. The human spirit and the basic character of the
spiritual attitude are breathed into the entire soul as its profoundest and most divine element. This spirit is able to
prove itself extremely independent of the body, and superior
to it, as soon as it has experienced a decisive liberation.

Such a liberation remains an impossibility, however, unless it embraces all areas of the soul. The human spirit is inevitably affected by any lack of freedom and any defilement
of life. The soul embraces all manifestations of life. It is the
bearer of everything that is alive in us. The soul is the total
consciousness of the individual: the combination of all the
sensual perceptions as well as the concentration of all the
higher and spiritual relationships. There can be no other life
for the soul than in this consciousness with all it encompasses. In this consciousness, all we experience with our feelings, thoughts, and will becomes reality and knowledge.

Our consciousness is that undefined place where all functions and organs become a unity. Unity of consciousness is the secret of organic life. Unity of spirit is the secret of our calling. As a living whole, we can recognize the body by the finger of the body pointing outward, the soul by the finger of the soul pointing inward, but the spirit we recognize by the finger of God pointing to his kingdom.

The life of our physical frame – that which makes it into a *living* body – is its soul. Being life, the soul encompasses our spiritual existence just as much as our physical existence from birth to death. Just as our physical frame without blood has no life, the body without the soul is dead.

The physical body that has lost its blood has given up its soul. Mephistopheles makes Faust sell his life with a drop of blood because blood is streaming and flowing life. The evil spirit wants to have the whole of a person – the life, the soul. For this reason he has to get hold of blood. "Blood is a sap of quite peculiar kind."* Therefore, according to an old version of *Faust,* just as Faust is about to use his blood-filled quill to sign the contract with the Devil, the blood congeals on his scratched hand to give a warning. It congeals in the form of the words, "Flee, O man!" This cry to take flight is forced from the blood by the imminent danger of being gripped by evil. The divine life demands more. The spirit demands that the soul resist to the utmost: "Resist to the point of shedding blood in the struggle against sin."

Resistance unto death is exceedingly rare because the blood is bound up through the soul not only with the higher, spiritual life but just as closely or even more closely with confused feelings and the basest impulses. There is

*Goethe, *Faust.*

something in the blood that weakens. Emotional people in whom the blood is not ruled by the spirit are easily led in their sympathies, becoming weak and unobjective. Because of their lack of strength for vigorous action and their limp, unsteady compliance, they are easily led astray. Once on the wrong path, each successive emotional weakness causes the soul to wither away.

Whenever the individual or the nation is roused inwardly by an appeal to the blood or by an insistence on blood ties, the enfeebled soul is swept along. That is why mass suggestion is so successful. Whether it turns the sexual life into degenerate licentiousness, incites the masses to war or civil war, or shatters business habits of trustworthiness and entices people to luxury and extravagant living – whatever it does, the surprising result is explained by the weakness of the emotionally impressionable masses. Each time that such weakness of life stirs the blood, it reveals the tyrannization of the emotional life over the nobler life of the spirit – thus revealing the ignoble servitude of our highest possession to our lower nature.

An effective renewal of life can come about only when soul and blood are gripped and penetrated by the highest life, coming from the spirit. This new life must come from the spirit because only in the spirit can freedom and clarity begin. It has to penetrate into the blood-life of the soul if it is to be a reality in life. For blood builds up the human body. Without the soul or life in the blood there is no organic connection between the spiritual life and the physical existence of the body (Rom. 8:11).

For this reason, according to ancient mysticism, everything that has gained power over my blood has gained power over me. Here is the link between the inner world and the outer world. If we want to master things we need to muster courage and take heart – to quote *Faust* again, "Blood is the sap above all saps. It can nourish dauntless courage in the heart." The soul reveals the fact that the blood is the natural element of all our urges and feelings, including – not least among them – the sensual ones. Because the blood communicates with every center of power in the body, a state of excitement in the blood is often an indication of an unspiritual life guided by natural instincts and impulses. The blood stream is the nitric acid that tests whether the spirit or the body rules. Whichever of the two comes through this test has won the battle.

However precious our blood is to us and however sacred our blood ties must be, we need a life that is guided and determined not by our senses and our blood but by the spirit. The life of the blood can be as thoroughly decadent as it can be noble. It bears within it the seeds of corruption. Everyone who builds on the blood is building on shifting sand. Blood is unstable and perishable. Only the spirit remains alive. The storm of the spirit is stronger than any other wind. The life of the spirit alone stands firm when all other life is doomed to destruction.

In these critical times we need more than ever a testimony to the truth that God has given an eternal life – one that cannot ebb away with the blood because it is God's life and therefore independent of the blood and the senses. According to the true testimony of the spirit, this life is in the Son. It comes to us through the Holy Spirit. It gives our spirit testimony of another homeland, different from the land of our blood. It makes us sons and daughters of God so truly that we can represent no other interests save those of his heart and his kingdom. The spirit leads us to a people quite different from the people of our blood. God's eternal life unites us with the people of God whose bond is not one of blood but of the Holy Spirit.

Only those who are prepared to risk life and blood can find this kingdom of the spirit, for others can and will not tolerate the attempts of this people to conquer the land. The path this people treads is strewn with the dead. By what he does to God's people, the god of this world reveals himself as the murderer from the beginning. The spirit of Jesus Christ has never allowed his church to kill even one single person. His people, however, have continually been murdered just as Jesus himself was brought to execution by the best state (from the military and judicial point of view) and by the most outstanding nation (from a religious and institutional point of view), yes, even by the majority vote of those of his own blood.

Today also, people and nations, the state, and the institutional church will not tolerate witnesses to divine truth. It is not only Israel that cries out, "Away with him!" Voltaire's *Écrasez l'infâme* is the cry of the West. Whoever wants to represent the witness of Jesus in word and deed must be ready for death anywhere. The reason is clear: any witness to the truth must tear down the disguises that have been put in place to conceal the workings of the prevailing powers.

Jesus brought a revelation that destroys all delusions. It exposes the true state of the world and its kingdoms, its principalities, its god and spirit, as well as the true state of every single human being. It is only under his influence that

we become free of the false idea that life consists in politics
and economics, in power and property, in violence and the
struggle for existence, in eating and drinking, in clothing
and shelter, in pleasure and variety, in honor and reputation.
The body is more than clothing. The soul is life and therefore more than food. The kingdom of God is more than all
the kingdoms of this world. The spirit is more than the soul.
What does it profit us to gain the whole world if we forfeit
our life?

Life during the last war [World War I] and its aftermath
of escalating need and distress freed many from a narrow-
minded, bourgeois misconception: that the creature comforts
of a pampered mode of life (faster transport and communication and better incomes) are necessities of life. Moreover,
many consciences have been awakened from their torpid
sleep and kept awake as if by a constant thunderstorm, real-
izing that in the face of the increasing distress everywhere
they had no right to hold on to a privileged way of life. They
have realized that they must come out of their castles and
villas in order to search out and bring in those who have become destitute in the storm, without work or home.

Yet a life of true community with God encompasses the
inmost fortification of our stronghold as well as the outer
fortifications. When a soul has been fully awakened to the
kingdom of God, the spirit who rules from that kingdom
will not only tackle its current mode of existence, but shape
it according to his will, down to the details. His goal is
brotherly and sisterly love. This transformation will be so
thorough that very few people can even imagine it.

However, before we can think of a new form for our outward existence, body and soul must be taken possession of

by God. They must be changed to accord with his image. We have experienced in the history of our times how impossible it is to reconstruct an outer existence and build it up when inner strength has gone into a decline. It is not only in the Russia and in the Austria of pre-World War times that we can see how little even such great empires signify when their inner character begins to break up. What is a kingdom that is divided in itself? "What does it profit a man to gain the whole world and yet suffer harm to his soul?"

Nothing is more necessary than an inmost renewal of life. In this renewal our destiny, independent of all alien influences, shall unfold like a seed growing into a strong, firm tree, allowing our soul and its whole sphere of activity to become as it is intended. It is not in ourselves that we find the strength, inner peace, and freedom for the growth of this true and genuine life. Still less do these prevail in the world around us. Only the truly living one can give them to us. Only he brings life, its fulfillment, and with it the active inner peace of his works. Only when he has become the loving, caring overseer of our soul can it find the strength it needs for a new, free, and active life. Only he leads to a life in which the soul, freed from turning around itself and circling around false planets, can live and work from the center of life.

This life is God and his rulership. The light of the life given in Christ shines more brightly on our weak, selfish existence than the sun into our night. And just as the sun gives life and nourishment to this planet, Jesus alone gives his us the strength and nourishment to begin a real life and build that up in place of our previous sham existence. Jesus is the bread of life for which we hunger. He has the water of life for which we thirst. His life, which far exceeds all other possible ways of living, merits our dismissing once and for all our own weak, selfish life and all ideals restricted and determined by our blood. We must turn away from all the will-o'-the-wisps that flit around churchyards. We must hold his burning light firmly in the hands of our heart because he wants to bring life into every grave. Nothing should be in our hands but his radiant life, because it alone is victorious over all the worlds of death.

There is a legend about a soldier who for a long time seemed to seek nothing but murderous battle and vainglory. He devoted himself wholeheartedly to war, and even when he joined a crusade, vainglory seemed to be all he looked for. It so happened that he was the first to scale the walls of Jerusalem. He had the privilege of being the first to light his candle at the altar of the Holy Sepulcher.

This flame transformed his life, though. He forsook the princedom that beckoned him. He took the candle. It became everything to him. He rode and traveled roundabout ways to bring this flame to his people without letting it go out. He was looked upon by many as a madman, for he held the burning light in his hands wherever he went, never taking his eyes off it. In the depths of loneliness, fallen upon by thieves, in want and exposed to storms, in hunger and privation and mocked at by the crowds, he concentrated on one thing: shielding the flame. From then on he could never have another thought but to protect each tiny flame of holiness. His life became a vigorous light of love that spent itself for others.*

*Selma Lagerlöf, *The Sacred Flame.*

Whoever wants to protect the flame of God's love and guard the light of life will have to show the same attitude. Once we have kindled our life from the flame of the crucified one, his spirit with all its powers expresses itself in an undreamed-of way. We could never learn it elsewhere. It is the torch of his spirit that shows the way then. If we want to reach the goal of our destiny we can only do it by letting his divine love flood us with its radiance.

Wherever God's fire is kept burning in our hearts, it means life for the whole world. It stands as a light on a candlestick set up for everyone. It represents the complete community of faith that will bring light to the whole world as the city on the hill. Its innermost life gathers all members around the carefully protected central flame, as around a bonfire. Only those who protect this grail of the church know what wealth of life God sends out into all lands from his city.

Once we have come to recognize God as the only element of true life, all inner powers of the soul seek to unfold in order to come fully and completely into action, concentrated on him. The soul that is filled with God embraces the whole of life with all its activities, inner and outer, intellectual and physical. In order to bring life completely under the authority of God's vital power, its inner aspect must be brought under his influence first of all. The power of infinite life sinks its roots into the innermost depths of the soul before it has a strong and active influence on external life. The confession "Thou givest my soul great strength" can be made truthfully only when this strength has begun to reign in our inner being.

The inmost heart of the believing church, in which God dwells, is like a well-watered garden, full of quiet, peace, and security. Enemies cannot find the way in. A living wall of tall trees rooted in fertile ground protects it from the storms raging outside. The noise of the world outside does not penetrate into the secluded center of this garden, in which God's heart has its dwelling. And yet the gates of the garden stay wide open so that all that is living can go in. They stay open because all the powers and capabilities of the soul are sent out to share in the world's distress and to bring help wherever possible.

When we speak of the life of the soul, we usually think only of the innermost part of a believing spirit. But we have to remember that the soul embraces the whole of life. That is why the apostles of old exhorted the believers to become new in mind and spirit. What the believer must do, therefore, is search his innermost being, because his life in Christ shall be hidden in God, so that from the bottom of his heart he can say, "I live, yet now it is no longer I but Christ who lives in me." The spirit is our inmost treasure. When it is illuminated by God's spirit, the Holy Spirit, our own spirit will be able to recognize what is in us. When it is led by the spirit of Jesus Christ, our spirit can become a lamp of God that searches the innermost reaches of the soul by lighting them up.

By and large, the heart embraces the inner aspect of life. Therefore we find the manifestations of life in the heart – our thinking, feeling, and willing, our disposition and the character of our heart – ascribed to the soul as well. For the soul by its very nature includes the heart as the inner core of life. We can imagine life as concentric circles of different colors superimposed on each other and enclosing each other. Our external, material body, part of nature as a whole, forms a comprehensive gray circle. A blue circle denoting the organic life we have in common with plants is just as big. The third circle, a red one, has the same dimensions and stands for the life of the soul in the blood, which, as a human person, embraces the whole consciousness. This last circle of life is characteristic of the animal kingdom as well.

With the smaller circles it is different. In contrast to the large perimeter three times covered, the heart forms a smaller concentric circle, perhaps best indicated by fiery coloring. This is made up of the life of inner feelings and thoughts and activities of the will, that is, the deeper part of a character. This alone is enough to distinguish us from all other living creatures. The spirit, however, forms the center that dominates the whole. It is a secluded, inner circle, which in view of our destiny should be colored white. This spirit is given solely to humankind. Schiller refers to this when he says: "Once I have searched the core of man, I know what he wants and what he is doing." It is this core that is all important. God's spirit wants to make his dwelling among us, beginning in our spirit.

The higher will of the soul is spirit. The spirit is the active and creative genius. The spirit is reason working constructively to meet the demands made by religion, ethics, and society. It is the spirit that directly perceives and experiences what is divine in the human heart. The soul on the other hand gets its feeling for life more through what is physical and determined by the blood. It includes all desires and longings and also what is purely receptive. The whole reception of all the outer stimulations of life takes place in the soul. It remains more sensual, more closely related to the body, more strongly rooted in the body, and more firmly bound to it than the spirit. The spirit lives in the activity of the highest and freest relationships and aims of the will. It dwells in the most royal of all the chambers of the consciousness. For the spirit, the highest destiny will be infused with the Holy Spirit.

The consciousness of the soul is a living mirror of all the relationships into which the life of humankind is woven. The influence of these relationships varies greatly according to their intensity. It is in the life of the soul that the decision is made as to which feelings, desires, ideals, and thoughts we allow to cross the threshold of our innermost being.

As long as the feelings of the soul in the blood (which work in darkness) are controlled by the power of the spirit ruling in our hearts, they cannot grow into base intentions or evil deeds. Yet we see in all the excitement of our times how these feelings wait for a moment when the image of God and his influence grow weaker in us. From that moment on, the lusts and false ideals of the blood (allied to other powers of darkness) can cross the threshold of our heart. They become the will to do evil, and then they unite in evil action. Sin has come. "Lust when it has conceived gives birth to sin; and sin when it is full-grown brings forth death."

Joyless lust for murder and hate, poisonous readiness to accuse one's opponents and use lies to disparage them, loveless joy in property and other personal privileges, impure and unspiritual lusts of the body – all these lie in wait for the will with insatiable greed. They have to capture the will with the dazzling temptations offered by stolen and pseudo-spiritual virtues before they can work their evil.

The soul is able to ward off these temptations, but only when the will that is good has found strength to resist, coming from a firm foothold. It finds this foothold when the content of the soul, what fills the soul, is clearly and definitely of the Holy Spirit. The will can reject all the enticements of seductive mental images; it can overcome all the temptations of murky ideals and aims; but it can do this only when –through being constantly reminded by the Holy Spirit – the soul's consciousness is firmly and clearly ruled by the unity that comes from the heart of God, by the unity of all the thoughts of his love, by the unity of all the pictures of his future kingdom and its powers, and by the image of Jesus with all his words and deeds. "Strength of character depends on this, that a definite unity of images and ideas continually occupies the conscious mind, weakening any opposing images and not allowing them to enter."* If the seductive powers of other aspirations are not to gain admittance and rule over our will, then the innermost chamber of our soul must always be filled with the spirit of Jesus Christ. The chamber where our spirit is enthroned must always be filled with all his thoughts and with his will; that is, with every impulse of his heart.

Satan, the archenemy of our soul, always has a powerful band of accomplices at the ready to shatter and destroy it. But in the hush of night God speaks clearly and unmistakably to the soul to draw it away from destruction and make it his follower. He awakens our spirit and shows us the way

*Johann Friedrich Herbart, 1776–1841.

to life. He wants to fill our awakened soul with his peace so that dark powers have no room. When the soul cries out for God, driven by the distress of our time, it will be led to the goal – to the church and to the kingdom – if by the will it is lifted up to Jesus Christ and stays concentrated on him alone.

THE CONSCIENCE
AND ITS WITNESS

L ife resists everything that threatens to destroy or kill it. It tries to build up its strength. It protects itself instinctively against all the influences of death and everything hostile and harmful. Only in a life that is going to rack and ruin – in one that has already come under the power of death – do the instincts fail and allow poisons to come in and destroy it. Every organism endowed with a soul tries to ward off what is harmful to body and soul.

The innermost part of the soul – the spirit – has also an instinct for life. This is the conscience. As a first sign of inner life, it has become a watcher at the threshold. It is the quiet, impersonal confidant of the human spirit. "For no one knows what is in anyone except the spirit itself, which is within" (1 Cor. 2:11). The conscience is one of the most primeval stirrings of life. The human spirit, as the profoundest part of us, has to represent our innermost calling. The most necessary tool for this is the conscience, an instrument that warns, rouses, and commands.

The conscience is the spirit's sensitive organ of response. Its task is to warn the character against degeneration and destruction. It is there to preserve moral order. The conscience has to show the character where it can find healing, strengthening, and the direction in life it is meant to take. Every time the soul is deeply wounded, the conscience makes us painfully aware of it. It is a warning bell that sounds every time the spiritual life falls sick. Above all, it gives warning of the deadly misery of isolation, when the soul has separated itself from the core of life, from the destiny of its being – when it has separated itself from God. Therefore with all the urgency of love, it demands reconciliation with God himself and, as part of that, a uniting with all people. For unity is the hallmark of life. Unity finds complete fulfillment in God and his kingdom.

The conscience in each individual arouses a longing to come out of all constraint and isolation and to have community with the highest consciousness, the all-embracing consciousness of God. As a result there will be a unanimous accord and unity of life with all who believe in God. This urge toward God and his community of life and faith accords with the nature of the human spirit as it was originally. Leibnitz described God as the only object directly perceived by the soul that can be distinguished from the soul itself.* God is in direct living contact with the soul and demands absolute love and community.

The conscience awakens a direct consciousness of good and evil – a knowledge of what promotes life and what destroys it. As such, it can never be separated from the spirit's direct consciousness of God. It plays a part whenever the certainty of an absolute "thou shalt" or "thou shalt not" penetrates the consciousness. In the absoluteness of "thou shalt," God works directly on us. Our conscience urges us to stand by our consciousness of God. It demands obedience to him. With every warning it gives, the conscience tries to help our consciousness of God toward free and willing obedience in faith.

*Gottfried Wilhelm von Leibnitz, 1646–1716.

It is God who wants to determine our life and lay obligations upon it through the conscience. The conscience has been compared to a mountain range along which God's thunder echoes a millionfold. The further away the receiving heart is from the one who calls, the weaker will be the echo. The nearer we are when we receive the call of God, the more powerfully will our conscience be struck and impressed. There is always, however, a necessary distance between God's truth and our response. The conscience drives the anxious, hesitating heart nearer and nearer to the thunderous judgment of evil and the lightning-lit revelation of good. And yet at the same time it keeps us at a respectful distance. There can be no echo if there is no distance at all from the mountain wall.

"No one is good," Jesus tells us, "save God alone" (Matt. 19:15). One alone is truly good. Those who blasphemously identify themselves with him cannot hear the voice of God. If in the soul there is something of the breath of this one and only being who alone is good, then even in depraved and irreverent souls there will be a live witness. This witness will demand a distance and yet press closer because it judges evil and engenders good. It is the conscience of the human spirit. When we do evil, it warns and insists; it smites and punishes. It makes clear to us how far we are from God. But it does still more. Even though there may be nothing good about us, this witness lives in our souls to make it possible for us to recognize good as good, to assure us that God is the only source of good, and to urge us on toward it.

Even where consciousness of guilt seems to have died out, we cannot feel at home in our selfish existence. We are well aware that we lack inner unity and the community that takes shape as a result. Even the hardest heart yearns for this. We were created for community. Our conscience fights against things being turned so upside down that life is destroyed by selfish isolation. It protests against every attempt to sever the living cohesion of things. Whenever a thread of life is broken, the conscience shows that it is wounded. Every time our inner being is divided and, just as much, every time the community that must come to outward expression is disrupted, the conscience gives a warning – life is being threatened by destruction. To the conscience, disharmony seems terrifying and deadly because the very nature of the soul demands unity of life.

Any separation from God is bound to lead the human spirit to a deadly division within itself and cold estrangement from others. When the conscience makes us aware of the urge toward God hidden within us, a conflict arises between the true calling of the ego and its actual condition. Every time we resist this urge and act against it, our conscience blames no one but us.

Julius Müller calls the conscience, even when it is utterly ruined, the divine bond that ties the created spirit to its origin.* It is the conscience that shows us we belong to the people of God, although we are degenerate and depraved members. It is the longing for God that rouses opposition to evil. This longing is for community in his kingdom of active love, brought about by him alone. It opposes the divisive power of the kingdom of mammon with its lies, murder, and impurity. The conscience makes us think about ourselves and our depraved condition and, at the same time, about the

*Julius Müller, 1801–1878.

revelation of the higher truth of our original nature, our true nature. It shows at the same time our wretchedness and our greatness.

The conscience is an inextinguishable part of human consciousness. As such, it gives bold witness to the fact that the origin of the human spirit is noble and divine. It never lets us quite forget that as humans we have been called to be images of God, however weather-beaten our spiritual coat of arms, however deeply rusted, however thickly over-grown with moss. Even in the most erring offshoots of the human race, the memory of this image is never so irretriev-ably lost that it cannot be brought back to the light once more through God's intervention.

For this reason Paul, the apostle of Jesus Christ, testifies expressly that even peoples estranged from God have a con-science. Paul is so deeply convinced of the divine origin of all living souls that he sees the works of the law written in the hearts of so-called heathen. In everything they experience and undertake, their conscience too gives witness through the conflicting thoughts that accuse or excuse them.

After all, the living book of God's creation lies open for all to see; it points constantly to the divine calling for which we were placed in nature. Nature is a continual admonition to us, for nowhere has God's creation departed so far from its origin and primeval purpose as in the human race. This is made obvious by the history of the human conscience.

Human beings were called to God's love. But once they gave themselves to murder and rebellion and refused to let themselves be judged and ruled by God's spirit, the pure, free spirit gave up pleading with them (Gen. 6:3–13). He no longer even wanted to plead with them. Violence presupposes a lack of freedom. Therefore God sent man the law and conceded him the death penalty, at first in the form of the appointed blood-for-blood revenge: an eye for an eye! A tooth for a tooth! "Whoever sheds the blood of man, by man again shall his blood be shed" (Gen. 9:6).

Again, in their servile spirit, the children of those who were meant to be God's people wanted a human king instead of God's rulership, instead of his dominion. God in his wrath thus gave them a completely human authority to enforce severe punishment for murder and acts of wickedness (1 Sam. 8). Today we have long forgotten what we have lost through these historical facts. Yet these measures to check still worse instances of evil will remain as long as men refuse to let God's spirit judge and rule.

The inner acquiescence of the conscience can be seen in our attitude to legal authority. For the sake of the conscience, everyone must still be subject to legal authority as to an appointed servant of God. For this authority judges and punishes evil as the conscience demands. Yet as soon as the conscience is roused through God's spirit, it demands – even in the face of authority – that we should obey God rather than people. God's kingdom claims recognition over and above all the kingdoms of this world. However, there is a prerequisite for this all-inclusive demand of God and his spirit. It is fulfilled only when this spirit who rules in God's kingdom really and truly rules over us, when he can actually plead with us and determine our whole life in an objective way according to God's kingdom.

Through the judgment and power of governmental authority, the conscience is punished and sharpened. Through God's kingdom and his spirit, it is set free and fulfilled. It looks everywhere for the source of the guilt that separated us from the rulership of God. In everything, the conscience wants to become clear in its judgment over the boundary between good and evil, because evil has separated us from God. Evil is its enemy. It sees the enemy everywhere – waiting to the right and to the left, besetting us behind and before. The most dangerous outpost of all is in our heart. The evil that surrounds and pervades our life is more than our enemy. It is God's enemy.

Murder, deceit, lust, and possessiveness – these are the faces of evil. Jesus called the evil spirit the "murderer from the beginning" and "father of lies," and he called his subordinate spirits impure spirits. Finally he has confronted us with a decision: "You cannot serve God and mammon." God's rule is incompatible with killing, with lying, with sexual immorality, and most of all with the rule of property. Therefore God's kingdom is diametrically opposed to the powers of death and sin. This is true not only for personal life but also for human society in general, which may try to subjugate evil and yet is mired in mammon and property: it cannot cut itself loose from lying and impurity, and is therefore driven to greater evil – even to mass murder.

Detection of the enemy, however, achieves nothing more than a reconnaissance before the battle. Even the progress of the battle, even the annihilation of the enemy does not mean that the victory is consummated. It is only positive reconstruction that gives triumph its value. Therefore the con-

science longs for vigorous work at what is truly good in order to be able to celebrate victory over evil.

The life of Jesus had nothing to do with killing and harm-
ing others, with untruthfulness and impurity, or any influence of mammon or property. And Jesus went even further:
in dying he defeated this hostile power in its home territory
and shattered every weapon of the enemy. But he did still
more. He brought the kingdom of God down to the earth;
he roused body and soul from death; he rose as the living
one; and through his spirit he laid the foundation for a kingdom of complete unity for everything in heaven and on
earth. He broke down the barriers between nations, and he
created the unity of the body of his church as his second incarnation. This new unity and bodily reality of Jesus lives on
our earth and in our human race.

We are called to this way as soon as we accept the call.
When through Christ and his spirit we believe in the unity
of God as the one and only good, when we live in faith out
of his strength, we lay aside everything that is opposed to
perfect love. We fight it to the death on every front; we live
as believers in the church of full community, ambassadors of
God's kingdom, representing Jesus Christ and commissioned by him. In this fight for the recognition of God's rule,
in representing the final kingdom in opposition to all governmental authorities and powers of the kingdoms of this
age, the conscience is the quiet ally of the Holy Spirit.

The conscience is that faculty of sensitivity in our inner
being which responds with pleasure to every good deed and
with displeasure to every evil deed. It exposes evil as alien
and hostile to our nature as it originally was, and as it is ulti-

mately intended to be. Therefore no quasi-superior point of
view and no knowledge that sets itself up as progressive can
reconcile it to evil. As soon as God's spirit takes possession of
the human spirit to make a common witness, the conscience
develops a resolute firmness. It revolts with a revulsion that
becomes almost unbearable every time love is wounded, every time love's obligations are neglected, every time love's
justice is clouded, every time love's truth is betrayed, and
God's kingdom misrepresented.

Whenever human self-preservation seeks an advantage, a
pleasure, or an influence that is contrary to the pure, absolute, and all-embracing love of Jesus Christ, the conscience –
being now an instrument of the Holy Spirit – raises its voice
in sharp protest in the name of the sovereign God and his
absolute rule. With just as much intensity, it furthers every
fulfillment of justice and social obligation, every disinter-
ested act of devoted love, and every brotherly and sisterly
uniting in full community.

The impulse of joyful agreement and inner satisfaction in
our conscience when we have acted rightly in the works of
love (at least as far as motive and aim are concerned) implies
an assessment of values. In the same way, when evil and godlessness gain the upper hand in our life, the conscience experiences qualms of shame, disquiet, and silent self-accusation.
These challenge us to evaluate our actions.

The conscience is the organ constantly at work evaluating
and passing judgment. It evaluates by feeling. It has joy in
what is good, for what is good is also just. It has joy in love,
for love is also pure, and in genuine unity and community. It
feels pain and revulsion against evil, for evil is injustice. Its

pain over all that denies love; that is, everything that destroys community, everything selfish, impure, ungenuine, and untrue.

The conscience speaks as the divine voice within us. It strives to bring home to us what we are (although we should be different), what we are not (although we ought to know how we should be), what human society is like without community, and what the nations are like without the unity of the kingdom of God. The more the heart is touched by God's holy nature, the more clearly does the conscience indicate what the church of God is, and the more clearly does it also point out how, from the basis of this church, the believer should represent love, unity, peace, and justice, all of which bear fruit in community.

When we examine ourselves in the light of the destiny God has ordained for us, we become aware of the sharp contrast between what we should be and what we are. The conscience belongs to human consciousness and yet represents a "thou shalt" that is quite different. The conscience is a decidedly subjective feeling. Yet it is based on and aims at an absolutely objective "thou shalt." Only when the demands of the conscience agree with the objective "thou shalt," do subjective impressions gain weight and meaning.

The conscience must represent an objective power that wants to take possession of us from within. It needs the Holy Spirit because within itself it does not have the power to rise above all that we are subjectively capable of. Without God's spirit it is unable to represent clearly the cause it wants to serve. And yet in remotest paganism also, the conscience remains active even though, without the spirit of the cause, its

accusations and demands are distinguished more by unbridled ferocity than by shining clarity. Like the Furies of pagan mythology, it pursues those who flee and seizes those
who resist, so that even such masters of evil as the emperor
Nero must undergo tortures of conscience.

The comparison of the conscience with the Furies, those
relentless spirits of doom and vengeance in ancient history, is
all the closer because the Furies served just as much to protect the good and pure as to atone for crime. They cannot
point anywhere to God's rulership because they know nothing of his Holy Spirit. They represent the conscience that is
not yet illuminated by Christ, that does indeed know of
good and evil but misses the way to the goal. They are
handmaids of the holy order of natural life, which they strive
to represent. Without it, the life that lives and moves in our
blood inevitably destroys itself.

The Furies are keen-sighted huntresses armed with whips
and spears, bows and arrows. Shrouded in mist, they lie in
wait for evildoers, ready to distract their senses, derange
their spirits and suck their blood. For they too represent the
old order – "blood for blood." Thus they correspond to the
merciless authority of the criminal court, about which God
spoke his awful word after the flood, when his spirit no
longer wanted to plead with a perverse people: "I will demand your lifeblood. Whoever sheds the blood of man, by
man again shall his blood be shed; for God made man in his
own image" (Gen. 9:5–6).

Throughout all ages, sin against the blood of a soul endowed with the breath of God has struck the conscience as
the gravest crime, the capital offense against God and his order. Therefore avenging it is seen as the first duty of human

authority. The avenging authority (representing human order) and also the wild raging of the Furies (representing the unredeemed conscience) are far removed from the spirit of the heart of God, and nothing can be found in them that reveals anything of the gospel of Jesus Christ. Yet hidden within them lies a corrective justice, a justice of wrath. It is the wrath of God, which through his judgment wants to make us ready for the perfect justice of love.

In this way the old Furies, as handmaids of punitive justice and as executioners of necessary law, are the strictest avengers of evil. But they are more. Like the authority of the state, they are intended to uphold and protect upright and law-abiding hearts. They hold their threatening snakebites in readiness for evildoers, but the good they meet with friendly eyes, bestowing their blessings as goddesses of the earth.

The Furies are more tormenting than any judicial authorities can ever be, for they are an objective personification of the conscience that has not yet been gripped by the gospel of perfect love. They symbolize the same punishment of conscience that Pestalozzi describes so vividly when his character Hans Wüst rolls on the floor in torment over his perjury – howling like a dog whose entrails are torn.* When Hans tears his hair out and draws his own blood with his fists, the cry is wrung out of him: "Satan, cursed Satan, has me in his clutches!" Abuse, shame, and imprisonment are nothing to him compared with the horror, the despair, and the fear that God might never be merciful to him again in all eternity. Here, with the eyes of the modern world, we see the Furies come to life again as agony of conscience.

*Johann Heinrich Pestalozzi, 1746–1827.

The same agony of conscience made Luther cry out, "Oh, my sins, my sins, my sins!" It is the same indescribable torture about which he said:

> I too know someone who declares he has often suffered this punishment. True, it did not last long, but it was so severe and so hellish that no tongue can tell of its severity, no pen can describe it, nor can anyone believe it who has not experienced it. If it had reached its peak or continued for half an hour longer – yes, for only a tenth of an hour longer – he would have been utterly destroyed and all his bones burned to ashes. Here God appears, mighty in his wrath, and all creation too, so no one knows where to turn. There is no comfort and everything is full of accusations.

Still at that time, Luther's conscience stood in the midst of this deadly fear of wrath and punishment, outside the gate and outside the grace of God, and yet he pursued the positive goal of divine justice. The conscience is more than a protection for what is good, which has to be guarded from evil. It is more than the terrifying discovery that there is nothing really good in us. It is more than the punishment of evil through the justice of God. Rather, through the devastating judgment of evil, the conscience must prepare our inner vision for the restoration of what is good. When the conscience is gripped and illuminated by the spirit of God, it must prepare the way for faith and rebirth through deep repentance and a complete change of heart. The darkened inner eye must become like the sun so that it can see the kingdom of God. The conscience that is breaking down under wrath must be led to justice – making it possible for a new life of active love to arise from faith.

As part of the human spirit, the conscience can never reveal the kingdom of God of its own accord. It can only strengthen the echo when the call to repentance reaches the heart – a call from God, piercing the heart and directing it to the kingdom of God. The call to life can come only from the origin of life, from God's heart. God's heart revealed itself in the voices of his prophets. In Jesus Christ it reached man as fullness of beauty, grace, and truth. The conscience is a God-created organ that is part of the life of the human soul, but it can do no more than answer his call as a call from the Holy Spirit. What it can do from its seat in the human spirit is to accept, affirm, and represent the demands made by God, that is, by the divine life of Jesus.

The divine spirit wants to penetrate and rule over all areas of life. Consequently, the awakened conscience cannot be restricted just to the area of morals. As the aesthetic conscience, it promotes joy in what is beautiful, edifying, and pure. From deep within, it cleanses our taste – also as regards the creation of art – from filth and ugliness, from artificiality and ungenuineness. As an intellectual conscience, it is the instinct for honesty and integrity; it has an understanding for what must be acknowledged as the truth, and expresses it in accordance with the facts. As a social conscience, it demands the dedication of the whole of our life, with all our faculties and possessions, to the service of love – to brotherliness, to justice, and to full community with the poor and oppressed. As a spiritual conscience, it desires all this for the sake of God's truth, for his love and justice – that is, for the supreme demand of unity with God himself and unity with his absolute sovereignty. Everywhere, the conscience is revealed as the heart's will for truth, justice, and unity. In everything, it demands obedience in the face of the objective absolute. It is the absolute will of God that challenges the conscience to let him become acknowledged as lord over all that belongs to life on earth.

Jesus Christ alone, in accord with the divine word of the Jewish prophets, proclaimed that the will of God's love is turned toward the earth and its peoples. He alone has brought the authority and reality of his kingdom to the earth.

The social yearning for brotherly justice and the longing for peace (which is born of active love for the enemy) are possible nowhere but on the ground of Christ, or under his influence and direction. This is why some individualistic anarchists argue that communism and atheistic socialism are secularized expressions of Christianity. And indeed, the assertion would not be thinkable without Christianity's love for one's neighbor, equality of birth, faith in the future as faith in a kingdom of peace and justice, and a social conscience awake to the stirrings of the divine.

When the conscience has found God's justice in Christ, it recognizes human injustice as the opposite of his love and of his aliveness. God's justice, which comes to expression in Jesus, is greater than the justice of the best human court, system, or code; it is greater than the religious and social justice of theologians and moralists. Like salt, like a light, like a tree, it is a real and living power of radiant warmth, strength, and protection – the real power of life in all its fullness. Therefore the life that God's justice gives birth to as perfect love must be completely different from the life born of any other justice, however socially admirable.

Even the social conscience of the believer does not exhaust the truth of this life (although this truth remains the most important expression of the social conscience). Christianity has shown that honesty with oneself is the most basic prerequisite for a Christian life. Even its bitterest opponents have to admit that the inner history of Christianity has produced an increasing exactness in the conception of truth. They can see that the sensitivity of the Christian conscience has been transferred to the scientific conscience, at times producing the finest intellectual integrity. The continual sharpening of the instinct of truthfulness has meant such a growth in scholarly exactness that Friedrich Nietzsche had to admit: "Conscientiousness in small things – the self-control of the religious person – was a preparatory school for the scientific or scholarly character and, above all, for the attitude in which we can treat a problem seriously without taking into consideration how it affects us personally."

The intellectual conscience of the believer also does not exhaust the truth of life. The conscience in Christ recognizes that what is untrue is the opposite of what is alive and essential to life. Truth means more than the intellect being indisputably right. Truth must seize onto the ultimate reality of life in all that is genuine and essential to it, all that is unadulterated and clear, all that has effective strength and power. Consequently truth, in unity with justice, must show itself as the very marrow of life, as vital energy and courage, as a productive joy in creative work, and as the power of love. Truth, as love, is master of the essential nature of things.

The activity of the conscience is not exhausted by the condemnation of what is evil, unlovely, and wrong. It works toward the acceptance of all the life-energies of love, for they are the very core of life. Just as love itself never ends, so the conscience that works for love can never come to the end of its activity. The conscience can never put a stop to its working. Even though it may not always have to suffer to the same degree from the consciousness of what is evil, ugly, and untrue, and even though there may be nowhere any good in need of its protection, the work of the conscience will never come to an end.

A good conscience is more than just a conscience that is not bad. It is not only a witness that condemns or approves but, above all else, a voice that impels us to loving dedication. We can see it perfected in the apostle Paul, when his heart beat for his people and demanded a readiness for the ultimate sacrifice. A good conscience never waits in passive silence; it always longs for action and drives toward it. It impels the will toward a truly loving life – ultimately, toward God and his kingdom.

Something of the demands made by the active conscience can be traced in all pagan peoples. Four centuries before Christ, Socrates was not only saved from making false steps by his inner voice, but he was also driven to constructive action. Above all, he was led to the search for truth through inquiry and discussion with all and sundry. Yet his inner voice was only the instinct of his soul, as unclear as it was strong, and just this inner voice gives proof that the human conscience, when it is not renewed by the spirit of God, remains clouded in confusion in spite of strenuous efforts to find the truth. The fact that Socrates called this inner voice a demon points much more to the dark rays of the other world than to the bright revelation of truth in the pure and perfect love of God's righteousness. It is dangerous and misleading to think, as many do, with the great Christian poet Dante: "A conscience stands beside me, pure and true, an authority in whom I trust completely and without reserve."

To regard one's conscience as an infallible authority is always questionable, to say the least. In and of itself, it cannot ever become pure and incorruptible, because it continues to have a part in every degradation of the soul. It is rather like a ship's pilot who has lost his bearings because he has sailed into unfamiliar waters. Whether he admits his own helplessness with honesty and shame or whether he steers the ship this way and that with apparent confidence, he cannot do what he is meant to do until he has found his way back to his own familiar waters. The conscience would naturally always like to steer the right course. But it has lost its way. It longs for the home port, but thick fog has clouded its vision. The land has disappeared into the distance as if forever – the land of clarity. The conscience asks the same alarmed question again and again: "My poor, erring soul, will you ever find the way home? How far must you go before you are given a guiding light?"

But just when danger becomes obvious – when immediate disaster threatens because the head is perplexed and the heart faint, when visibility is poor, destructive icebergs or rocks loom ahead, or collision with others whose course is just as erratic seem imminent – just when there is utmost need, the conscience becomes disquieted and is nearest to fulfilling its task. Therefore a bad conscience – a conscience full of sin, an evil conscience – is all that many people are aware of. This fact remains, and it must be recognized again

and again in all the confusion today: the witness of the conscience shows itself most sharply of all in the face of guilt
and threatening destruction.

The heart is like a secret chamber of justice in which the
conscience, as the judge within, challenges all that
takes place. A shadow of God's will remains printed, as it
were, in the heart, even if it is only scarcely visible. The judge
within has to pass a verdict in accordance with these faint
lines. He is busy day and night. He seeks judgment and
atonement uninterruptedly. And yet one thing is always
clear – the conscience does not give atonement. We ourselves cannot still our conscience. Consequently it testifies
with unquestionable authority to the God-fearing of all ages:
burnt offerings, sacrifices of things and even sacrifice of life,
make no one perfect.

Splendid ceremonies and symbols of the utmost devotion mean nothing to a tortured and burning conscience
unless the source of its distress is removed. In spite of the
most earnest piety or the most genuine idealism, the conscience never ceases to condemn sin in all its heaviness as sin,
which of itself it can never expiate. Even if we sacrifice our
very lives for our ideals, the conscience still speaks to us of
sin whenever we do something in the course of our sacrifice
that offends God's truth and purity; that is, his unity and
love.

Only through the knowledge of good and evil can this
unremitting accusation of sin arise. This knowledge became
part of the first man when he joined forces with sin. Like the
child today, he had no awareness of a conscience in this
sense, that is, in the sense of a bad conscience. Like every

true child, he knew nothing about evil. In his innocence he was unable to discriminate or choose between good and evil. For it is only possible to "discern" spiritual powers, good or evil, by becoming one with them in will and deed.

It is true that the first man, like a child, knew that he had to do the will of God. Yet he knew as little as any child to what extent God's will stands in opposition to evil. Without a doubt, he had the deep urge, as does every childlike soul, to do the will of him who gave him life and breath. This urge was in no way strengthened when the utterly new and completely different knowledge of good and evil came to him as a bad conscience about sin. It could only hinder and paralyze this basic yearning of life.

Man became a coward and a weakling. His conscience realized the evil he had done, but he was held captive and powerless. He still had a little will left, but this will had become sick and paralyzed through choosing evil. He could of himself no longer do good. His conscience recognized good, but it did not lead him to God; on the contrary, it drove him to hide in shame and fear.

How could it be otherwise? A defiled conscience does not have within it the power to purify itself. The knowledge of evil has plunged it into derangement and confusion, and it sees no way out. It cannot achieve its goal until rebellious humankind has returned to the life that it has deserted – a life in God. God must be served again with a free will and a clear conscience. Freedom and purity are to be found nowhere except in God. They are not to be found among people. Diametrically opposed to things as they are, they depend on a break with all existing conditions, and a turning to the life of God's coming kingdom. It is only here that the conscience can be released from its association with evil. Only here can community with God be found – a complete transformation of the inner and outer life to correspond to the childlike spirit and the origin of the first man.

God in his loving-kindness will do everything possible to move the heart to this conversion. In every event, whether in the history of the great world or in our own small world, God seeks through his loving-kindness – and through the wrath of his judgment – to lead us to radical repentance, a repentance that leads to rebirth and to the kingdom of God. In the composure of prosperous middle-class life, man has hardened his heart against this message from God. Consequently, the iron plow of bitter need must now tear open our consciences. Need and distress must awaken our consciences so that they might again condemn all evil and search out all good, learn again to listen to the word of truth, and establish God's future in the present.

Ultimately, the task of the conscience is to represent the truth. The closer it comes to converting people and all that relates to them, the more it thirsts for the ultimate truth and the life that truth brings, a life that changes everything and makes everything possible. The conscience responds to the truth. The writings of the apostles and the prophets testify that every genuine proclamation of the word, every unadulterated revelation of the truth, speaks to all consciences. The conscience recognizes the objective truth of the word and the subjective honesty of the confessor for what they are. Beck's saying "Christianity looks to our consciences for authentication" refers first and foremost to the inner testimony of this objective truth.* But this testimony also includes the

*Johann Tobias Beck, 1804–1878.

authentication of all God-ordained proclaimers of the gospel as to the sincerity of their intentions and the harmony between their words and way of life. The word brings truth and is truth. From those who proclaim it, the word demands the integrity and reality that befits the truth.

When God's message awakens us, it tries to strike our conscience in such a way that we can never seek or long for anything but what God is saying. From now on, we seek the kingdom of God and his righteousness. In all the things that fall to our lot, God's purpose is to give us the same task as the first people – we are to cultivate and preserve what God entrusts to us; we are to penetrate it in spirit, designate it clearly, and proclaim it. Our conscience must become free for this life task.

Just as God once gave the first man and woman the peace and community of the old garden, he gives this task to the believer in the new garden of his peaceable kingdom, the Christ-church of the new spirit. It is, therefore, for the task of cultivating the earth for his rulership that he wants to purify the conscience from its self-willed and hostile separation. The curse of this separation lies more obviously before the eyes of people today than any other generation. God's garden is more remote than ever before. The separation is constantly increased by frenzied travel. We rush with headlong speed over an earth deprived of God. At the same time though, God and his kingdom draw near in secret to win back the garden, here where it was lost.

The contrast between the kingdom of God and the kingdom of mammon has seldom come to light so clearly in the history of humankind as in our time. We are in a similar situation to that of the Reformation. At that time the radical reformer Jakob Hutter worked throughout the German territories of Tirol and Moravia, from 1529 until his martyrdom in 1536. He proclaimed anew the entire gospel of God, founding and establishing for thousands the complete community of the united church based on faith in the kingdom of Jesus Christ. Among other important letters of the year 1535, he wrote the following one (delivered from Tirol to Moravia by a fellow reformer), in which he vividly testifies to faith in the showers of living water from above – faith in the constructive and strengthening power of the Holy Spirit and the healing mercy of Christ:

> May God shower these blessings upon our hearts and bless his garden so that it may become fruitful with all good works. This garden is the church of the living God. May God fence this garden for you and make a wall around it, shield it, and protect it so that the fruit may ripen; for the Lord's garden blossoms now! The children of the Lord thrive and grow in godly righteousness and truth like lilies and flowers, as a lovely garden flourishes after a gentle May rain. Yes, their hearts burn with the fire of God's love. Their hearts are alight and kindled by the eternal light and fire of God. Therefore they are justly called a garden of the Lord, or a paradise of God. The holy city cannot remain hidden.

The same divine community of peace and the same work of love for the earth is entrusted in our time to this same church, this same garden of God, as it was once entrusted to the first man and woman. The building-up of the same justice that will conquer the whole world in the final kingdom of Jesus Christ is entrusted into the church's hands. The lordship of the spirit over soul and body (and therefore over all that belongs to the earth) shall be revealed once more in the church as the image of God, as it is given in Jesus Christ. The gospel of God wants to awaken our consciences for this task, given to the first man and to the last Adam. Even though we are not equal to it, we have to accept this task.

Sickness of soul and spirit has eaten so deeply into our conscience that it is no longer able to be a clear mirror of good and evil. Least of all can it give a clear picture of God's image. In spite of the testimony it gives again and again, it is stained by evil in the soul. Just as it is unable to keep itself from being besmirched, the conscience is also unable to purify itself. Of itself, it is not only incapable of producing a clear picture, it cannot even reflect in clear outlines the radiant image of God that shines out so wonderfully in Jesus.

The only way the human conscience can be purified is through the sacrificed lifeblood of Jesus, the only pure image of God. His sacrificed soul brings God's life to us, and thus represents the only stainless human soul. The life of his soul, like ours, was in his blood. His blood and his body were also bound together in one frame. But his body was without sin; his blood was pure; his conscience was undefiled. When he sacrificed his life for us, his blood was free from any guilt of his own. His blood was free from all impurity, all ungenuineness, and all covetous desires. It was free from every guilt, including the heaviest that can lie on our hands: that of shedding blood. No matter the circumstances, no matter how lofty the ideals, Jesus would have nothing to do with this gravest of crimes, the crime against life given by God alone – life that only God is entitled to take away. No social critic, no criminal court could condemn him. He commended his spirit into the hands of the Father free from the stain of this guilt, as of all guilt. His was a living spirit uncorrupted by any traffic with the powers of darkness or death.

From God he once more sends this quickening spirit down to us. The souls and consciences of those who receive it will be purified from all former guilt, and their lives will be protected from new offenses. For the life of Christ, the bearer of the Holy Spirit, who was sacrificed for them, is purity itself – the purity of a love that is perfect unto death. The blood that was sacrificed for them in death is mightier than death and more powerful than all its deadly, poisonous, and divisive powers. It has a life within it that remains free from all the elements of death and decomposition, which are hostile to life and to God. Purification through the blood of Christ means that in his spirit his spotless, surrendered life unfolds its powers here and now. Therefore it is able to set our consciences free from all impurity.

Through the complete uniting of his life with ours, his sacrifice has the power to purify our consciences from all guilt and confusion. It gives our consciences the highest and purest of tasks. For his sacrifice created unity: the new unity, and the only unity there is among us. It created the organic unity of the kingdom and the church, which does not tolerate a single barrier between the nations. For it has broken down the strongest barrier between peoples – the barrier that stood between the Jewish people and other nations. Whoever tries to erect this barrier again – and whoever insists on the erection of other walls between people – is a traitor to the blood of Christ and his sacrifice. All that takes place as a result of this attitude is bound to show itself as the work of death, because it is inimical to the spirit of life. All works that establish self-willed boundaries are and remain dead works.

In spite of its profound weakness, the conscience is in this respect true to the origin of the soul in God, the source of life – it fights against all dead works. Through the blood of Christ, the conscience strives to do away with all works done in our own strength. Such works can never create life anywhere, for they are undertaken without the spirit of Christ and without the power of God. When works are born out of our own strength, arising from our own motives and pursuing our own aims, they are dead works. When they deny the origin of life and God's goal in Christ Jesus, they are dead works.

The gospels would have us rest from all our own works so that God's work can begin through his spirit, just as it did in the first church in Jerusalem. God begins his work now. The Holy Spirit establishes it. Jesus Christ completes it. In God it is consummated. When the conscience is purified from all that belongs to evil and death, it sets to work more zealously than ever before. Now the mystery of faith has to be kept safe in a clear conscience. Now the new life must set to work, as God's love and God's work, in deeds of love that are born of a pure heart, a good conscience, and a sincere faith.

The awakened conscience exerts its humble strength more and more so that all available means and gifts are used for the fulfilling of God's will – for the work that only God can do. Perfect love longs to express itself in God's work everywhere so that justice is done to every human, and so that as many as possible reach an awareness and fulfillment of their highest destiny.

The conscience expects us to put into action the dignity we have rewon in God, and to let it bear rich fruit. This new nobility bears the image of God on its coat of arms. It accepts the responsibility of working for God's kingdom of justice in the joy of love and the unity of peace. The conscience purified in Christ, as a conscience enlivened by the Holy Spirit, seeks the image of God. Only in the church of Christ and in the kingdom of God can it be truly established anew.

The image of God appears wherever the spirit of the church's master is, for it is the spirit of the king of the kingdom. There the features of God's character stand out more clearly, more radiantly. The conscience illuminated by the spirit recognizes that it is its vocation to be the image of God. Once that has happened, it has nothing to do with any other witness. It has become the finger in Grünewald's altarpiece, unceasingly pointed toward the figure of the crucified one.* The image of humankind, which has already been repainted a hundredfold, has been renewed in the image of Jesus Christ as the image of God.

---

*The reference is to Matthias Grünewald's "Isenheim altar" (ca. 1516), a triptych that portrays, among other scenes, John the Baptist at the crucifixion of Jesus.

THE CONSCIENCE
AND ITS RESTORATION

The conscience is a center of extraordinary delicacy and sensitivity. It represents the deepest feelings of the human spirit. Like a supersensitive recording instrument, it is influenced by every change of weather and liable to be seriously damaged by any shock. When life becomes more and more superficial, when every door is thoughtlessly left open to the atmosphere of the times, to its changing winds and temperatures, the conscience is in danger of being thrown off balance. But not only then: it can be led astray just as much by mental and intellectual development. Even an increase of religious activity can cause serious derangement. The conscience is an uncertain factor even in the holiest spheres of life.

The conscience is diseased as long as it is not healed by the power of Jesus' surrendered life. Bound to false ideals, that is, to erroneous human thinking, the conscience is unreliable and degenerate until it experiences freedom – and asserts its freedom – in the true and vital word of God, in the living spirit of Jesus Christ. It is only in doing the will of God that the spirit is given health. Jesus declared this with unmistakable authority; he put it into practice and sealed it with his death. Any other idea, however strongly represented, makes the conscience uncertain and ineffective.

The conscience craves for the very essence of truth. It demands an ultimate, indisputable goal. Strength of conscience, growing certainty and clarity, is to be found only where peace rules as unity, justice rules as brotherliness, and joy rules as pure and all-inclusive love. Every other ideal, no matter how praiseworthy it may seem, has disastrous and even fatal results if it aims at other goals even for a short time. The one way leading upward has both solitary paths and wide, well-traveled highways branching off. Every one of them leads us further and further away from unity, justice, and love. They bring us into darkness, uncertainty, and division. Finally they plunge us into the abyss. The conscience, as a supersensitive faculty, is all too easily brought into danger on false paths and then corrupted and destroyed.

The unhealthy state of an erring conscience comes to expression in annihilating self-accusations and hateful reproaches so violent that they derange the mind. Dissension and hate undermine the health and vitality not only of individuals but also of nations. Most of all, sickness shows itself when the conscience reacts in a very sensitive way in the wrong place. It is typical of all false ideals and goals that they rob the conscience of certainty about the essential thing. They all bind the conscience to secondary issues. They all serve dissension. They all shake trust in the spirit who unites and purifies. This is because they all wish to set arbitrary boundaries to limit the cause they should be representing. On the one hand they blunt the conscience, and on the other hand they incite it to wild exaggeration and injustice.

The conscience starts to go wrong when we lose trust in the uniqueness and absoluteness of the goal. In the end, confidence and clarity are given up as lost forever. As long as other points of attraction compete with the magnetic pole, the needle jerks unsteadily here and there without any accuracy. This restlessness gives rise to a wavering judgment, looking for a victim like a bird of prey. There are cases in which a sick conscience lets no thought arise and no step be taken without submitting it to serious misgivings and harsh judgments. Such a sickness fills the whole of life with grievances and dissatisfaction, with self-laceration and injustice.

Only when the conscience that inflicts such suffering on itself experiences the remission of sins through Christ's spirit can healing can be given. When accusation comes to an end, impure fires are extinguished and their unsteady flickering dies out. As soon as the pure light of loving grace breaks through, hostility and injustice sink into ashes. The fire of evil dies away in God's air. Those love much to whom much is forgiven. Those who experience love forgive much. When the power of all-embracing unity breaks through, division and destruction vanish, and all their misleading and subsidiary aims vanish with them.

It is a fact that anyone willing to become healthy again begins by speaking about his or her malady openly and without reserve. Those who frankly expose the accusations and inhibitions of their conscience have already begun to recover. They recognize the power of their censured urges as a reality, they bring to light the morbid repression of these urges and make known their self-laceration and hostility and all the injustice that goes with it. To conceal these exhausting struggles is to sap the energy of life, as the Jewish psalms testify with superlative clarity. By disentangling conflicting forces in a matter-of-fact way and exposing all the aims and motives behind them, anyone can knock the bottom out of this exhausting conflict.

Yet here too, disclosing the harm is only the first step. The next important step will be to show the corrupted and repressed urges the way to healing and the sphere of action that God intends for them. The conscience must find God's land, in which joy in life – which is God's will – takes the place of the despondency and despair to which all human unrest is doomed.

For this reason, any attempt at pastoral help is bound to be inadequate and futile as long as the conscience is not entirely freed from soul-killing accusations and self-accusations, from the sweat of its own desperate efforts. Nothing that is reaped from the accursed soil of self-appointed efforts or goals can stand before the conscience or before the final judgment seat. The conscience must be freed from our selfish spirit, from our self-will, our own goals, our own works. All of life's energies must be directed toward the one and only task in life that is truly active and positive: carrying out God's creative will and working toward the goal of his new creation. Even though the conscience is not clearly aware of it because of its seriously sick and degenerate state, subconsciously it does have this one goal before it.

In times past, there was a tendency to call even the healthiest reactions of the conscience a sign of sickness that should be ignored. But that must be repudiated most decisively. The conscience must never be silenced or despised. Instead, it must be led to splendid health by being freed from false aims and directed toward the kingdom of God. This never means that the conscience is silenced or despised – rather, it gains positive recognition through being filled with new clarity and new content. This freeing and fulfillment leads to lively activity in all areas of life embraced by the conscience. It is truest of all for public responsibility and vocational activity: in these areas, plain for everyone to see, completely new ways and unheard-of possibilities will be opened up by the conscience that is bound to Christ and his kingdom.

One and the same thing is true for all areas of life filled with new meaning and attained to new purpose; they are freed from selfishness, violence, deceit, and immorality. Human existence as a whole is at stake. It must be won completely or given up as lost. Many are so bewildered by the utter confusion of life today they cannot summon enough strength and clarity of conscience to have a decisive effect on even one area of their character. They are and continue to be at a loss.

Even in circles that had long shown a certain sureness of moral instinct, shady business practices gained ground during and after the war in more than half the German nation. Any effective defense the conscience might have had against the powers of hell had been destroyed – by political murder (lightly interpreted as self-defense) and by thoughtless readiness for a repetition of war and civil war.

Whoever can read the signs of the times will hardly be surprised to find that there is scarcely any real uneasiness about the injustice of mammon and property – an injustice that in fact kills every bit of love and the whole of life. In the obvious confusion of conscience, it is not surprising to find a lack of restraint over covetous desires and a brazen unfaithfulness that is growing beyond all bounds. The masses are in motion. The human race is gravitating around a turning point. In all probability this critical and turbulent state will lead to destruction. Ominous signs gather on all sides. The greatest danger in all the different areas that are corrupt today is this: spiritual leaders explain the ever-increasing confusion in such bedazzling ways that no one feels uneasy.

Nowadays what is most abnormal has become the norm, or at least put into currency as an ordinary necessity of life for almost everyone. The present-day confusion of conscience with regard to sex must be mentioned here as a typical example, one that is characteristic of all areas of life. In the circles influenced by Sigmund Freud, people attempt to draw all kinds of sexual perversions out of the slumbering subconscious mind regardless of whether they are committed on themselves, on the opposite sex, or on the same sex. They regret that these perversions have been repressed into the subconscious by the conscience.

Followers of Freud probe into the earliest experiences of childhood and into the most spiritual relationships, trying to prove that even such pure feelings as those between parents and children are based on and defined by erotic drives. And what Freud himself saw as a general principle applying to scientific research has been used by some of his followers for practical orientation and guiding principles in personal conduct. This is bound to have harmful effects.

People try to bring into the clear light of consciousness images that can only be recognized as morbid. They intentionally try to bring these images back into channels from which they had been diverted by a healthy reaction of the conscience. In all this, there is a marked tendency to attribute all emotional disturbances to repressed sexual desires – desires that were actually hardly noticeable or that were long since inwardly overcome. What is most dangerous of all (and even seductive) is that these impulses that have been driven into the subconscious and forgotten there are supposed to be cured by being brought back again as consciously willed images. It amounts to an attack on the conscience – an attack that distorts everything. It is impossible to imagine a worse attack – one that leads people more astray. The would-be cure leads to a sickness and poisoning that grows progressively more widespread and more serious.

And yet even these circles had to admit that "culture" and "true humanity" are possible only through a repression of sexuality, which can never have a cramping effect when it takes place through the pure spirit. Even these circles must recognize the repression of impulses by the conscience as the necessary link between sexuality and spirit. Without this link, the spirit would be cut off from our life.

On the other hand, the word "repression" is enough to deprecate the whole activity of the conscience and throw suspicion on it. It is wrongly understood, however: this dangerous word does not apply to a healthy conscience. Yet it is not without significance. There would indeed be a fatal repression, a morbid suppression of vital impulses, if the active conscience were not able to point to a responsible way in which all the powers of body and soul could be led to a positive and creative task.

Here lies the real reason why this dangerous misconception is so widespread in our sick age. In the concept of the family almost universally accepted today, the responsibilities and tasks of family life no longer correspond to God's creative will. What is true of parents is true of children. Count-

less young people and just as much their parents lack that
sense of inner responsibility in their mutual relationships
which puts the whole of life into the hands of God's faithful
spirit.

Large numbers of our contemporaries suffer no pangs of
conscience when the soul's deepest need for faithfulness is
destroyed. They are affected just as little when the smallest
souls that want to be called into life are prevented or annihilated. Little souls wait in vain to be called out of eternity.
Living human souls wait in vain to be called by constancy
and faithfulness. There seems to be an ever smaller circle of
people in whom the conscience protests clearly and sharply
against contempt for the creative spirit, just as it protests
against any profanation of the longing for unity, faithfulness, and constancy.

This inner protest is also a stirring challenge to us to shape
our love life responsibly and faithfully. Anyone wanting to
call it "repression" casts suspicion on creation itself. In actual
fact, this activity of the conscience provides us with our only
safeguard against the fall that threatens us, a fall that would
make us lower than the animals, lower than the beasts of
prey. A comparison could be made with a war-veteran who is
emotionally disturbed, or with the morbid excitement in a
smoldering riot or civil war: in both cases, the conscience has
to repress the passions that urge people to shoot others in the
streets of their home town. In the same way, it is a healthy
sign when a person represses uncreative and life-thwarting
urges toward his or her own body, sex, or life companion. It
may be that in one or the other area of our life we are not
given the opportunity for responsible and constructive action. Then we should be thankful that "repression" – a term

so often misused – has led to the complete forgetting and
wiping-out of sterile or murderous desires.

The enlightened person will see to it that the sultry, natural urges of his unthinking subconscious mind are not
allowed to influence the thoughts of his soul. He will condemn sinful urges as irresponsible. No one can regard a sense
of responsibility as morbid suppression. Every clear spirit
must feel that it is a sign of a healthy mind when the conscience wards off each degenerate impulse or sterile activity
through feelings of dislike and embarrassment, shame and
disgust, or horror and fear. A conscience working like this is
a psychic mechanism on its way to recovery; it helps us overcome everything that would destroy the holiest powers of
life. It is a question of what these powers are meant for. In
the conscience regaining health, the creative spirit awakens
an awareness that all life-energies are intended for the greatest and noblest tasks, tasks that we cannot allow to be hindered or desecrated.

The sensual person, on the other hand, crushes under-
foot all threats of conscience. Without any feeling of shame
or disgust, he or she wants to become one with every orgas-
mic deity, wanting undisturbed to say to each passing moment of desire, "I am lust itself." Such lust is devoid of spirit
and meaning. It is altogether lacking in purpose and moral
content. Such a person is not a victor but a miserable slave to
the lecherous god. The pagan satyr is a symbol of the violation of all noble-mindedness. It desecrates the human spirit,
and it is the enemy of the divine spirit. When this grinning
pagan god who threatens everything holy is banished to hell,
the creative spirit does not in any way spurn the body or its

psychophysical powers. The pagan god is dead, and all he can do is to embrace death.

To be sure, this pagan god is not the only enemy of the creative will for life. In his presence, the conscience is stifled; but also in the "grumbler" against God's will, in the sanctimonious hypocrite, the conscience is trained to a morbid aversion to life. Such would-be Christians want to reject all the urges of the living senses as alarming and embarrassing. They ought to call themselves Buddhists rather than Christians.

The attitude of Christ is utterly different: his life and death remain devoted to the earth. His will is that God's kingdom comes on earth! It is important that the conscience is so restored to health that the natural urges go in the direction meant for them. Then they will unfold without further harm in a way that corresponds to the will of creation. This healing can take place only in faith in the coming kingdom: faith in a power that is present here and now. Weighty reasons can be brought forward to support the opinion that this healing has become an impossibility for people of today. It takes an absolute transformation of the whole of public life to develop these vital powers in the one and only living direction. To many however, this seems impossible in our present times; it has become too remote for their small faith.

Moral philosophers may demand that the sexual life is purified by insisting on purity before and during marriage. But even the best of them become insincere and unjust if they do not make clear the actual basis for the fulfillment of such high demands. Even destruction of the life that is waiting to come into being – a Massacre of the Innocents intensified a thousandfold today – remains unassailable without faith in the kingdom of God. The supposedly high culture of

our days will continue to practice this massacre as long as
social disorder and injustice prevail. Infant murder cannot
be overcome as long as private life and public life are allowed
to maintain their status quo.

Whoever fights against self-centered acquisitiveness and
against the deceit in unjust social distinctions must fight
them in a realistic way – a way that demonstrates a different
form of life as a possibility that actually exists. If this is not
done, purity in marriage and an end of murder cannot be
demanded either. Not even for families with the soundest
morals can anyone wish the blessing of many children, corresponding to the creative powers of God's nature. Christian
marriage cannot be demanded outside the whole context of
life that is called the kingdom of God and the church of
Jesus Christ.

Only marriage fulfills the demands of the sexual conscience, through the will to have children. It is a fulfillment
in the picture it gives of the unity of God with his people
(Eph. 5), an example of the rule of the spirit of unity, and as
a community of life and community of goods. It symbolizes
the rule of the spirit over body and soul. In all these ways,
marriage is a picture of the church. The place for marriage is
nowhere but in the church. Only where the unity of the
church, filled with the spirit, creates community in material
things through inspired and united work, can these demands be made of marriage. Only in the church can these
demands be fulfilled at the right time and given their true
value.

The unity and purity in marriage taught by Jesus and his
apostles are unique. They have nothing to do with the old
nature. They belong to the new church order, which as

brotherly justice lets the spirit of love rule supreme. Unity and purity in marriage do not belong to the unredeemed. They can be realized only in the new church of the spirit of Jesus Christ. They belong to the kingdom of God. They are symbol and sacrament of that kingdom.

It is to God's love and to the fruits of all the gifts of God's love that the conscience leads us. Through the invasion of the spirit into every area of life and his rulership there, God's love leads us to this unity of the spirit. God's will is that we put this love into practice with all the strength of our body, soul, and spirit. God is love. Whoever abides in love, abides in God. God abides in them. A life lived in love is lived in God. It is on the earth that the love of the father of Jesus Christ is bestowed so that love shall reign supreme here, so that what love dictates shall be done in everything here on earth. Only in this way will God's name be truly hallowed.

God is unchangeable. His name is "I am that I am." His heart embraces everything and remains the same for everyone. It was revealed in Jesus Christ. Jesus Christ is today and forever the same as he was in all his words and deeds. He is here and now the same as he will reveal himself to be in his kingdom. His words of love point to the same way for all things. What he said for the future members of his kingdom holds good for all his disciples at all times. Everything he said for his disciples' instruction belongs together, just as the sap belongs to the tree, the savor to the salt, and the flame to the candle. They belong together.

For this reason, what Jesus said about marriage must not be isolated from any other saying in the Sermon on the Mount. In marriage, Jesus represented the will to love as the will to unity. But he represented it just as much in not having property, not bearing arms, not insisting on rights, being free from a judging spirit, being forgiving, and loving one's enemies. Poverty born of love is a protection from a bad conscience because it guards against injustice. Perfect love strides on to voluntary poverty because it cannot keep for itself anything that a neighbor needs. Perfect love does away with weapons because it has given up self-preservation and has nothing to do with revenge. It remains steadfast and for conscience' sake bears evil and injustice. It keeps in mind the Sermon on the Mount and knows that this attitude is God's greatest gift because it reveals his heart. The love that conquers everything is revealed by a firmness that is not upheld by weapons.

Love gives up everything it owns. Like the elders of the early church, those who guard the mystery of faith in a pure conscience remain free from involvement in any legal or hostile action. Christ's justice conducts no lawsuits. It does not carry on a middleman's business or any business that is to the disadvantage of another. It foregoes all its own advantage, it sacrifices every privilege, and it never defends a right. Christ's justice never sits on a jury, never deprives anyone of freedom, and never passes a death sentence. It knows no enemies and fights no one. It does not go to war with any nation or kill any human being. And yet when this justice is at work, it is justice in its most active form, peace in its most energetic form, and constructiveness in its most effective form. The sum total of all we are commanded to do is to love: to love with a pure heart, a clear conscience, and a genuine faith. In order for perfect love to flow freely, Jesus showed the conscience the way of responsible community in

God. This is the essential nature of his kingdom and his church.

The way of Jesus is love, agape. His love tolerates no unclarity. This kind of love is unique. It gives a very definite direction. It is a way, and this way is very clearly marked out. In the experience of God's love, Jesus Christ leads us up to the purest and loftiest peaks of willpower, clear recognition, and strength of heart that is joy. He does not do this for our sake. His will is that we pass on the streams of this power of love that is poured into our hearts. These streams are meant to flood the earth. They are meant to conquer the land, reveal God's heart, and establish God's glory.

God's glory is his heart. His heart is love. It devotes itself to everyone in the joy of giving. God's glory is love. Love is his justice. When our seeking for the kingdom of God and his justice is single and undivided, we are filled with such a love for all that everything we want for ourselves we want for everyone. That is the only justice, the only righteousness, when we give our lives for love.

The highest goal of this pure and unadulterated love is the kingdom of God. This love alone fulfills the longing of our conscience. All other objects of our thoughts and inclinations prove to be either weak representations of the pure service of God's kingdom or distorted caricatures of it, a hostile antithesis. Nothing is conceivable to the purified conscience without the thoughts of perfect love. Unity is its first and last thought.

From first to last, life is called to unity with God, expressed as the unity of the church, the unity created by his spirit of love. In this community of love, the conscience gains a strength that goes beyond the rejection of what is wicked and evil. It becomes the driving power behind joyful, constructive work. The conscience fettered to Christ is bound to the king and lord of the coming order of God. Therefore it demands and creates everywhere the one form of life that strives to correspond to the order of the kingdom of God down to the last detail. In Christ, we are concerned in all areas of life with the greatest and highest that can be entrusted to us: the eminence of God, the rule of his heart.

However, the apostles of this Messiah-king also know of an enfeebled state of conscience, in which the conscience is influenced from another side and chained to dead objects: a conscience bound to idols. Even a believing conscience can be critically weakened by the influence of other spirits, hostile to the spirit proceeding from God. Other kings – whether cultural icons or popular idols, heroes or political leaders – arise to bind us and lead us away from Christ.

The conscience is always weak when bound by an influence different from that of Jesus Christ. It wavers and goes astray. It is wrong in its judgments. It makes demands that have every appearance of decisiveness and manliness and yet arise out of weakness: they do not represent things as they actually are, they give no real help, they use weapons that are injurious to life, they contradict the truth of God's word and the spirit of Jesus Christ. They are dead and lead to death.

A conscience that pays allegiance to the wrong leader is bound to transgress constantly against the will to life characteristic of Christ's rulership. This fact is most painfully clear in all who combine the name "Christ" with an alien name and goal. In this futile undertaking, Christianity today – more than ever before – is deprived of the spirit of the one they still want to confess. The pure spirit does not allow itself to be mixed with any other spirits. His kingdom does not tolerate any rival power structure.

What do idols and the house of God have in common? Has goodness anything to do with wickedness? Can the one join forces with the other in the same undertaking? Does light associate with darkness? When has the kingdom of God made an alliance with a state built on human power? Did Jesus ever mix other watchwords with his prophetic message? How can the word of Jesus tolerate rival human commands? When has God shared his sovereignty with human rulers? Can the city of God go hand in hand with Babel? Can one equate Christ and Belial, God and the Devil?

Yet it does no good to hit out at a conscience that is sick and feeble. Even an erring conscience deserves consideration and respect. There must be some influence that frees it from all vacillating emotions and from all the ties of the Antigod, without striking it dead to the ground. Surely it is the radiant light that overcomes all gloom and shadows. Faced with the rising sun, night is powerless. The spirit of life is victorious over the spirit of murder. No other authority can bring peace. It is the spirit of life, as the spirit of light, who sets the conscience free. This spirit conquers without destroying. God's rule takes command over the heart. The spirit of his rulership transforms hearts and nations. It is the church of Jesus Christ here and now that shapes an order of communal life with the same character as his future. The church's will to unity and her spirit of love transform everything. But they never kill anything that has life.

The conscience is at peace only when it is in perfect accord with God's will. In the conscience of a believing and loving person, the will to truth dwells as the spirit of Jesus.

In this dark hour of world history, it is of crucial importance that this news, this answer, is carried to the four corners of the earth. Then the conscience will become free from all legalistic ties, from every influence of the spirit of the age, from every human opiate, and from all demonic magic. The distress in this hour demands a supreme strength – a strength found only in the healing brought down to mortally sick humanity by God's kingdom of life and love. This mission goes out to every nation. The task is clear. The message runs: "Let yourselves be united in God!"

Only community with God and Christ's redemption gives healing. Without God's justice, the conscience remains evil. Only through faith in God has a good conscience any stability. The unity of the church gives this faith the most definite confirmation. All stimulation from outside, all flames of human enthusiasm that leap from one person to another, leave the anxious question behind whether it was really God who gripped us. There is only one criterion to apply to this alarming question: the agreement of all believers, the unanimity of their judgment, and the full accord of their consciences in the tasks set before them. The unity between the church and the words and lives of the apostles and their prophecy is proof that the voice speaking in human hearts is God's voice. The conscience is robbed of all certainty if the believers do not come to unity among themselves and to unity with the life and spirit of the early church. Certainty about the message leads to a uniting of believers and uniting with God.

Only from within can the conscience reach this certainty. Community in all things is inmost certainty. The state of the conscience varies according to the degree of community with God and the acceptance of his will. The closer the community with God, the more does the conscience thrive. Only in this way is unanimity achieved. The more deeply Christ dwells in our hearts the more sharply, delicately, and carefully does the conscience insist that truth means unity.

At first, what the kingdom of God demands appears not only too sharp and strict but downright impossible. But the perfect will of God gains recognition more and more as the will to joy, the only thing that is good and living. The more God's will gains ground, the closer the conscience comes to unity with God and his church. Therefore we can say that when a conscience is healed it is in fact sharpened, purified, and clarified for the unity of complete community. To be sure, the conscience loses its clarity to the same degree as we refuse to serve the will to unity. And finally: the conscience can never acknowledge a community supposedly in God and a unity of the church that is not constantly proved in deeds, that does not show a fitting attitude and way of life. For basically the conscience is always intent on action. God is action.

Through the unity of the church led by the Spirit, a right way of life shows that it is in reality a community in God. When the attitude of the believers is purified and unified through the Holy Spirit, unanimity and unity of life come into being. In Christ, their attitude to life becomes one with their way of life. With its renewed sensitivity, the conscience strives toward this immediate goal, upholding the influence of the spirit of Jesus with unmistakable certainty and perseverance.

As the moral function of the human spirit, the conscience has to say yes to everything prompted and inspired by the spirit of God in the human spirit. It has to take a prophet's place in the human spirit – the place of one who is the mouth of God and has to repeat and pass on what God says. The conscience that is on the way to recovery calls out, "God says it; God wills it; therefore it will come to pass." As the keenest instrument of the human spirit, the conscience has to represent in the liveliest way the uniting of the human and the divine spirit. God's holy spirit wants to unite with the human spirit to witness to the truth together. Our spirit's conscience will be clear and healthy to the same degree that our faith has accepted the spirit of Jesus Christ.

When our conscience is on the way to recovery, the only attitude that will keep our inmost spirit pure and give it strength is the attitude that Jesus had. Keeping a good conscience depends entirely on keeping the holy faith. The redeeming and healing grace of God nurtures a purified and healed conscience in us. As a gift of this grace, faith denies godlessness in every thought, desire, and action. It denies all the worldly lusts that belong to godlessness and are harmful to life. Only in this way can we justly and with deliberation affirm the life of Jesus and accept it. We can do it only in community with God, that is, in community with his Holy Spirit.

Faith and a good conscience are so closely bound together that rejection of the one means shipwreck to the other. For this reason, baptism of faith testifies to the bond of a good conscience with God. The conscience is made good by faith. Without faith, it goes astray. It becomes a bad conscience.

Therefore the apostles of Jesus Christ say about those who do not have faith that they are tainted in mind and conscience alike. This is inevitable because without faith the conscience has no anchor. And the opposite is just as true: if we ignore the compass of the Christ-directed conscience, the ship of faith will be dashed without warning on the next reef.

If we want to fight the good fight to the end, it is just as important to protect our faith as it is to protect our conscience. Faith in the freely given love of Jesus Christ needs to be treasured. A good conscience needs to be protected with the utmost watchfulness. True faith demands a tender and delicate conscience as a fruit of the spirit. Faith gives birth to a death-defying and victorious decisiveness against all evil. Faith is served by a sound conscience. Faith demands deeds of love. It is, in fact, love of God, love of Christ, and love of the Holy Spirit. When we take pains to keep our conscience free of offense at all times, then we are given growth and activity in the grace and knowledge of Jesus Christ, then our inner life becomes anchored in God and in all the powers of his spirit. Only love is without offense.

Yet we should not make the mistake of thinking that when our conscience steadily gains health and purity in love, we become sinless! Sinfulness remains characteristic of our nature. But the grace of his blood – the grace of the sacrificed life of Jesus – continually purifies our conscience through the Holy Spirit. Again and again, grace purifies it from all dead works and all offensive actions, from everything that violates the justice and love that go hand in hand with faith. The spirit of Jesus Christ leads believers to a life that steadily increases in clarity. And yet the believer continues to be bound to all others by a common guilt.

Nevertheless, however clearly it shows itself to be common to all, the guilt has been wiped out. People have the freedom to do good and to further it, to avoid evil and to fight it. Step by step, there is an advance toward the kingdom of God. In the life of Jesus, sacrificed for us and brought near to us, God has freely given us the gift that takes one burden after another from our conscience. It makes us free, without making us sinless. We become – not gods – but those who allow the kingdom of God to come to them.

We can accept God's will in our life only when we are freed from the curse of a bad conscience. We can be one with God's holiness only when our hearts are unburdened, sprinkled, and consecrated. The heart is in a condition to come before God and become united with him only by being in touch with the sacrificed life of Christ in the closest and most intimate way, by being met by Christ himself and united with him as he was and is and will be. Therefore there is no entry into the holy of holies except through the blood of Jesus: Christ's stainless life, his dedicated soul, his sacrificed body, his quickening spirit, they all unite us with God – the whole Christ with all the power of his life and death.

Jesus is the way to God. There is no other God than the one who is the God and father of Jesus. Wherever we may seek him, we find him in Jesus. Unless we are freed in Jesus from all our burdens, we try in vain to draw near to the Father of all as he is brought near to us by the son. We have no access to God without forgiveness of sin. Jesus gives it to us by sacrificing his life – by sacrificing his body, his soul, and his blood.

Through Jesus, Satan, the accuser of our brothers, is silenced. The conscience also is no longer allowed to accuse. Even the most murderous accusations that human blood can raise are stilled. The blood of Abel has been erased. The better blood of the new brother speaks louder than his. The blood of humankind has found a new representative and leader; by him, the better one, it is absolved and liberated. Murdered like Abel, he nevertheless speaks for his murderers instead of against them. He, the guiltless one, has become one of them, because he is the only one who has become truly theirs. If he, the Son of Man, is for them, no one can condemn them. From now on, no accusation has the power to prevent them from approaching God.

The conscience that used to be our enemy becomes in Christ our friend. Before it was in Christ, it had to condemn our life; now it says yes to the new life given in Christ. Freed from all impurity through community with Christ, the spirit accepts the assurance and certainty given in Jesus Christ. So the conscience, as a Christ-conscience, becomes a representative of God. It becomes the voice of the one who is sent, representing our covenant with God. In the inner land of our soul, the conscience begins to do its task. In the church, our covenant with God comes into force. In the task of mission, the embassy steps forward to appear before the world.

It is the church that in baptism confirms the covenant of a good conscience with God. The believers are united by the bond of faith, and baptism is the banner and battle flag of this unity of faith in the face of the whole world. There is no such thing as baptism without the church. The water of baptism is the pure water of the spirit of unity, just as the wine of the Lord's Supper proclaims the unity of the pure blood. Nor without the church is there any such thing as a meal celebrating unity of conscience. The common meal of love and thanksgiving confesses and proclaims the new covenant: the sure victory of unity given through the life and blood of Christ. The bread and the wine in remembrance of Jesus Christ are living symbols of the unity that has made many grains and many grapes into one whole. Only on the basis of the church can community be built up in the unanimity of all consciences. Only from the church can there be sent into the world a mission that is authenticated before all men in their consciences. From the church, unity will be proclaimed as God's freedom. Where her spirit is, there is freedom.

It was to the unity of the church, that is to the unity of the apostles, that Jesus gave his spirit with full authority to represent his kingdom. Their authority to loose and to bind, that is to forgive and leave unforgiven, makes it possible for all to be completely freed so that they can enter the kingdom of God. No conscience can live without forgiveness of sins. No one can see the kingdom of God without it. United in faith and in life, the church of God is entrusted with the power to forgive sins, valid before all consciences; as her charge and prerogative for this day and age, she is given the life of Jesus and his future rule.

False prophecy forgives without authority. Such forgiveness is null and void because it changes nothing in life: peace is proclaimed where there is no peace. Freedom is proclaimed where everything remains unfree. What is unjust is called just. The joyless are comforted with counterfeit joy and stolen happiness. Unity and community are betrayed. In the atmosphere of false prophecy, the conscience becomes dull and blunt and loses its commission. False prophecy robs the conscience of every reason to go to the attack.

Yet where the truth of the spirit of God proclaims forgiveness and peace, the conscience will be roused to action more and more. It advances to the attack: where there was no peace, peace must be made; where everything was in chains, freedom must dawn; where injustice ruled, justice must take its place; where love and joy had grown cold, the joy of love breaks through; and where each one lived for himself, community comes into being. An all-out campaign against evil is launched: no area of life can escape being attacked. Resistance breaks down. The conscience of the world wakes up. The conscience of the church is on the march.

The prerequisite for this missionary attack is the effective working of consciences in the heart of the church. All growth in the gifts of God, every task given by his truth, and every deepening of community with him sharpens the conscience and intensifies its activity. In the presence of Jesus, we get to know ourselves more and more clearly and judge ourselves more and more firmly. The longer we go the way of the church, the more we know ourselves dependent on forgiving grace. That in the church the conscience gains equally in tenderness and in strength is a proof of the working of God in our midst. The conscience condemns and puts away not only everything that offends against love and community – however small or subtle – it even attacks all weariness and neglect. It punishes all dead works, for they actually prevent the spirit of God from filling our hearts with the breath of life.

As long as God's spirit is at work in his church among believers, consciences work and speak without respite and without delay. A conscience that is as still as the grave is not a good conscience. Everything would be lost if this voice were to fall silent. It is only by a twofold deception that false prophecy can bring the conscience to the point of being deathly quiet. First of all, the conscience is lost when we allow ourselves to be persuaded to the false belief that evil and all consequent injustices are unchangeable – that their supremacy is inviolable. Educated to false humility in the face of evil and to false submission to alien gods, the conscience gives up the struggle and forfeits its fighting spirit. The god of this world and its zeitgeist has dazzled the conscience: he has cheated it of its goal.

If there is anything more dangerous than this submission to the influence of evil over the world, it is the second deception practiced by false prophecy: soothing the conscience with feigned self-assurance. It is another weapon, just the reverse of the first, but it is the same enemy. It attacks the front from the other flank. Through a morbid, imagined holiness it leads to the same result: the blunting and deadening of the conscience. Our conscience is inevitably struck dumb as soon as we see ourselves as sanctified and our own life as equal to Christ's. With such delusions we are farther than ever from God's kingdom. Being self-satisfied, we no longer have the hunger and thirst without which there can be no God-given life , without which the righteousness of his kingdom cannot reach us. In both types of deception, there is a deadly similarity in the end: we belong to those who are seared, as it were, with a branding iron and hardened to their own conscience.

Among the personal testimonies through which Paul gives us a glimpse into his inner life as an apostle, the most striking is that his conscience too did not rest: through the free gift of God, Paul's conscience became as active as it was good. Because of the lively activity of his conscience, it was made free of all offense through grace. The testimony of Paul's conscience is confirmed by the simplicity and sincerity of everything this apostle of Jesus Christ does and says. It is through the grace of God that this happens. The grace of God makes the one who is sent out able to carry out his commission among people. It can be carried out by no human strength or wisdom.

It is forgiving grace that frees us undeserving people from all guilt. Only this grace can give an active conscience the help that protects and strengthens it. It is only by being acquitted that the one arrested can find a new freedom for work. It is the same today before the judgment bar of the conscience as it will be on the day of judgment at the end of history: only grace that forgives through the blood of the crucified one, exoneration from all guilt through the deed of the innocent one who was put to death, will lead to acquittal.

This undeserved gift of an acquittal is given, not because of anything in the conduct or the inner life of the accused, but as a final, judicial pardon from the highest power. The life and blood, spirit and soul of Jesus must be accepted by the condemned, becoming part of their very nature. Only in this way can they expect new life instead of death.

It is quite different with Christ. With him, it is not created matter that is decisive but the spirit of the Creator. There is no transfusion of a material substance here: it is not blood that is given to blood. Spirit is given to spirit. The spirit who is God comes to the spirit of humankind. It is not a material thing but life from God. Jesus lived in the spirit of God. He brought his kingdom in this spirit. At the climax of his life, his soul, filled with the Holy Spirit, was poured out for us. This pure life of Jesus is the starting point from which his quickening spirit streams out to our spirit. The crucified one gave his spirit into the hands of the Father. From the Father, he sent out the Holy Spirit to his church. Now he who is lord and ruler is the spirit of the church. In the spirit Christ imparts himself to us. Through this spirit, we no longer lead our own lives but his life, and his life alone.

In this spirit, Jesus is in the midst of those who believe in him. In this Holy Spirit, he is present with everything he has accomplished by his life and death. In this spirit, strength comes to us – that strength with which he shattered all the instruments and weapons of death and exterminated all the poisons and germs of evil. The historical reality of the deed that blotted out all guilt brings us strength through the Holy Spirit.

From the death of Christ we receive the strength to break with things as they are and to die to the dead life within us and around us. This dying requires the utmost strength. It is given to us in Jesus. Then in all we are and do, what is decisive is no longer our life, or the life of others, but his life alone. Whatever we were and did before, we are now absolved and pardoned. Where the old life has come to an end, the new life begins.

The inner life is brought into community with God through the gift of purification – purification of the conscience through the death of Christ. The Holy Spirit does this. In faith, the innermost soul has access to God. The believing spirit has intercourse with the presence of Jesus Christ. Our spirit brings its witness into agreement with the spirit of God. Our conscience lives in the Holy Spirit from now on. Our spirit and conscience are led by the spirit of God. Christ proves himself as the risen and the living one in the powerful working of his spirit. Through him, the new life corresponding to the kingdom of God is brought into being in and around us. This life demands a supreme strength. It is given to us in Christ, the living one.

In the spirit of Jesus Christ, the kingdom of God as justice, peace, and joy spreads over the whole of life. Whoever believes in him in this way is able to exert himself to keep his conscience alive and preserved from offense at all times before God and man. When we have turned resolutely and steadfastly away from evil, we can turn again and again to loving justice and to peace-making unity – to the purity and truth of God's kingdom. This life in Christ is possible. Wherever we believe in Jesus Christ, it will be given through the Holy Spirit.

Once it is bound to Christ, the conscience has found its goal and its destiny. In the word and example of Mary's son, the picture of the longed-for justice and righteousness engraved on the hearts of all people finds its perfect original. In his work it has found its consummation. This holy truth does not want to be a mere onlooker outside the conscience. The life and work of Jesus is planted into the heart and all it does. Those who have faith become a living letter from Jesus Christ: the truth of Jesus has become an inner word written on the pages of our hearts. Deeds are what make this handwriting legible to everyone – deeds that are imprinted on a life as they spring from the heart, one letter of the spirit after another. The conscience is made clear and new, in that the holiness of God's will is alive in every heart and becomes a reality in every deed. Our whole life is illuminated by the indwelling Christ. He transforms every sphere of our life from within to without. He makes everything new and different.

The soul has received the truth into its innermost depths, into its spirit. The conscience honors the truth by being obedient to it and gaining support from it. The conscience can be compared to a tender climbing plant: without a support it sprawls on the ground and withers. It needs something high and strong. No matter what it climbs on, it does not change its nature. Ivy never adopts the form of leaf and growth that belongs to the tree it clings to in order to live. And yet its laborious climbing serves to glorify the object to which it is attached. Its destiny is that of the object it clings to. Should the tree fall, the ivy is inevitably involved in its fall.

The conscience seeks the Rock that cannot fall and can never change. It seeks God. It longs for Christ; it presses on toward his spirit and his truth. It can never find peace and it can never find stability in other ideals, especially when they whip up emotional enthusiasm to the point of racial fanaticism. Certainty of conscience dwells in absolute truth alone.

Within itself, the conscience has no guarantee that it is right. It is like a pair of scales that has no weights. Give them false weights, the more accurate and sensitive the scales are, the bigger will be the lie. It is more deceptive to weigh with false weights than to lie and deceive in other ways. Only true weights give the conscience any value. Without them it keeps on vibrating and wavering unsteadily, deceiving and misleading in the most dangerous way. Only absolute truth gives the conscience any authority or guarantee of being right. The truth and what the truth demands in life is all the conscience can represent with confidence.

The *Vehmgerichte* – medieval Germany's secret courts – did untold harm. What they lacked was the clear foundation of an authoritative standard that had been objectively determined. We have experienced what confusion of conscience is caused by contradictory orders and their unforeseeable consequences, even when they have been issued by well-meaning governments and authorities. If it cannot prove itself before the conscience to be an objective expression of absolute justice, the most carefully thought-out legislation is pernicious.

The horrors of the Vehmic courts have been directly brought home to us by the murderous commands of courts-martial, by the unbelievable opinions of excited reporters, the appalling injustice of misinformed journalists, and the confusing slogans of fanatical parties and civil war organizations. The murders committed by secret courts in our day are no mere coincidence. They have revealed the evil spirit of our day. Fanaticism is uncertainty run amok. That is the only reason why it out-Herods Herod in senseless and exaggerated hate. It has forfeited all light and warmth. It has no heart. The conscience has lost its criterion. Without any objective reason, it rages against everything that goes counter to its morbid obsessions.

After a recent election I read of one man who had to be taken to a mental hospital as a result of his desperate efforts to make up his mind in the utter confusion of his po-

litical ideas. That was more than a grotesque and isolated in-
cident. He had made the daring attempt to go along with
the convention policies of all parties and all factions. It may
well be that he was more sensible and reasonable than the
blind mass of voters. How much weaker are the consciences
of those who cast their vote without ever having recognized
the real nature of party candidates and party platforms.

How many there are who make no attempt to go into the
policy or motives of the party that is overthrown by their
vote! People throw their votes into the scales of world history
without being able to weigh up one party against another.
Conscience has been thrown to the winds. People have in-
curred responsibility for incalculable guilt. Without looking
for guidance from their consciences, they have presumed to
make weighty decisions of worldwide importance.

Our conscience warns us: do nothing without sufficient
reason; never act without a firm basis of fact; go into action
only when you know what you are doing! The only way to
safeguard our lives from the curse of irresponsible action is
to accept the unfalsified weights – truth. God's justice, alive
in the heart, is the only criterion that carries authority in every decision. Otherwise there is no ground under our feet.
When God's nature – his unchangeable righteousness – is
firmly imprinted on our conscience, then, and only then,
can our conscience pass judgment and give witness.

Conflicting human opinions of relative right and relative
wrong do not help the conscience to make well-founded decisions. It can take a clear stand through the weight of God's
truth only. It is only on the rock of the genuine Christ that
the conscience finds any stability. Christ alone is the example, guide, and liberator. He alone gives the conscience

the foundation, the basis, and the reason for responsible action. There is no other righteousness – only that of his coming kingdom.

Everything else fluctuates, uncertain. It changes its nature, for it is inadequate. It has no stability, no adequate foundation. Even in the most educated families and the finest schools, human ideas totter and fall. Everything that is human fluctuates between limp docility and rigid opposition. Nothing is certain. Everything is relative. The result is clear: in this relativism, which gives equal recognition to quite irreconcilable opposites, humankind loses all sense of values.

In the face of all this confusion, Jesus Christ remains today and forever exactly the same as he was in the time of Augustus and Herod and Pilate, no matter how many thousand times his clear picture is changed and falsified by this relativism. What his will brings about today is exactly the same as he will establish in his final kingdom at the end of time. Only he who is immutable is decision – everything else is delay and displacement. The relativism and fickleness of our own opinions can have only one result: the will to live sickens and breaks down. Life gains health only through the absoluteness of Christ's will, which is always and forever the same. Health is strength to act and power to create, born out of a sure instinct for life and well-considered decisions. It calls for something firm and constant to fill the whole of life.

Only when it is completely bound to Christ will the conscience become healthy. True life is not to be found anywhere else: only in this divine influence, which is immutable. Only when Christ, unlimited, has become the anchor for our consciences can life recover. Only when the inner life regains health in Christ can the distress in our time be tackled. The conscience looks to Christ for healing. It is Jesus who heals the people of our day and age just as he healed the sick in his day. It is Christ who shows our generation the way of salvation. It is the same way along which he, the king chosen by God, will lead everything to the goal at the end of all days. The tremendous tasks facing us today can never be accomplished by the hopelessly confused spirit of our times – only by the spirit of the future, the spirit of Christ's kingdom.

Just as he was the spirit of the early church, Christ's spirit of the future wants to be the spirit of community here and now. It is in the living Christ of the prophets and apostles that the stream of future riches comes to us. It is in the apostolic word that Christ comes to us. It is in the prophetic word that his spirit purifies our conscience. He wants to submerge us in the truth as in a bath of invigorating waters. In the spirit of the prophets and apostles, the spirit of Jesus Christ reveals himself always and everywhere as unchangeably one with himself. What he instills into our conscience today is no less than the substance of this constant accord with himself. He brings unanimity to the church today in one and the same way as to the prophets and apostles and to the church in all ages, inscribing on their hearts the one way of truth and of life.

In all ages, the spirit of Jesus Christ proclaims the same things of the future. He brings the powers of the same future world to all generations. All those who accept these powers are able to live by them at all times. The spirit constantly reminds us of the eternally valid words of Jesus Christ. They can and shall be carried out by all generations on earth. The conscience of all believers becomes firm and sure through the direct uniting with the word of the Spirit, which is spoken into the conscience and is always the same as the word of the apostles and prophets. In this supreme unity, the conscience is equal to any new and unexpected event.

The conscience becomes lively and firm through this spirit, who glorifies Christ as the unchanging lord in the entire church of all times: past, present, and future. Out of faith, the spirit of God awakens courage to do unflinchingly what this spirit wants done. In this way, faith becomes joy in fruitful work and activity. This work corresponds to the kingdom of the same Christ who was and is and is to come.

In the very beginning, the conscience got its voice from the vital fact that the first man was a living soul whose breath came from God. Since the fall of the soul, the conscience can do justice to this divine origin only when the quickening spirit has taken possession of souls who are slowly dying (Rom. 5:12, ff.). The old conscience – the conscience given to every human soul by nature – is by no means an authority for the apostolic task. The apostle of Jesus Christ bases his conscience on his witness in the Holy Spirit.

The witness Paul uses to prove the truth of his statements is not a divided one. On the contrary, the uniting influence of the holy, quickening spirit heals the conscience that stands before God from all the dividedness it has fallen into through the corruption of the soul. God's spirit purifies our spirit to such a clarity that the one can unite with the other to make one witness. In the Holy Spirit, the conscience regains health to form a unanimous witness with this spirit-above-all-other-spirits, who is the spirit of God.

When the conscience lives in the Holy Spirit, it is so completely immersed in him that it breathes no other air than that of the Holy Spirit. From then on, the nature and character of this spirit determines the conscience. As a conscience in the Holy Spirit, it glorifies Christ, brings to mind all that Jesus said, and leads to the active expectation of his future. In this way, the conscience rouses people to a most intent watching and praying so that they might not succumb to other spirits in times of danger nor be tempted again by foreign influences to a new downfall. To fall again would mean not only the loss of their living soul but also the loss of the quickening spirit.

Yet this spirit is stronger than all other spirits. The sole purpose of the Holy Spirit in waking and protecting the conscience is to win a conclusive victory over all the powers that enslave people. The Holy Spirit is at work when Christ is glorified, when God is revealed, and when his rule is recognized. God's power liberates the conscience from all other spiritual powers. No one but God himself, the Omnipotent, can win this victory.

When the original Greek speaks of "the conscience that is bound to God," it relates the conscience so firmly and closely to God that to be accurate we would even have to translate it as "God's conscience." The inner life has the same feeling: "the conscience that is bound to God" is a conscience before God, toward God, and in God: a conscience of the spirit of Jesus Christ, God's conscience. In God and through Christ, it has become free from every false direction and from every tie that enslaves. It lives in God and has become God's. God is the freedom of the conscience.

Today when all the impassioned movements among peoples take their stand on the struggle for freedom, what they have in mind is one of the ultimate thoughts of God's will. Freedom is God's thought for humankind. Without freedom, no one is a *real* person. Only those are free who are not compelled to do what goes against their consciences. Emancipation gives back to the conscience the possibility of working without restrictions. Only when life as an integrated whole asserts the freedom to fulfill its destiny in every area, spiritual and material, can we speak of freedom.

Only when it is lived in accordance with the deepest and ultimate calling is life free. This applies not only to religion and morals (the more specific area of the soul's activity) but also to public relationships in society and economic life; not only to the innermost life of faith but also to vocational and family life. The last battle for freedom is waged for a conscience that embraces all aspects of life. Any other fight for freedom is a delusion. Any restriction of the goal of freedom brings unfreedom. We should know that true freedom consists in the unhindered development of the whole destiny of the whole person. Freedom lives in being whole.

Before the call to battle for freedom goes out, against the danger of permanent subjugation threatening our spirit and working strength, it should be made clear first and foremost that the destiny of the human spirit is universal freedom of conscience. Only then can steps be taken leading to freedom. The task must be clear before we can devote ourselves to it.

The call to freedom stimulates freedom for everything a healthy conscience wants; otherwise it is a lie and a delusion. We must know what we are freed for before we can be told what we must be freed from. The question is, "Free for what?" Freedom without a goal is bondage. What must become free is the will for the good; what it must become free for is good deeds. It is the purpose and meaning of a deed that make it good. A conscience cannot be called to freedom as long as it is lying bare and fallow, aimless and empty. Truth alone will make us free. Only the task that truth sets us gives meaning to our free dedication. Half-truths are untruths. The tasks they ask of us are worthless. Only the whole truth is freedom.

If we want to fight through to the freedom of our ultimate destiny, we must put aside all dependence on human beings and human standards. Only this freedom gives purpose and meaning to our conscience. To the healthy conscience, voluntary subjection to human powers is bondage. It demands a dedication that is in fact purposeless and meaningless. The apostle of Jesus Christ challenges us never again to become slaves to people. Only in the one freedom, the freedom for which Christ has freed us, can we throw off once and for all servitude aping freedom and slavery hiding beneath a mask. The obedience springing from faith in Christ is freedom. It leads to a life that is in harmony with the holy "thou shalt" coming from the healthy conscience. God's holy "thou shalt" is our holy freedom. It is the true essence of our soul and conscience.

Jesus Christ is the only leader to freedom. He does not bring bondage in disguise. He does nothing against the free will of the human spirit. He rouses the free will to do what it must be challenged to do by every truth-loving conscience. The Lord is the Spirit, and where the Spirit is, there is freedom. It is power that is free to act freely.

Anyone who wants to hand over the responsibility for what he or she does to another – anyone who wants to obey a human leader – has betrayed freedom, become enslaved. And when this leader, this seducer, calls to a freedom that is no freedom, it spells complete ruin for enslaved consciences. Consciences are ruined by all leaders whose authority is human. It is for this reason that Jesus said: "You shall not call each other leader. Only One is your master, but you are brothers." The foundation of freedom on which the conscience can regain health is brotherliness, sisterliness, and equality before God. This alone guarantees that love – the pure love that springs from faith – is put into practice.

When the church is free, it means healing and health for the conscience. This freedom is given by the only spirit that is free: the spirit of God. It is God's rule that brings freedom to the conscience. The kingdom comes. The healing of all hurt begins. The conscience bound to God becomes free and healthy. Then it becomes active – then the way is cleared. Work begins. The whole of life becomes free. The work of the Spirit will be established. Those made free by Christ are indeed free.

The freedom of Christ masters reality. Through him, the conscience becomes healthy in this freedom coming from clear and objective decisions. The gift of creative powers is the result of this instinctively sure way of life. The conscience has found substance and meaning in the will of the Spirit. The healing of humankind is the kingdom of God.

The more shaking the events in the world around us, the more necessary it is to recognize the forces at work in them – that is the spiritual powers that determine their course. Outward events as violent as those of our day call for an insight into this ultimate will and its aim. But the more agitated the times, the more temporary matters push to the fore; the more tense, the more impossible it seems to get clear about the ultimate answer. Issues are utterly confused. Mounting pressure leads to emergency measures – imperative, or so it seems. Limited to the times, they are not able to turn the tide of need and distress. One attempt follows another, misery increases, and nothing can overcome it; people go under in the day-to-day struggle and lose all hope of a change.

Some think they have to give priority to patriotic ideas and the historic task laid on the nation. The longed-for freedom of the national community seems the only goal, demanding that everything else is subjected and sacrificed to it. Others, however, believe in a historical development in every nation to raise to power all those oppressed and exploited by competition and private enterprise: They are to be given a power that for a time is unlimited. In comparison with both of these, the champions of liberty and freedom for the individual retreat into the background. No state protection preserves them from the approaching insignificance. In the end, a classless society based on justice and peace and uniting all extremes falls almost completely by the wayside in the struggle for quickly-won power.

Not one of these three directions with their struggles and fluctuating hopes expects anything from the prophetic power of the Christ-proclamation. Those of the third and middle way between the first two extremes have no fears that their egotistical life might be shattered by the kingdom of God. And where an individual tries to comply with the economic system, his or her conscience becomes too dull to be aware how universal need and distress are. But to the right and to the left, people think more seriously. To the right, in contradiction to Christ, they want religion to uphold unconditionally the power structure they have fought for. Christian consciences are meant to surrender to it in willing submission; the conscience becomes the slave of political power. To the left, all they see in the Christian confession is their most hated opponent and the social power of class privilege. All they know of Christianity is a power which, contradicting Christ, covers up social injustice with a hypocritical mien and refers the tormented to a better world hereafter. The Christian conscience represents the height of injustice. Therefore it should be exterminated.

To all this, Christian confessions in general, apart from a few rare exceptions, have nothing to say. The prophetic clarity of intense and confident waiting for a final kingdom – a kingdom of loving community in God – has given way to feeble imitations. People no longer believe that the peace, justice, and brotherliness of the kingdom of God are a present reality, eclipsing all other hopes of the future. And yet all these prospects of a better future are borrowed from the hopes of prophetic early Christianity. They would not exist without them. But not even the historical significance of early Christian prophecy is taken seriously. In practice, the general run of Christianity just accepts existing conditions of social order, or disorder, including any new ideas people come up with. The early Christian expectation is being forgotten. Because it is no longer seriously believed, it has for present-day Christianity lost the dynamic to overturn and transform everything.

True, there are still some who point out seriously that God is quite other than humankind, quite other than all they of themselves want or do. But there are very few who so really and truly believe in this quite different God that they see the approach of his reign and comprehend it. Only these very few lend a hand in faith so that a fundamental change, affecting everyone and all conditions, actually begins. The inner thinking born of faith in God's kingdom is completely other than the thinking of human religion: those with faith in God's kingdom approach everything with a certainty from God himself that the impossible can become possible, in outer circumstances just as much as in the innermost. This faith in God may be as small as a grain of seed, yet it will remove obstacles of the weightiest nature.

Such faith lets the future and the beyond penetrate the present – this earth. Out of the strength it derives from this source, it sets to and gives everything shape and form. The believer has realized that to leave God in the world beyond is to deny Christ. For Christ has said and proved that God draws near, so near that everything has to be changed "from the very foundation (Mark 1–15). Yet Jesus knew that this triumphant joy would be accepted by only very few. People are readier to believe in the autonomy of things than the message of God that overturns everything. They experience things more forcibly than they experience God. They are idolaters, for they serve the creature more than the creator. But faith has to step in and unite our life with the creative power. This alone remains superior to any created power.

God stands above all that happens. Only when we are one with God can our faith withstand all powers that storm it. It is not we who stand firm. Only God is invincible. In him alone is freedom of soul found, saving us from being enslaved, however mighty the power. God has drawn near. We can be in God. God wants to be known and experienced. Yet we quake before it. It is terrifying: truth is disclosed as a consequence. Because God's light shows up our darkness, we are afraid of it.

God begins – that is the end for us. When in fear and trembling we know God and are known by him, we are shocked, and God draws near. When the Most High descends to us, the degraded, all cloaks and barriers are torn away. God is revealed only through this fearful experience. When we experience God, we appear before God as we are. As long as we shrink from being exposed for what we are by God's unhindered recognition of us, we remain hopelessly lost and helpless in the supremacy of the world outside. As long as we submit to things as they are and remain their slaves, terror of God repels us and keeps us at a distance.

God is indeed other than we are. It is true that to our unbelief, he is far removed. We have lost sight of his image. But it was not always like this and must not stay so. We were once created to be near to him. God began – that was our beginning. There was a time when God's drawing near did not spell terror. God's image was once entrusted to man and woman so the Spirit would rule. This rule of God's spirit was to be recognized as the creative power of unity, as love and community. We have forfeited all this. We have lost God. Only God himself could give us back what we have lost: he himself and his image. In Jesus Christ he did this. In Jesus, God's heart has come into our midst once more. Once more it became clear in him what will and spirit God is. He revealed afresh what purpose and what reality of unity and love live in God. He came to do the will of the Father. He brought the Father down to us. He carries out his decree. He and the Father are one. In Jesus, God is near once more. This message has to be believed.

When Jesus brings God near, God can be recognized as God, and men and women become men and women. God's approach changes us, without us becoming God. We stand in terror before God who is quite other; even in the gift of his presence, one decisive thing remains unchanged: we cannot become God. We remain other than God.

Therefore, although we might understand it, we cannot embrace the sort of mysticism that deifies nature or people. Such deification is a delusion: it leads people to the mistaken notion that human life can be subsumed in some grandiose conception of a divine All. To a follower of Jesus it is clear that the spirit of the living God comes not only to save but to judge. As the law and the prophets testify, he is the good *and* the just, the pure and the holy one. But we are not good, not just, not pure, and not holy. God's nature is the opposite of our nature.

God is spirit and will in a way we are not. He is the will of what is good and perfect. This we are not. Yet his judgment is our salvation. Out of the rubble of our degenerate lives he wants to salvage the life of the creation. God demolishes our nature as it is and with it the way we have lived and carried on. Out of these ruins, he wants to bring to light the human race as it originally was and is finally meant to be. We are lying under the mountain. The boulders are being blasted. The debris must be cleared away. The vein of gold cannot be laid bare unless the mountain is blasted. This freeing is love. The place for gold is in the sun; without the sun, gold is as black as coal. God is merciful to us in our poverty, for we are suffering under it, burdened by it, and buried in it in spirit and in will. He releases us from every need and supplies all we lack.

God has drawn near as power, liberating and drawing us close. He accomplishes this in Christ. He is the God of uniting love for people who were not free, not united, and not loving. He leads to a future that allows his will, as his spirit, to rule over everything else. God's future wishes to rule over us here and now. Through this we will be transformed and made true. His kingdom of unity shall take possession of everything that has been disunited. Here is Christ: God remains God, we become God's people.

We cannot be merged with God as a drop is merged with the ocean or a spark with a sea of fire. For we are not part and parcel of his nature. There is no "we" between us and God. There is only "thou." But there is this "thou," and that is greater. God goes out to us, and a personal community is the result. It is a moral relationship of unity in will and deed between God and his people. Just this is so unspeakably great in Jesus Christ: unity becomes a reality in that the truth is unveiled. The light of truth shines on us in all its sharpness. When we experience God in Jesus Christ, we experience his nature as holiness – a holiness that judges our sin yet draws us into unity with him. God makes us conscious of our corrupt state as unholy unrighteousness yet leads everything to holy righteousness.

Because God is a creative spirit, he cannot let his works come to a standstill when he has brought us to realize with horror our own unrighteousness. It is quite a lot, even a great deal, to know ourselves condemned and absolutely opposed to God and hostile to him in our very nature, in our actions, and in all the relationships that condition what we do. But it is still not enough, not nearly enough. First it has to become clear that we (with all we have and do) are absolutely different from God and his works, absolutely different from how he wants us to be. Then his spirit, who makes all things new, insists that we with all our doings become at long last as God means us to be. Our own works have to stop in order for his to begin. In us his work has to begin. With us it has to be established.

Some reject faith in the intervention of God in his creation here and now as a mystical faith based on personal experience. Others cannot believe that God makes himself known as a living God in the hearts and lives of those who receive him. They have forgotten the gospel as Matthew, Mark, Luke, and in a special way John passed it on. They deny the power of God as it was revealed in Jesus. Some want to exalt the limited theological thinking of the human brain and elevate it as the only faith to be experienced. But they reject unity with God and the works of love springing from faith – not only for our time and our contemporaries. They reject the apostles of Jesus Christ and therefore Jesus himself. And whoever rejects Jesus rejects God who sent him.

By bringing God near to us, by coming himself with power, Jesus exposed our smallness and hostility more clearly than all human dialectic can do. So one thing is and remains right about these theological reflections, something fundamental with regard to the gospels: faced with God's greatness we become terrifyingly aware of our smallness. This absolute feebleness and smallness applies as much to our feeling, willing, and doing as to our thinking.

In God's light our baseness and smallness, our weakness and darkness, must constantly be exposed to him and to ourselves. Before him, we can appear only as we really are. In his presence, the last shreds of self-idolatry, self-redemption, and self-seeking vanish. His sunshine reveals our life as night. His clarity opens our darkened eyes to see the mountains of filth that bury us. His loving justice shows up the injustice of our rule with its mammonistic nature. His all-inclusive will for peace reveals the will to murder and the urge to set limits that characterize all our ideals. Whether they are based on individualism, patriotism, proletarianism, or any other "ism" makes little difference. God's truth and God's essential nature throw into sharp relief the untruthfulness and insignificance of our lives, private and public.

The experience of God unites and divides at the same time. The deeper his love leads into community with his heart and into brotherly uniting, the more sharply do we become aware of the absolute difference between our sin, which is separation, and his purity, which is unity. There is all the difference in the world between God and us. God wants unity without glossing over the differences.

Uniting with God is possible only through the radical destruction of all powers that oppose God, of everything in conflict with him or done in antagonism to him. Therefore, fundamental in any experience of God is forgiveness and the taking away of sin (remission and freeing). Forgiveness is the taking away of what is present (that is, sin). When God unites, what is against him cannot be present. He wants absolute purity in uniting. Therefore everything that opposes purity must first be given up and then taken away. That is forgiveness. God's kingdom will not come without it.

Whoever accepts God in Jesus, or receives in Jesus the forgiveness and the works of God, embraces God himself directly. God is embraced by the faith of the heart. For the heart has been gripped by God himself. But God never divides himself when he gives himself. He gives himself completely. Acute consciousness of our utter insignificance, dividedness, and sinfulness makes it possible to accept the utterly different and eternally indivisible one. The believer is completely one with God, because only God is completely one. Faith is truth, because the object of faith is God. Because God is truth, our self-deception vanishes. The heart knows only too well: my small "I" has not been merged into the great "I." Still less has this very small "I" been puffed up into something great. Lightning from above has shown up the tension: the human heart remains a very small "I," and that very small "I" dedicates its will to God completely and worships the great "thou" that gives itself to us in ineffable loving-kindness.

The believer does not surrender his or her feeble consciousness to the almighty consciousness. In experiencing God, Christians are not seeking an opiate for their intelligence. They do not see in the spirit of God a fading-out of human senses. But just as little do they presume to comprehend the spirit of God through the powers of understanding. They do not believe they can know God through the insight of their own powers of thinking. Believers do not presume to think they can grasp God through the intensity of their inner life, their emotions, or their willpower. Their faith places God's greatness before them as something so inviolable that feeble human strength has no chance of touching him. All human efforts to achieve union with God are in vain. If faith were a human function, it would be nothing. It could have nothing but a human object; it could never grasp God.

At this point, however, God intervenes. The union so impossible for us ever to achieve takes place through his intervention. If the word "faith" is to keep its meaning, it must be a certainty about what God – not people but really God – is and does. Faith belongs to God; it does not stem from people. It is God who gives us faith and brings it about. That is where we are one with God.

In the soul, faith is expressed in a heart-to-heart relationship that God brings about. In this uniting through faith, God is the one who wills, God is the one at work. Faith is expressed in an active and effective love in outward circumstances and public life, but it is God at work. God is the loving, the active one in these new works of love.

The believer acts according to God's nature, what God wills, and what God is. Without God, faith is nothing.

Wherever community is given through faith, its works are vital and effective because they are God's works. Through faith, God's power is made clear by our incapability, God's greatness by our smallness.

In every decisive experience, our insignificance is confronted with God's greatness, our inadequacy with God's mightiness, our incapacity with God's power. This experience of God runs through the whole history of humankind: God's supremacy overpowering us. When we stand in reverence before God, our first, intuitive experience of him is of an almighty power, before which all human strength is a mere nothing.

Like Elijah, the first prophets veiled their heads in shuddering awe when God was about to draw near to them. The thought of seeing God fills all genuine people with terror. In the times of the prophets, the sight of God cast the beholder to the ground, dead. In all ages, the mystery of God's greatness has been awesome beyond measure. Whenever an overpowering sense of this comes over us, all human powers are conquered. We are bound to shake with terror whenever God draws near.

God's greatness, majesty, and might are beyond all powers of our imagination. If we were to see God, we would perish – God is so far beyond our capacity to see him face to face. With whom could we compare God? How could we give a picture of this inconceivable greatness and power? God is unattainably great and glorious. The prophets know very well that beside him no other power can endure. His divine decree can never be fulfilled by anything human. No human power can stand before him. The life of God goes far beyond all boundaries of beginning and end. It towers immeasurably above all created things.

God has power over all nations on earth. He gains authority over all human powers. He will eventually rule over all worlds. Such an overpowering greatness of majesty makes corresponding demands that are unspeakably serious. Those gripped by prophecy sense with awestruck reverence the inviolable and adamant nature of this overwhelming will. As Job had to lay his hand on his mouth, we have to be silent before the greatness of this power.

The greatness and majesty of God is so overwhelming that the whole earth along with all humankind will become his footstool – the footstool on which God's foot rests. Under God's feet lies everything that is visible and invisible. In human eyes, creation is overwhelmingly great and supremely powerful, a shatteringly magnificent prospect through which God draws near to our small human hearts. In the childlike minds of primeval people, God is never confused with nature. Even the earliest beginnings of faith are far from deifying nature. But childlike people do not experience God's majesty and greatness without nature. They cannot disregard creation when they stand before the creator. In the mysterious coherence of created worlds, as believing creatures we sense the might of the creator, which gives all created things their greatness, life, coherence, and unity. In nature, we in our smallness have an intimation of God in his greatness.

Here we have to pause for a moment. In the rush of a life cut off from nature, we must remember – stop and take it in – how overwhelmingly God's power comes to meet us in nature. No scientific progress has changed this mighty fact. The whole history of humankind proves it. Through the great and visible creation, the infinitely greater and invisible nature of God dawns on our insignificance. Creation makes known the power and divinity of the creator.

If we live on the land, the terrors of the powers of nature above all else bring us to quake before God's might. In earthquakes and volcanic eruptions, huge mountains melt like wax beneath God's feet. Thunder and lightning, storm and tempest, scorching desert wind and blazing fire are powerful signs of the awe-inspiring approach of his greatness. Whatever the mighty phenomena of nature, it is the greatness and majesty of God that shakes us. The created world has elemental power. But we sense that over and above it all stands God, the creator who is infinitely greater and mightier than the greatest powers of creation.

As God's creations we quake before these superior forces, but no less before the tremendous mystery of life. Truly reverent people sense an ultimate mystery in all living things, aware that the living, creative spirit must be greater than all created life. Full of wonder, they stand in awed reverence at the tree bursting with life; at the lively, bubbling spring; under the light- and life-dispensing constellations of day and night; and in the midst of earth's fruitfulness and life. How great and powerful God must be to create and sustain all this life! Every deeply shaken and moved heart is struck by the challenge that God the great creator must become undisputed sovereign over all this power and life.

In the midst of nature, history reveals the overwhelming power of God, both as violent wrath-filled terrors and as the life-giving, uniting power of love. Awaking with trembling awe to a sense of this, we can look back to the beginnings of our own history. The profoundly mysterious beginning of the human race comes from God. It is God who has in his hand also the end of the human race. Without God, the end is shrouded from human eyes in the same darkness as the beginning.

The mystery of God the creator is experienced in all living things, but particularly in the life of human beings. It is the same in the middle as it is at the beginning and the end of the way: God is always drawing terrifyingly near when death and catastrophe break in, as in the destruction of the world in the Flood, or the division into nations at the peak of Babel's civilization. In the history of humankind, as in the whole of nature, it is God who is breaking in with mighty power when people are shaken by terrifying events. When God's greatness strikes nations to the ground, empires and world powers are the instruments of his wrath. All the nations of the world must come to fall at the feet of the God of all worlds.

The creator of the universe rules over all ages with his decree. In history as in nature, coherence of life, community of life, peace, unity, and life itself shall be revealed (in spite of all opposition) as God's nature and God's power. So God appears to the prophetic eye as the leader and shepherd of history. He guides the actual history of humankind toward the one goal: that all nations are united in one fold.

Thus the people of Israel experienced God as the God of history in all world events, in all the whirlpools of international politics, and in the collapse of whole peoples. Only God the creator has right and might over all peoples. Whatever happens, God is arising and claiming the world dominion that is his right alone.

As humankind develops, its dawning perception finds the same traces of God in history as in nature. When the conscious mind wins through to greater clarity, it turns to history. It cannot find peace until it has wrested the ultimate meaning from past and present events and those yet to come. So it is clear that nascent faith never confuses God and history (as if the course of events could be God himself), yet God is never experienced without history. Behind all the shattering events in history, awakening humankind senses God. Gripped by faith, they see God at work, intervening and ultimately determining everything, behind all the mysteriously tangled threads of history, behind every event, great or small. God is at work in all that happens. His majesty towers above all history.

In all this, Jesus Christ shines out in prophecy and in the apostolic mission: Jesus, the decisive point of all history for the whole of creation! Through Christ, the eye of faith is opened and a discerning eye for history is given. Then we see how far creation and history belong to God and how far they are estranged from God and even hostile to him. Faith catches sight of the coming hour of decision. In Jesus Christ, prophetic truth becomes reality. Those illuminated by him see the approach of the kingdom of God as a historical event. The creator breaks in upon his degenerate creation. The Lord of all worlds draws near to history with all its devious ways. Jesus Christ intervenes in history and turns it into the history of the end time.

The end goes back to the beginning. The Morning Star of the new beginning appears. The secret of life is the sun of the future. God's aim is not the destruction of all things; his ultimate will is the resurrection of life. Resistant humankind must go through judgment, death, and annihilation. In the fire of judgment, the beginning of the new shines out as the end of the old. Renewal and restoration are revealed as the goal of all that happens. The experience of God is resurrection from the dead.

The small world of the individual is meant to mirror the great world of God's history. To experience God means to give ourselves to the goal of his kingdom in such a way that we accept his death sentence and believe in his resurrection. Strength from the future comes to the believer. The spirit of the coming Christ is at work and charges us now with the task of the future. In the reawakening of faith, the prophetic spirit works toward the establishment of God's kingdom. New life begins at this given place, at this very moment. The nature of the coming kingdom shall be represented in the course of history itself and on this very earth.

Through the experience of God, people living today will be drawn into the end history of creation. The fire baptism of God's judgment will raise the phoenix from the ashes. The dying of the old world announces the rising of the new. Just because life comes to the heart when it is touched by God, it is near to death. Christ's death brings resurrection. The false life, which in any case bears the seeds of death within it, comes to an end. Life that rises in God begins and presses on to the future.

In Persian mysticism, those who become sacrifices to the passion of love destroy their lives forever, as the dying moth surrenders to the singeing flame, leaving nothing but ashes. It is quite different in Christ. In his flame, no loving believer shall perish in silence. In him, the weaker life is not meant to lose itself in the stronger. The stronger has no wish to overpower the weaker and swallow it up. Christ kills the old in order to give life to the new. Self-will, which is sick unto death, must die. A renewed and transformed will shall come to life. The old will, already turned toward death, falls prey to it. The new will becomes free – to belong to the other life. It is roused in order to live. In God, strength is given to the will to serve this life in deed and in truth.

God's will is for our resurrection so that we can live to the full extent of our powers. Basic to the new life is its voluntary nature. Resurrection from death leads to a life of freedom. When this becomes a reality, it means that the greatest of tasks has been effectively assigned. Whoever proclaims judgment and death without commitment to life turns God into a judge pronouncing the death sentence or into a cold, indifferent stranger. The living God has been denied. The quickening spirit of Jesus Christ does not allow himself to be relegated to a distance. In him, superabundant life, with all its powers of renewal through love, remains concentrated on the earth and its inhabitants. God's creative power, calling forth new life, draws near to all who want the life that is in God. This life is the worldwide rule of God.

The life-creating spirit blows where he wills. He comes as he wills. He knows where he wants to go. Everywhere, he seeks out anyone with a determined faith who accepts no other spirit than this one and only spirit of life. To such he reveals himself as a power that breaks in across all distances. He proves himself as almighty power; our strength, compared, is a mere nothing. It is not we who awaken him: he awakens us.

In the face of his direct breaking-in, all our delusions must give way, vanquished by ultimate reality. Truth dispels all illusions. The sick and misguided spiritual life will be cast aside. The selfish psychophysical life, going headlong to ruin without light or warmth, is overpowered. Selfish life, in and of itself already condemned to death, is destroyed in the consuming fire of God's approach. Severed from the divine core of life, it was lost before it was abolished.

Even though it had died long ago, the life of the individual in its own nature was still wrongly called life. The madness and deathly stupor that makes an individual think that he or she is "the only one" must be shattered. In morbid presumption, those individuals who think they are "the only ones" claim as their property what belongs to God. This self-conceit must die. The other life, God's life, has to begin. The individual is freed from his or her own life and won for the greatness and power of God – received into the sphere of God's power. What was dead wins community with life.

Here in this personal contact with God's life, an existence begins that encompasses everything. It cannot become sick and cannot pass away. The life that has its source in God puts its boundless energy to work in a practical way: all its members and powers come to life in the service of justice and righteousness. Then we are received into the sphere of God's kingdom. The nature of this kingdom is the rule of love. God's life is love. It is the social and moral life of perfect love. Divine love in believers brings it forth. It wants justice and righteousness first and foremost. Anyone set free in this way experiences a transformation. He comes nearer and nearer to the perfect image of love's radiant power, the reflection of the Lord and creator of life alone.

Such an experience of God brings about a new birth that lifts us high above all deadening enslavement. Rebirth is the gateway into the kingdom of God. From a new relationship with God, an absolutely new energy and joy in life begins. The beginning of life is birth: new life begins with rebirth. Only in God can life, real life begin. Life is free to unfold only where God has absolute rule. God is life. Because he was one with God, Jesus could and had to say, "I am the life." Because he fills us with his life, the fountainhead of strength, he had to say, "He that believes in me has life."

We are able to and should live his life because he sends his spirit into our hearts and he himself, with the Father, makes his dwelling in us. Through his strength, we keep his word and do the deeds of his love. Whoever claims that he abides in him is duty-bound to live as he lived. Because he brought God to us as working and unhampered life, Jesus alone can satisfy the hunger and thirst for living righteousness. Only Jesus, in his human existence, has put into action the vital energy that comes from perfect love. Only he can reveal God to us as life. Only Jesus, who is one with the Father, who made the life of love an historical reality on earth – only Jesus can disclose to us human beings the mystery and the power of life.

Through the power of the indwelling spirit of God, by which Jesus drove out all other spirits, the rule of God has come to us. Through the life of Jesus, we shall know what it means to belong to the kingdom of God. How dare we speak of this kingdom if we are not prepared to live here and now, in deed and in truth, as Jesus lived, to place here and now all circumstances of our life under God's rule? When we pray for God's kingdom to come, we ought to stop and ask ourselves whether we are prepared, whether we want to accept and represent all the changes that God's rule involves.

Jesus shows us that the kingdom of God means recognizing the absolute supremacy of the highest will, the will to love. The final kingdom is the perfect realization of the will of God, who is life and love. The unconditional nature of God's life and God's love will not let itself be restricted. God's will does not allow any other will to stand. The rule of love will not ally itself with anything that curtails love, restricts it, or limits it. God's rule will not tolerate any rival authority. The kingdom of God is power because it is the righteousness of God, the peace of Jesus Christ, and joy in the Holy Spirit.

For our day and age, God's rule can already begin in hearts where he and his peace reign because Christ has made his dwelling there. God has sent the spirit of the Son into our hearts. That carries an obligation and an authority with it – all those gripped by this spirit must drive all other spirits from every sphere of life. The kingdom of God means power to make its spiritual laws valid, also for the outward form of human life. The justice and righteousness valid in God's eyes rules so effectively through the Holy Spirit that it can build up social justice – spoken about by the prophets – in the entire surroundings of those who let their lives be governed by it. All spirits of human privilege and social injustice are cast out by the Holy Spirit.

Peace ruling in people's hearts as God's unity enables them to become builders and bearers of outward peace. From the church of God as the center, the driving-out of all spirits of unpeace, war, and civil war, like the spirit of competition and private property, will take place. Joy in the love of God fills the believing heart with such overflowing joy that it must go out to all in love. As recipients of this faith and joy, one after another shall be drawn into the circle of love and complete community. The spirit of the church is the spirit of justice, peace, and joy, for it is the spirit of the kingdom. It is the church of Jesus Christ that brings the kingdom of God down to earth here and now.

The spirit of God is a power working within our hearts, but it has outward consequences. Its effect on society is to break off all existing relationships and build them up completely new. Whoever denies this betrays the innermost nature of this power. For the spirit of unity wants community in everything. He achieves unity among us because he brings us into unity with God. The oneness he brings about expresses itself in such a way that all the evil and unrighteousness in us is overcome through the goodness and love of God.

To every situation, such a spirit brings a superior power that is in God alone; it can never originate with people. The will of faith strengthens life and increases works a thousandfold. This faith is the confident trust that radiates from hearts gripped by God. Love is poured out into a believing heart. This takes place through the spirit, through the living and objective spirit, who brings with him God's life and God's cause. Faith is something so clear and definite in content – in a personal way and in an objective way – that it cannot be separated either from the believing heart or from the object of faith. Christ himself is this faith, so that Paul declared: "I live, yet not I but Christ lives in me. For the life I live now in the flesh I live by faith in the son of God, who loved me" (Gal. 2:20). There is no other life of faith than that lived in the unity and community in which Christ lives.

Faith lives in Christ. The believer is in Christ, and Christ is in him: that is the power that transforms the whole of life from within. Luther expressed this mutual relationship between Christ and the individual heart in the most challenging way. He went through years of struggle, striving in vain after the righteousness of God with all kinds of human efforts; for this reason, his experience of God has such an unprecedented historical importance. The consciousness of sin that characterized him had thrown him into agony before the face of God, an agony so great and so severe that many cannot understand it today. Anyone who has lost the feeling of terror before God's might will never be able to understand this agony. And those who do not know Luther's distress can also not grasp his faith.

God seemed so full of wrath to Luther that he did not know which way to turn. He could find no consolation, either from within or from without. His agony of soul rose to such a pitch that it was infernal: no tongue could express it, no pen describe it. He felt he must perish utterly; he had to admit it. God's greatness and might threw him to the ground. Fear before God's justice crushed him. Only through the experience of love could help come to him. In the righteousness that springs from grace, he experienced it. By the word justification (grown so alien to us), Luther understood the experience of God that gives us in Christ a "being good through faith" without our own efforts or works; without this we cannot live before God, before ourselves, or before our fellows.

The new element that put Luther's heart and life on a completely different foundation was the relationship of mutual exchange between him and Christ. As he put it in a letter to a friend, Georg Spenlein:

Learn to know Christ, that is, the crucified Christ. Learn to sing his praises and to despair about yourself. Say to him: "Thou, Lord Jesus, art my righteousness, but I am thy sin. Thou hast taken upon thyself what was mine and given me what was thine; thou hast accepted what thou hast not been and given me what I have not been." Yes, you will learn from Christ himself that, in the same way as he has accepted you, he has made your sins his and his righteousness yours.

This mutual relationship, this receiving and giving of one to the other, is Luther's understanding of the words: "I live, yet not I but Christ lives in me" (Gal. 2:20). He understands with this confession that the bond between the believer and Christ is so complete that it is impossible to separate faith from Christ. This certainty of being one with Christ is based on his surrender to us. Brought about by Christ, it lives in our surrender to him. Faith gives us everything we are and have. Paradoxically, when this surrender takes place, it becomes the strongest power of will that can be brought into being. Our own will is never capable of it. To say about myself that I no longer live is possible only when my will has become one with Christ's will to die. Everything I have ever been or experienced or achieved must die there where Christ gave up his spirit. Only from Christ's grave is there resurrection of the free will.

The hours in which we come to this experience are hours spent, as it were, in the Black Tower.* It is the loneliness of the crucified one in his death that gives us freedom from our self-importance. It is the step taken by faith, into death and through the grave, that leads to certainty of life: Christ has accepted me in such a real way in his unity with me that he

---

*The reference is to the Wartburg Castle, where Luther stayed after being outlawed in 1521.

can say, "I am this poor sinner; that is, all his or her sin and death is my sin and my death." In this unity in death in spite of the most terrifying consciousness of sin, we become free from all sin. We have life in the risen one.

New in this experience is having Christ in us: he has taken our life upon himself. Our old life is taken away. Through his life, we share all that he is. Everything he possesses will in him be given to us. The same Jesus who said: "All power in heaven and on earth has been given to me" (Matt. 28:18) gives us his authority. The same Christ who takes as his own the seat at the right hand of power and confesses his unsullied unity with the Father makes us become in him partakers of divinity. Because he has made us his brothers, the Son of Man, who is called the last Adam, has become *our life*. In Christ, the power of him who can give everything to everybody is in us. The throne of all the worlds is his. His riches are infinite.

It is often forgotten what Luther recognized as faith: taking hold of the precious and costly treasure itself – that is, Christ. Only Christ himself could give substance and content to Luther's faith. Only Christ, "comprehended and dwelling in the heart in faith," is righteousness. Here is no human definition of faith; it is simply a matter of Christ. Christ comes down to us and becomes our life. His coming is faith; what he does is faith. With all their understanding and good intentions and church services, the human forces of piety, wisdom, and religion have no faith. Their efforts to rise up to God are futile. Believing in Christ means that he, Christ, has become one with me. It means that he abides in me. The life I have in faith is Christ himself.

This fact that Christ lives in me is what is new in my life. Where Christ is, the law that condemns is forever canceled. Here is Christ, who condemns sin and throttles death! Where he is, everything that destroys life must withdraw. Who shall separate us from the love of Christ? Christ is here! No power can sever us from the love of God in Christ Jesus as long as he, the most powerful, is our master. If I have lost Christ, there is no help, no consolation, and no counsel to be had anywhere. The terror of death is all I know. Life is dead without Christ. Only he is life. To be with Christ means life and peace within and without. The life of Christ is energy. God is dynamic power. Luther says expressly: "A believer has the Holy Spirit; where he is, however, he does not leave us simply idle or lazy but impels us to all manner of good, in which we can exercise our faith and prove our Christian character." Here we must go beyond Luther, for here he goes no further.

Christ living in us means he unfolds his powers in us. Christ wants his power of love to come alive in us with his will to serve and his abundance for giving to others. With all the diversity of his gifts, he wants to be at work in all those who have accepted him as their life. Christ living in us means a wealth of serving and working to be measured only by the need and distress confronting it. When the vials of wrath are poured out over the world, when misery reaches unbearable heights, then a justice must be proclaimed and put into practice that will be mightier than the injustice over all the world: all the punitive justice of judgment will be fulfilled in love.

Through faith, Christ lets the justice and righteousness of God become our justice and righteousness. God's justice cries out to be revealed to everyone as the goodness of love. Wherever this justice and righteousness is, anything to do with injustice or selfishness has to withdraw. God's greatness is revealed as the power of love. There is nothing greater than this. When Jesus Christ is the whole content of faith, this faith must be as active in his perfect love as he was. What Jesus accomplished has to be represented by the believer personally and in actual practice. The love born of faith is urged on by the consciousness that the unity of Jesus with the Father was so complete that he said, "What is mine is thine, and what is thine is mine." The unity of faith that binds the human heart to Christ is so completely clear that what Christ says to him, the believer also says, "Mine is thine, and thine is mine."

Such community of complete sharing must reveal, out of each heart that has experienced it, the same essential nature and power in all things. A love that is active on behalf of all sees to it that there is everywhere a sharing of the mine and thine in complete surrender, bringing everything unitedly to a common pool for the use of all. Then the believers, as those who love each other, say to one another, "What is mine is thine. What is thine is mine." The love of Christ impels them to act and live in this way. The justice and righteousness of a Christian is Christ and his life. The Holy Spirit urges toward the same good deeds that Jesus did. Those gripped by Jesus have, like him, a love that makes them let go of all privileges. When they confess that Christ is their life, like Christ they must choose voluntary poverty for the sake of love; like Christ they must sacrifice their life unconditionally for friends and foes, with all they are and have.

Jesus was given all power and might. His love, therefore, must rule unconditionally and unhindered in the lives of those who are equipped with his authority. Then from the throne of power he puts his spirit into their hearts and gives them his commission. This commission must fill the whole of life. It must transform all the circumstances and relationships of life in accordance with its objective demands.

We should not say that we believe in Christ and his kingdom or unity and community with him if we do not sacrifice everything and share everything with one another, just as he did. We should not claim that his goodness and his righteousness have become our goodness and our righteousness if we do not give ourselves to the poor and oppressed just as he gave everything to them. We cannot think we experience the Strong One, who exercises all authority at the right hand of the Power, if his works of justice and community do not come to reality in our lives through the Holy Spirit. If we have that faith that is Christ, the working of it must become obvious in works of perfect love. If Christ rules in us, his rule must go out from us into all lands. If his spirit is in us, streams of this spirit must transform all the land around us in accord with his promises about the coming kingdom.

For such deep-going and far-reaching changes to take place, we fickle and weak mortals need to be constantly renewed and deepened – all the more, the more we are threatened by increasing distractions and inhibitions. Indeed at all times our inner experience needs renewal and deepening. Constant renewal belongs to the realm of the spirit just as much as to the natural, physical life. When the sun is shining and our eyes can see the light, when the birds are singing and our ears can hear them, it is an actual reality only because our ears are not deaf, our eyes are not blind, and our spirit is not dulled. Above all, these experiences of our mind and spirit can be renewed only when something actually happens, when God's mighty power lets the sun rise again every day and lets the birds begin to sing afresh every year.

We are born again through the living word of God and the blowing spirit of Jesus Christ. The strength and power of God does not live in faint recollections. It is not at work in dead intellectualism. If our spirit is not to fall prey to death, the word of truth, which creates new life, must prove to be again and again a living power in our hearts. The spirit of life judges the thoughts and motives of our hearts; he wants to sever soul from spirit moment by moment so that we do not become subject to our emotional nature and unable to perceive the living spirit (Heb. 4:12–13).

The spirit of truth is always ready to fill us and unite us in his church again and again. Christ wants to confer his power and authority on his church so that through the Holy Spirit she can time and again win new victories over all other spirits. It is the work of the spirit whenever the word of God cuts our hearts to the quick and shows up all confusion in sharp relief. We need these experiences of the true life-giving spirit even more than we need our daily bread.

In the strength of this truth, the Master over all spirits rejected the encroaching power of the tempter: "Man shall not live by bread alone but by every word that proceeds from the mouth of God." If life is not to die out, we must accept God's truth constantly and let ourselves be renewed by it. Jesus says therefore: "My food is to do the will of him who sent me." God lives in deed and action. When we receive the word of God again and again, it brings forth in us the strength of God's life and God's deeds from the heart of God.

In this sense, George Fox was right when, in the formative days of his great movement, he emphasized his belief that it was the Spirit – the inner light, the inner word – that was all-important.* The living word is always waiting to be received into the innermost ground of our soul – to be grasped quite personally and so transformed into actual deeds. This is the only way we can be always steeled for the hardest battles, as John wrote to his church communities: "You are strong, the word of God abides in you, and you have overcome the Evil One." We will abide in the Father and in the Son in all we do – but only when the direct witness of living truth abides in us and is constantly renewed.

From the beginning, the word of God has led man in the atmosphere of grace. Every experience of God is an undeserved gift. By utterly exposing our incapacity and opposition to him, we have let ourselves be known by God. We have known him in the completely undeserved love he revealed by sacrificing his son. We have known Jesus as the healing savior of a life going to utter ruin. Through his death, we have received forgiveness and redemption from the heaviest burdens. Every time we experience God, we are led to a deeper consciousness of the deadly interrelationship of all guilt and to a deeper reverence for undeserved grace.

The daily purification of our hearts helps us to see more and more clearly what separates us from God and to take vigorous measures to set it right. God is faithful and just, and when we are ready to take the consequences right to the

---

*George Fox, 1624–1691, founded the Society of Friends, or Quakers, in 1647.

end, he is prepared to forgive everything that disturbs his unity and purity. When we sin, we need the Advocate, who reconciles and unites. Through this spirit Christ the mediator wants to set in order all that causes disintegration and division – all that mars the unity of life. The work of reconciliation blots out guilt and sets free the guilty for life in God – it restores unity.

No one can dispense with the renewal of this experience even for a moment. Community with God and the unity of his church are constantly attacked by all the powers of the earth. They are in danger of being broken up at any moment. The spirits of mammon, of lying, of unfaithfulness, and of impurity besiege and storm the stronghold of God's community without respite. If we allow them even the smallest foothold in the outer fortress of our being, they concentrate their attack on the very center. Their concentrated fire tries to numb the heart and destroy the unity of life. The soul in our lifeblood is constantly exposed to their destructive rays. As soon as the darkness that surrounds us gains power over our stand in life, we lose community with God. We deliver up the lifeblood of our soul to impure powers. We are separated from God and his kingdom by a barrage of dark rays. We are without God and without community in this torn and divided world.

Yet the light of unity outshines the darkness of decadence and ruin. We must follow the light. "If we live in the light as he is in the light, we have community with one another, and the blood of Jesus Christ cleanses us from all sin." The bright beams of God's light are stronger than the dark radiation of destructive demonic powers. Light cannot be overcome by darkness; but faith and the life determined by it must be focused steadily on the light. Rays of darkness cannot capture those turned away from them. Such rays are active in the area of the will and aim at destroying it. If the will keeps free from their poison, the battle is won. Light is victorious over darkness. The will that lives in the light repels the attacks of darkness and is free.

Living in community takes living in the light for granted. The life given from God has a clarity and purity that leads to perfect unity of life. It overcomes all powers of destruction and disintegration. When we are at one with the soul of Jesus, with his blood and his life, the purity of his sacrifice sets us free from all impurity, and the powerful, unifying deed of his death from all disunity. This power brings a life that radiates the same brightness and glowing warmth as that from Jesus. The light of Jesus Christ is the new life of perfect unity. Lack of community and opposition to community are darkness and coldness – turned away from the glowing light of Jesus. Isolation of soul and impurity of will are antagonistic to the life of Jesus. The will is impure and darkened when it mixes the clarity of Jesus' life with other elements, when it offends the faithfulness of perfect love or the community of perfect unity, and when it denies the surrender of all belongings. It forsakes the light and chooses darkness when it becomes a selfish, covetous, or possessive will. Every disunity and separation denies the power that radiates from the sacrificed life of Jesus.

In the spirit of the church – in which Jesus is among us here and now – he brings the community that is united. Only where there is unity is the life of Jesus actively at work. In his church we stand under the impact of the cross. Unity was created by the cross. The Spirit brought it. Without the witness of the blood of Jesus there is no witness of the spirit of Christ. Unity is preceded by the abolition of disunity. The Spirit brings death to the fiend. In the power of Christ's death our old life dies and new life begins. Those who lie buried in the churchyard are no longer to be seen at the tavern, on their property, or carrying on their own affairs. They have been taken away from the busyness of their old selfish nature.

Those who, with Christ, are dead to all they own turn their backs on all influences of self-will and self-interest. They live in the strength of the sacrificed life of Jesus. In this strength, they sacrifice their own old life just as Jesus sacrificed his perfectly pure life. They are prepared for the same baptism of blood that poured over the body of Jesus. Those who believe in the executed Christ are prepared for death in the strength of an inner dying. If for the sake of truth it has to be, they are even prepared for death with the shame of public condemnation and execution. As a sign of this readiness they are lowered into the grave of Jesus: early Christian baptism is the symbol of the power of dying and the power of resurrection. As a sign of the pouring-out of the Holy Spirit, baptism testifies to the break with things as they are and to the beginning of a new life. Unity in Jesus' death brings unity in God's life. It is only through sacrifice that we can find the courage to enter into the presence of God.

Whoever has experienced God in the holiness of his love, brought close to us by Jesus, knows why Jesus died. God wants us always to be one with the soul of Jesus' blood, dying the death of Jesus, rising in the power of his resurrection, and living the words and life of Jesus. This takes place through the presence of Christ, that is, through the life-giving spirit, and through Christ's love, poured out over us and filling our hearts. His love draws us into God's community through the Holy Spirit. Dead to everything that is evil and unjust, we live from now on for the good, in the justice and righteousness of perfect love.

God by his very nature can never deprive himself of his moral character, of his goodness; he can never enter into community with evil. He cannot end his own existence. God is the good. He wants to conquer the world for the good. The good can live only where evil has died. Our whole nature, which is shot through and through with evil, has to undergo the death of Christ as a dying to evil, as our death. With the crucified one, we suffer a death that frees us from all that makes community with God impossible. Delivered up to the judgment of Jesus' death, we become one with the heart of God in a new life: God breaks in. What is new begins. What is evil comes to a stop. What is good starts.

The love of Jesus' heart has turned the judgment of God into redemption. Unity with him who was executed on the cross brings unity with his soul, with the very essence of his life. That means unclouded community with the living God. Community of life means victory over everything that has anything to do with sin and death. The death of Christ brings us to his resurrection. The powers of his sacrificed life bring us new life from God. This new life proves, through the working of the Holy Spirit in the resurrection, that Jesus Christ is the living Son of God. In the Son, the heart of God has come to us. The spirit of God brings us his heart. We can perceive his hand and footsteps in nature and in world history. His heart is revealed in Jesus. And his heart is mightier than all his power.

Then the proclamation of the cross becomes a divine power; coming from the heart of God, it shows itself as the power for resurrection. Zinzendorf says his "rule and method" is "to make the glorious Lamb everything and to know no blessedness other than being with him and thanking him and being pleasing to him."* He is talking of the living sacrifice, which has its joy in the life and work of all-powerful love. The Lamb takes the rulership of God's kingdom on his shoulders because he bears the heart of God. If we accept the cross, come life come death, we take hold of the risen Christ in the crucified one. In him, we believe in the all-victorious power of love, which is God's heart. The cross is revealed as the victorious power of perfect love. It leads to resurrection and to the lordship of God. Jesus Christ, as the revelation of God's love, is life risen out of death. His death overcomes all the powers of the world and all deadly forces. Unless we experience (at least in some measure) the same readiness to die that characterized his love, we cannot experience his all-powerful life. Without him, nothing we can do has the power to withstand death and the devil. Only his divine life turns our actions into living work. Only the works of the living God are living.

We can sense things and experience them, we can move and be active, only as long as life is at work in us. There is no way of creating life apart from the power of life that is God, that is in Christ. When life flees, our eyes grow blind and our hands wither. Our ears stop hearing. Our spirit can no longer turn perceptions into experiences. Our will can no

*Nikolaus Ludwig von Zinzendorf, 1700–1760.

longer take on any work. In death there is neither strength nor activity. This power of life – this capacity to take in experiences – is decisive for being able to act or to create. Only God is life without any death. Only God's vital energy triumphs over death, degeneration, and decay. God rules over all spheres of life as creative life of infinite power.

Only the whole Christ for the whole of our life transforms and renews everything. Half of Jesus for half of our life is a lie and a delusion. The Spirit tolerates no choosing of principles or objects of faith such as a self-willed spirit selects from God's truth. Truth is indivisible. Christ does not let himself be taken to pieces. Those who do not take the same attitude as Jesus in everything have rejected Jesus. Not even the most ingenious explanation for their half-heartedness protects them from the words, "He who is not with me is against me."

Those who want to hear, read, or experience one or the other specific thing about Christ yet use weakening interpretations to wipe out what seems impossible will come to grief no matter how Christian the edifice of their life seems. Therefore Jesus must say that all those who hear the words of his Sermon on the Mount without doing them are like those who build on shifting sand. Their building is lost from the start. At the first attack of hostile forces, it gives way.

So Jesus commissions his ambassadors: "Teach them to keep to all I have commanded you." Whoever loves him keeps his word. Whoever believes in him does everything he has said. But whoever ignores any part – even a seemingly small part – of his living commandments cannot receive Christ's life. Organic unity is the essence of his life and spirit. Jesus' life is indivisible. It withholds itself or it gives itself –

completely. It is living unity. Those who want to cut Jesus into pieces and lay violent hands on his life are left with nothing but death in their hands.

Christ wants to be experienced as a complete reality who stands at the center of living action. His life is integration and wholeness itself; his life tolerates no mixing with anything outside its sphere. Thus anything contrary to the unity of his life and its living task has to give way before him. True life fights against all ungenuine life. Where Christ unfolds his divine life, all other life is extinguished. No other love can exist beside his perfect love. With divine jealousy, he annihilates every other image – often a falsified Christ-image – we set up beside him.

Over eight hundred years ago, Bernard of Clairvaux said, "When Jesus comes to me, or rather, when he enters into me, he comes in love, and he is zealous for me with divine zeal."* The whole Christ wants us wholly. He loves decision. He loves his enemies more than his halfhearted friends. He hates those who falsify him even more than those who are diametrically opposed to him. He abhors what is lukewarm and a colorless gray, the twilight, and the pious talk that blurs and mixes everything and commits itself to nothing. All this he sweeps away when he draws near.

Jesus comes to us as he is. He enters into us with his entire word. He reveals himself to our hearts as a coherent whole. In his coming, we experience the full power of his love and the whole force of his life. Everything else is deception and lies. Jesus Christ draws near to no one in a few fleeting impressions. Either he brings the whole kingdom of God for-

*Bernard of Clairvaux, 1091–1153.

ever, or he gives nothing. Only the one prepared to receive him completely and forever can experience him. Such a one is given the secret of God's kingdom. To all others Jesus cloaks himself in unrecognizable parables. Whoever holds aloof from complete surrender hears parables without understanding them. He has eyes to see and sees nothing. He has ears to hear and understands nothing. Whoever does not want the whole loses the little he thinks he has.

The experience of Jesus Christ is either a confirmation or a delusion. It proves true by holding firmly and with enduring steadfastness to the very beginning, to the whole way, and to the final future of Jesus Christ. So it endures to the end. When Christ is recognized fully, the invincible love of the Spirit overflows with endless insight and knowledge. It fills life with the fruit of steadfast righteousness; for Christ, the whole Christ, is its righteousness.

How we conduct our lives proves whether this experience of faith forms its basis. The father of Jesus Christ is God the creator. Every experience of God brings power to give life shape and form. Where it comes from God, a form of life takes shape in keeping with the complete picture of Jesus Christ and, therefore, with the kingdom of God. The weaker the life, the less able it is to give life shape and form. The difference between fleeting observations, which skim the surface, and experiences that go deep and remain steadfast can be seen in the power of their effect. Where God is at work, he goes into the depths while he reaches out into the distance. He is power at work giving life shape and form.

How many people travel in rushing vehicles from country to country, hastily skimming over the beauties of the whole world! Their eyes take a quick glance at everything. Yet nothing becomes a lasting experience. Their lives remain infinitely poorer than the lives of many of their neighbors who have never seen anything but the fields or woods outside their home town, but for whom trees and flowers blossoming and fading or nature stirring in any way becomes a fruitful experience.

Those who go rushing by in cities see nothing but the deceptive exterior of life. Their less esteemed neighbors, however, know deeply shaking realities in the joy of love, in daily work, and in the need of the world; they penetrate into all that life has to offer and to the very core of death too. True life is the all-embracing consciousness that sees deeply into the essential nature of things and, at the same time, far and wide into the distance. It bears the suffering of the world. It hungers after justice and righteousness. For it has heart and is heart. It is God's heart.

In some people, the shattering experiences of worldwide need, of war, and of all the subsequent catastrophes have only blunted the conscience. Others, though, see with new eyes what was previously hidden: the present as it really is and the future as it truly shall be. The new vision transforms life and animates every action. Only those who take in fully the true nature of all things and all events have a true and enduring experience of life. Truth demands hearts touched to the quick and the whole of life moved by the shattering experiences of God's wrath sweeping over the world today and making history; but beyond that it makes even stronger demands: that hearts and lives are moved by the love that appeared in Christ Jesus.

No matter how much we may hear and read of the life of Jesus, no matter how well we understand his words according to the letter of the Bible, our knowledge remains lifeless if the spirit and essence of his love does not grip us and our whole life. The letter kills. The Spirit gives life. His life is love. If truth as the essence of love does not become all-determining in our lives, its power kills the conscience. Without love, the new life dies before it is born. Truth also has a deadly effect when its life-giving works are rejected. Whoever hardens his heart to the transforming power of its living nature will be killed by truth.

The effects of an experience show whether it has been significant or empty, whether it has awakened life or killed it. Every experience of the unfalsified Christ means energy that proves itself in actual life. The renewal of our mind and nature brings about a transformation. Then we give up ourselves, and all we have, to serve God and his kingdom only. The results prove whether we have experienced God or whether we have become entangled in an illusion. For God has a power of life and love that his creatures are never capable of. The experience of God brings a superhuman love because it brings God's life. Love pours itself into the heart. The Holy Spirit transmits the divine power of this love.

The experience of God means strength for action. There is no love that does not come to living expression in deeds. To experience God as a life of love is to experience strength. A freeing from all unjust, loveless, and self-willed activity liberates abundant powers, leading to fruitful works of love. The love of God is experienced in the innermost heart and unfolds toward the outside. The more faith increases in

knowledge, experience, and strength, the more must we do
the works of love. To experience God is to be overwhelmed
by the power of love.

Our world situation calls for the kind of dedication that
lives in Christ alone, in the heart of the powerful God of
Jesus Christ. Only a heart filled with the superior power of
God's love will be able to check need and distress and allevi-
ate suffering. Only in the strength of the omnipotent God
can we carry the burden of historical responsibility laid on us
today, a burden beyond all human strength. The perfect
strength of all-powerful love, surpassing every other power
or greatness, is needed to penetrate our devastated world
with God's rule and Christ's message.

In the midst of the escalating power of injustice, in the
midst of today's widespread cruelty and coldness of heart,
love must be revealed: a love that towers above all the mountains of earth; that shines out more clearly and brightly than
all the stars of heaven; that is more powerful and mighty
than the quaking of the earth and the eruption of all its vol-
canoes; that is greater than all world powers and ruling authorities; that works more powerfully on history than all
catastrophes, wars, and revolutions; that is more living than
all life of the creation and its most powerful forces. Above all
nature and throughout all history, love proves itself as the
ultimate power of the Almighty, as the ultimate greatness of
his heart, as the ultimate revelation of the Spirit.

The experience of God is love – love that overcomes everything that withstands it. Love is the energy of the new
creation. It is the spirit of God's coming rule. Love is the one
and only element in the new building-up. It is the herald of a
new time. It is the organic strength of unity, the building-up

of a new humankind. This love is put into practice by the unity found in the church of Jesus Christ. The building-up of the church means a gathering. Whoever does not gather with her, scatters. Her life consists in uniting. Whoever does not take part in this uniting continues in death. In an age of decline, the life-bringing spirit of Jesus Christ establishes the work of the church. In her, God is experienced in Christ. In the church of perfect love, the spirit of God brings Christ's kingdom of perfect justice and righteousness down to earth. The experience of God means the reign of God in the church of Jesus Christ.

THE PEACE OF GOD

A deep-seated need makes people long for togetherness and harmony. Our inmost feeling tells us that the life ordained by God is one of organic unity, unity of all powers of the spirit and the will. In actual experience, though, the fate of unpeaceful humankind today is petty limitation, discord and disunion, inorganic confusion, conflict of spirits and aims. There is no unified center, no living point from which our entire thinking and doing can radiate. We lack this common point of reference, from which any effective unity must be determined if life is to prove itself strong and undivided. This dynamic integrity of life has been lost to individuals and to humankind.

Only where peace is alive and active – where its harmonious working embraces the whole of life – can a clear conscience acknowledge peace. There can be no talk of peace or harmony if a life does not show its integrity in lively activity and rich diversity. Impassive silence and unbroken quiet belong only to the deathly peace of the graveyard. Life is energy for enthusiastic action and reality in all its facets. Where the quickening spirit of God's peace fills and unites us, he puts his infinite energy into deeds of love. They are varied yet consistent, animated yet stable, diverse yet whole and undivided. The peace of God is the dynamic harmony of the perfect life, vibrant with infinite riches. "Whoever finds me, finds life" is the revelation it brings.

God's life is love. That is why he is the God of peace. His will is unity. In Jesus Christ, the revelation of his ultimate will, the supreme power of the Almighty brings a peace the world cannot offer. Jesus brings God's peace to us. In Jesus, God's countenance is so illuminated it brings an inmost peace of heart, a national peace that is justice, and an end to all warfare through love for one's enemies. The peace of God is unity in his creative spirit, who wants to bring a new peace and unity to the torn state of the whole world today. When God blesses his people with peace, we must never think exclusively of peace of soul or of a military cease-fire. It refers to the new order of a kingdom of peace that carries all before it inwardly and outwardly. The prince of peace makes faithfulness and justice the foundation of the land of peace he rules over. Under his rulership, justice and peace kiss each other. Where God has been at work healing and making whole, he grants perfect peace on a stable basis: constancy and faithfulness of heart, mind, and manner of life to the very end. Whoever obeys his spirit says with the prophets: "As long as I live, peace and faithfulness shall reign."

On the basis of a justice that can serve nothing else, God creates peace. The Lord of peace consecrates every aspect of our human life to his perfect purity and unity. He demands the surrender of all the goods of this life and of life itself. His new justice gives the poor and the wretched the land they never had; great peace shall be their joy. Without justice there is no peace. If the land of this stolen earth is not given back to the poor, justice will remain lost. For the poor who have been robbed of land, justice demands that everything amassed in self-will and opposition to God's will is handed back again. God's justice overcomes self-will and private property. What we own hinders God's unity. With the doing of good deeds, the peace of God supplants the evil of discord and unpeace.

Peace belongs to all who do good by giving up everything to love. It belongs to them alone. It streams out from the mercy of God and reveals his heart. Where his peace rules is goodness in abundance. The world peace of Christ establishes the order of love and justice for all and for all things. The peace of God, as the future of God's kingdom, is to have complete sovereignty over world affairs as well as over local churches. This takes place through the unity of the church of Jesus Christ, through the united nature of the innermost life. In the church of Jesus Christ, the peace of God reveals the infinite power and united nature of God's heart. His all-conquering supremacy will penetrate and master all things and all beings to unite them in God.

When God says, "Peace be with you," and Jesus gives his "peace" to his disciples, when the early Christians and the powerful Christ-centered movements of the Middle Ages and the Reformation greet each other with "Peace," we must acknowledge the joyful certainty and the power in this blessing of God's unity. The peace of God brings with it the grace of Jesus Christ and the power of the Holy Spirit. It encompasses the complete supremacy of God's rule, which as the unity of the creative spirit aims at bringing all created things in God. Whoever believes in the all-surpassing power of God is full of courage and confidence that his peace will be victorious. Faith in the peace of God is courage in a heart sure of victory.

P eace is the opposite of of fear. Peace, as unity springing
from life in God, overcomes the fear of dissolution in
death. The greeting of peace to Gideon was to encourage
him to live: "Fear not, you shall not die!" Discord belongs to
the kingdom of death. Peace allows life to triumph over
death. Unpeace bears within it the fear of death. Peace is
freedom for a courageous life of justice and righteousness.
Unpeace is slavery to injustice and to the fear of death arising from it. People justify preparations for war as security
measures because they are anxious in the face of oppression
and danger. They fear injustice and the loss of freedom. Yet
these very preparations bring nothing but injustice and slavery. The individual's fight for life, discord in the struggle for
existence, stem from weakness and fear and result in nothing
but unfreedom and injustice. Those who fear do not have
perfect love.

Fear for our own lives prevents us from keeping peace and
doing works of righteousness and justice. Enervating fear is
overcome by the power of love; then strength of abiding
peace enters. It builds up everlasting justice. There is no fear
in love. Perfect love casts out fear. An armistice with armies
lying in readiness, fearing renewed hostilities, cannot be
called peace. An armed peace is no true peace. Only the rule
of peace staying for ever and ever (as promised to the house
of David) is true peace. Only eternal peace is true peace.

God alone rules over eternity. We do not even reign over
the very small span of time allotted to us. There is no peace
other than God's peace. All peace treaties and all great con-
gresses and conferences among nations have spoken about
everlasting peace. They know temporary peace is meaning-

less. Yet they cannot achieve peace. A significant work written by Immanuel Kant in 1795, when he was looking back on his life from mature old age, bears the characteristic title, *To Eternal Peace*. A hundred years earlier, Quaker William Penn had also demanded peace for Europe for both the present and the future.* Both point to the divine character of peace. Only perfect life has no end. To us mortals and our undertakings only a brief span is allotted. Only God's peace and the kingdom of the prince of peace, who is arisen from the dead, have no end. Our works must retreat before God's works: "When he rules far and wide, peace will have no end."

Only from eternity, which is immortal, can lasting peace be guaranteed. It can never be established by time-bound powers. Only the infinite power of God can build up unity and preserve peace. Everything mortal falls prey to dissolution and decomposition. Life has to overcome death if unity of life is to be won and kept. When scripture says God will bless his people with peace, it as much as promises he will give the strength of his eternal and unchangeable power. God is life and strength. In them, he is the God of peace.

As creative power, it is God who brings about the productive life of constructive unity. His joy in peace delights in energetic action and demands active mutual help. It aims at a community of work that creates values. The peace of God is grounded in creative justice. Peace is God's work. There is no peace in creation without the Creator, just as there is no outward peace without the inner peace of social justice and no justice without community of creative work. God alone is love. Peace is created only when his spirit of love is at work.

*William Penn, 1644–1718.

We should not talk of peace if we do not do all we can to pass on to the poor and down-trodden everything we receive from God – all the goods and strength. Helping one another through deeds done in love to God – that is peace. Unless this power is at work, everything stays lifeless, nothing is at peace. Talk about establishing outward peace is false prophecy from those who do not build up active peace through loving work in community. What they call peace cannot be peace. The object of peace is missing: the building-up of unity through mutual help.

When foreign ambassadors came to David the king of Israel and spoke of peace, he said to them, "If you come to me peaceably (which can only mean to help me), my heart shall be knit to yours." Only mutual help and service in action is living peace. The lifeless peace that is all negation, such as the abolition of war, the peace that is satisfied when we lay down arms and cease to kill, is an empty nothing. The same is true when we claim we have peace in our hearts simply because the fire of inner conflict dies down.

The peace of God brings the strength of God's life. It brings the power of his love. It is active deed and service. To the first challenge, "Lay down your arms!" belongs the second, "Pick up your tools!" Depart from evil and do good! Turn your back on war, and with all your strength build at the communal work of peace. Peace is constructive work.

Peace is born when justice as a living body comes to the light of day. The church of Jesus Christ is this body, this organism of justice, peace, and joy of the spirit. This is why the psalmist says both things: "The mountains shall bring peace, and the hills shall bear justice! At the given time, justice and righteousness shall arise for you. With the rising of the sun of justice, the day of great peace dawns." This day has dawned in Jesus. In Christ, it draws near again. When justice shines forth, peace is guaranteed.

The land must be opened up to love. Starting from thinking and believing hearts, peace is making its conquest of the earth today through the church. If peace is to reign within city walls, true counseling of justice must be found for everyone and put into practice. The city that is the church of God is responsible for the carrying out of this counsel of peace. Whoever wants God's peace has to think the thoughts of peace, God's thoughts. The church, in thinking the thoughts of Jesus, is the bearer of God's heart. Hearts filled with the truth of Jesus know what counsel to give, and do what needs to be done. Where God is at work, faith is present. Faith is action. Faith produces love. Love knows what to counsel. When Jesus commands us to have the biting salt of truth, he is referring to the peace that the believers have among themselves and take out into the world.

Truth ends the disorder of unpeace so the order of peace can arise. The God of peace and order wants to stop the inorganic scattering of our thoughts and end the disorder of all things in our world that obstructs peace. Without Jesus Christ, people cannot find the way of peace because they do not recognize it. And they do not recognize it because their thoughts are bent on the divergent ways of unpeace. They are unclear about the main condition for true peace and just as unclear about its needed consequences.

If we are to recognize and avoid all other ways as leading to destruction, if we are to set foot on the way of peace and go with peace in our hands to those without it, then the spirit of wisdom must reveal the whole truth hidden in God's unity. Our hearts must become rigorously honest in the light of truth if we are to live up to the wisdom that comes from peace. The peace of God is given through the truth – but only to the upright. "Seek what is upright and you shall have peace."

Only to the upright is wisdom given; only wisdom opens up the way of peace. When God speaks about peace, he speaks against unpeace as folly. The practical wisdom of God seeks peace. Jealousy and strife are marks of worldly, emotional, and devilish wisdom. It is folly and brings nothing but evil and disorder with it. Wisdom from God brings peace, for it is full of mercy and good deeds. Directed toward everyone without any hypocrisy or partiality, God's wisdom is all-embracing. As long as we remain petty-minded and aloof from the oneness of the whole and put what is isolated and individual in the limelight, we remain torn by untruthfulness and sunk in confusion. We are not at peace. We get lost in superficialities, persist in folly, and remain in death.

Some want to talk exclusively about the peace of their own soul or the peace they share with another. They are incapable of representing the whole peace of God that belongs to the final kingdom. They remain sunk in narrow-minded folly, bogged down in the swamp of isolation. But it is the same with those friends of peace who make the opposite mistake and speak about world peace without peace with God and without the social justice of complete community. They want "pacifism" without fighting the spirits of unpeace, without battling the covetous nature of mammon, without opposing the accepted lies of social insincerity, and without waging spiritual warfare against unfaithfulness and impurity. Both of these false paths represent unpeace. It comes from folly, and indifference to all-embracing truth.

Where there is wisdom and faithfulness, peace is a reality. The kingdom of God is the union of love and truth. Therefore to unite outward peace with inner righteousness is the whole will of God's love. Only those hearts have peace and only those people bring it and work for it who love the whole truth. God's truth brings wisdom and uprightness – it begets perfect love. Love is the ultimate truth – it brings peace.

We keep peace only when the truth of God is in our hearts and our lives are upright, in tune with his perfect love. Only this truth in love and this love in truth makes for peace. When we do what God lays upon us, we shall – in the truth of love – bring salt and strength, help and loving-kindness to all people. In this love born of truth, peace is guaranteed by loving-kindness and faithfulness.

Out of the thoughts of what is good, peace is born. In the strength of peace, we want what is good for all people and all things. A heart that thinks evil cheats itself and everyone else: it becomes unhappy and spreads unhappiness. But whoever works for peace through the good – only love born of truth is good – brings the joy of life to people. Everything that offends love – the love that is the truth of God and his universe – is evil. Whoever represents the good for all with the unfailing power of perfect love puts into practice the peace of God: the ultimate truth of God's decrees.

The prince of peace is also called the wonderful counselor, the mighty God, and the eternal father. The kingdom that rests on the shoulders of the Son of Man is one of peace because it has the counsel of wisdom, the strength of might, and the divinity of the father of Jesus Christ. The creator of the new creation establishes the divine work of eternal peace: God's counsel leads to peace as the kingdom over which he rules.

The quiet and security of God's household of peace makes us free to dedicate ourselves to the task. Hands freed from defense should be active in building up the city of God. When the pickax is not used as a weapon, it serves as a tool. Those limbs not going to war on the side of injustice work for justice. Only then do we become true men and women. The faithfulness shown in dedicated work is God's peace in practical community.

The peace of God works like a stream, a wind; it is almighty power. Only God's peace can move all the mills that work for us, like a mighty river whose waters overflow, whose depths and force produce the greatest achievements. Whoever wants well-being of the people, building-up of the city, productive employment instead of demoralizing unemployment, and healing of human society must want peace as God wants it. As work in community, in a completely united society, peace is the only state that brings inner and outer well-being.

Love as God's peace is a bond of perfection; it unites everything that was split apart. It leads to complete surrender and common action. The Lord of peace wants to establish and maintain unity – in infinite diversity – for all things, however dissimilar. Peacemakers must represent God's peace as the solution for all problems, however remote. The strength of God's inmost nature copes with everything. It overlooks and neglects nothing: it is concerned with every-thing. God's heart is the mightiest power of all superterres-trial worlds, of all the powers of eternity. The peace of God's heart shall "have dominion from sea to sea, from the river to the ends of the earth."

Jesus proclaims peace to all, far and near, as part of the fighting equipment of his mission. The feet of his ambas-sadors must be shod with it for carrying his truth on long journeys into every land. The message of peace as a fighting commission shall conquer all countries for God's rule with weapons of the spirit. Only for this task will the Lord, the commander of peace, be on our side. The life of Jesus was sacrificed in the decisive battle to establish peace. So we too should be ready to lay down our lives. Whoever is not ready to fall in battle for the truth cannot live for peace.

When Jesus gave his ambassadors the commission to pro-claim God's coming reign, he wanted peace and its powerful effect announced to each house open to them. Their peace descended in God's full truth on each house they visited. If a house was not ready and willing, the peace, like a boomer-ang, would return to the hands of the warrior of peace. Peace is the salting power of fire, the spiritual weapon of the king-dom of God, the sword of the spirit.

Peace is the battle-song of God's heavenly hosts: "Glory to God in the highest! Peace on earth to men of good will!" In its strength the messiah-king entered the walls of Jerusalem. He rode no war-horse to a battle in which blood would be shed. The animal of poverty and peace was carrying him when he heard the cry, "Hail to him who cometh in the name of the Lord! With him is peace!" Defenseless, he rode to meet his death. Victorious, he sacrificed his life to lay the foundation of peace, carrying into all the world a bloodless battle against the power of the bloody sword, a battle for the complete dominion of the Spirit. Whoever glimpses the king of peace enters his kingdom in unsullied peace even though, like him, he must ford the terrifying river of death.

God's peace is the Spirit's victorious and death-defying battle against the evil spirit of devilish unpeace. In his defenseless death, Jesus destroyed the deadly weapons of the enemy just as the God of peace will soon crush Satan under the feet of the Spirit. He establishes peace in an all-out battle to the point of dying a defenseless death. He does not bring that flabby lack of hostilities we call peace. He brings the sharp sword of spiritual warfare, but those in his spirit sacrifice their lives without killing the enemy.

Jesus went to his death to bring peace. He killed no one, but he was killed. Without defending or sparing his life, he let his body be broken on the tree, welding hostile nations into one united people of peace, one single and united humankind. In the death struggle of his body, he gave humankind a new body: his living, united organism of peace – the church of Jesus Christ.

Anyone who wants to belong to this new united body must be ready like Jesus to suffer the most shameful and cruel death, to accept the same cup of poison from enemy hands, to be baptized by the enemy in the same bloodbath of the death sentence. Anyone who wants to live for the peace of God has, without sparing his or her own life, to take on the same fight to the death that Jesus fought to the end for the kingdom of peace. This is why the human heart is terrified and shakes with fear when the risen one stands before it with the marks of death to pass on his peace and the message of his mission.

The militant peace of Jesus Christ is unknown to humankind. This world knows only hate with its murderous preparation for war or the insincere and uncreative flabbiness of peace without struggle and without unity. This world knows only blind rage leading to the mass murder of war or the untruth of false prophecy, sparing the individual life but unable to represent an effective peace.

B ecause we ignore the sacrifices that lead to peace, we know nothing of God's will to unite or of his well-considered thoughts of unity. Peace blooms on the soil of genuine truthfulness that is shown only in a life sacrificed to the utmost and spent in unarmed but out-and-out combat against all opposition to unity and constructive peace. The heart that makes the perfect sacrifice – the mightiest power of all worlds – is the only strength that can bring peace.

Love fighting for unity makes this perfect sacrifice, which demands inmost purity of heart, making our whole life pure. Because Jesus poured out the soul of a pure life in his sacrificial death, because Jesus commended an unstained spirit of divine love into the hands of the Father, he triumphed as the pure one over Satan, the prince of death, and his impure spirits. Purity atones and must rise again. Impurity not atoned for leads to death. Not even by sacrificing its life can an impure life gain peace. Unity demands purity.

The unbridled passions of youth bring the deadly unpeace of impure spirits. These passions undermine trust and destroy faithfulness. They break up the coherence of life. Peace born of living unity exists only in the pure air of trust and faithfulness. Purity, trust, and faithfulness make up the atmosphere of life and of all viable community. Those who want to devote their strength to a living peace must strive for that sanctification of dedicating their whole lives to God's pure cause.

The purity of a life dedicated to God's unity lies hidden in the long-suffering humility of Jesus Christ's sacrifice. It wishes to take command of our lives in the pure spirit of Jesus. God's peace is unmerited grace. Only through a direct gift of God is our life at any moment pure and blameless in the absolute peace of God's heart. All the gifts of his spirit are gifts of peace, to be used in the service of the pure unity of his church.

The house of God upholds peace. It tolerates no breach, no irritation and strife within or hate and enmity to those without. All unpeace is banned from this house. Joy in all God's gifts, in all the objects of his love, lives in it. Where God grants his gift of joyful hearts, born of love that includes everybody, his peace gathers a people in creative unity. God brings about his righteousness of faith that grants peace with God, which is his will for all. The Holy Spirit who fills the church of faith means life and peace from God for all. The fruit of the Spirit is love and peace, the joy of a life in God.

Peace is the daughter of faith. It surpasses all human understanding. As an offspring of the spirit of Jesus Christ, peace keeps the heart and mind in him. Unity born of the spirit of God can accomplish what the thoughts and demands of the understanding never can. Faith conceives this unity, just as Mary conceived. Now as then, it is the body of Jesus Christ, the united church, that is born of God's creative spirit through faith. She surpasses everything that is human. Starting with the hearts of believers, she has power to rule and direct them; and she brings peace into all the world. Like the birth of Christ, every commission to the church of God is given in peace and unity. Her ways are ways of peace, just as the ways of Jesus Christ were, are, and always will be peace among all nations. Therefore the sons and daughters begotten of God delight in creating and in bringing peace alone. The kingdom of God belongs to peace.

God himself is in his sons and daughters; for they carry his blessing as peacemakers, carry out God's commands, live to give him joy, and do their utmost to keep peace with everyone. Yet they know that peace on earth can only be the fruit of faith in God and Christ and that the godless cannot keep peace, as long as they remain far off from true life. The goal of all Christ said and did, and the goal of his ambassadors, was unity with God and peace among all people as a way of life.

The ambassadors of Jesus Christ proclaim a peace that rules over all areas of their life. They bear the name of the prince of peace because Christ is the lord and king of divine peace, and because he holds the universal kingdom of eternal peace in his mighty hand. For them, his kingdom does not exist in sterile words but in the strength and power of unity, creating the peace of his future world. Sent out from the spirit of the church where peace rules, they carry its power into all the world. They fight and make every effort to improve conditions to help build up the holy peace of God.

For them, peace is the hope of their faith, their expectation for the future, and a power here and now. Peace is for them the sum total of all God's wisdom and decrees. God as the Lord, Christ as their expectation, and the Holy Spirit as the power that reveals all future things fill them with the most confident joy and inviolable peace. Their peace is not of the moment, for it comes from him who is, and was, and is to come.

Peace as God's future is proclaimed by the whole prophecy of the old covenant and the prophetic mission of the new church. All war and hostility are to come to an end. The old prophecy and the new prophecy are one. The prophets of the old covenant and the new covenant bring to bleeding humanity the divine kingdom of God's peace, putting an end to the violent, predatory nature of all ruling powers. Bestial malice and ferocity will be completely banned.

The predatory nature of brute force is overcome by long-suffering with its sacrificial nature. The reign of the Lamb replaces espionage and violent killing. The love that lays down its life fills the new person and replaces the injustice of the old one, who alienates God and destroys life. From the time of the first Adam and the first fratricide, our true image had been forgotten. The Son of Man, the last Adam, leads the way to our ultimate state, in which we are truly God's people. The heart and soul of the Bible is filled with this certainty. All of divine history in the Bible and all the history of humankind lead to God's goal.

The book that reveals God in history begins and ends with peace. The inmost depths of the Bible, its life and soul, is and remains peace. Loss of community with God always leads to murderous unpeace. Yet Christ, the morning star of the coming peace and unity, is never extinguished.

After the breach with our origin in the first kingdom of peace, the next step follows immediately – fratricide, which must not be avenged. The descendants of the man who murdered his brother proceed to found cities. The fellowship of the metropolis – as in the soaring structure of Babel – leads to dire confusion, disintegration, and warlike tensions between nations. Revolt against God leads nations to insurrection and war. Yet God revealed his heart once more: the deluge of his judgment swept over humankind, disunited and resistant to his spirit; but under the colorful symbol of the rainbow, he established the covenant of peace.

Abraham, the father of faith, is consecrated as a prince of peace by a mysterious priestly figure who belongs to the united dominion of peace. The faith of the patriarchs turns again and again to peace because the faith of Abraham, Isaac, and Jacob in the one God shows itself as a uniting power. So the greatest blessing of these patriarchs and later of Aaron (the first priest of atonement) is the blessing of peace. Even in the war years of the lawgiver, the blessing of the first high priest culminates in the peace that the last high priest was to turn into reality: "May Jehovah establish, work, and give thee peace!" Through Moses the law comes to God's people. In its wake come war and the sword. The military power of the Israelites reaches its zenith through the kings, given them at their demand by God – in his wrath. But despite all battle songs, at the heart of the psalms of the people and the songs of the kings there lies a longing for the peace that shall come from God.

The prophets proclaim peace as justice from God that shall take possession of the whole world. In the midst of the storm of devastating historical events, the prophetic message of peace stands like a rock that cannot be broken. The coming helper and leader of God's people will calm the raging sea of nations. As the bringer of peace, Jesus is given the name "Our Peace." Faced with his strength and truth, every illusion vanishes. The Old Testament prophet sees the contrast between the conditions of his time and the divine justice of the coming one who judges and saves. It must shine relentlessly through all the evil of the present time; it is love at work, and its fruit is peace.

When God is involved, so is his creation. Where God's peace appears, human unpeace is struck at the root. Social discord is revealed as human injustice – enmity to God and an obstacle to peace – which must be identified and ruthlessly exposed. Whoever sins in this way commits an outrage against God. The spirit of peace demands justice. The divine spirit in prophecy strikes society at the root of its poisonous growth. It exposes the economic injustice of hardworking people shamefully robbed of all meaning in life and condemned to a life of unhappiness.

Through the toil of the poor, unearned privileges are piled up, only nourishing strife and discord. Social distinctions and class consciousness rob us of soul and spirit. The injustice committed daily arouses the wrath of the God of peace until it reaches white heat. The prophets of God expose the depravity of assessing human beings in terms of money values. We are all responsible for those who have hardly any dignity or joy in life or vestige of peace left. As outcasts from the love of human society, they are delivered up to discord and unpeace.

The prophecy of peace is directed against this debasing of human love, this degeneration of the social conscience.

Prophecy rises up against the loveless will to possess. The prophet of peace attacks pride of rulership, making slaves of others. The rich person's cold love of money and heartless will to possess – which results in economic exploitation of the poor – summon the prophet of peace to the Spirit's battlefield, where it fights all greed, force, and wealth. The prophet recognizes that one who gathers possessions at the expense of others, often violently, is nothing other than a cheat.

The prophetic spirit calls to account all who helped trample the poor, who sided with the rich against those with nothing. The prophet Amos says every luxury is won at the expense of the poor and needy. The wealthy enjoy expensive furnishings, rich food and drink, and spacious rooms only through tyrannizing and crushing the poor and needy. Other prophets too hurl their "Woe betide thee!" at those who, by amassing clothing and furniture from the poor through seizure, become enemies of their own people: "You tear the skin from the body and the flesh from the people's bones." "You feed upon the flesh of my people."

The prophet exposes the enormous outrage of people planning to gain new land and houses to consolidate and increase private property. Isaiah cries "woe!" to all "who join house to house, lay field to field until there is no place for others." Moses had spoken the word of the Lord: "The land is mine." "The whole earth belongs to me." It must not become heritable property. Taking interest, like owning land, is unmasked as godlessness: they are the two hands of greedy mammon. All taking of interest is condemned by Ezekiel through God's word: "You have forgotten me!"

Ezekiel proclaims God's justice at work only where no one is harassed by poor wages or demands for money, where goods are not seized for debts, where people give their bread to the hungry and their clothes to the naked, where money is borrowed and lent without interest: that is, where the right to own property has been supplanted by love.

All prophets want economic oppression to be overcome, slavery's yoke removed, freedom for the degraded, the homeless led home, and the ill-clad given new clothes. Hosea puts the prophetic demand into one brief sentence: "Hold fast to love and justice and wait steadfastly for God!" All prophets know that for this a new spirit has to come over humankind. The spirit of God must be poured out over the crushed and downtrodden also to remove their suffering. The God of the stars and all their heavenly hosts will rule on the earth. He has laid his spirit on one whose righteousness and justice will never be exhausted until firmly established over all the earth as peace: it shall begin with one and shall come upon all. The spirit-bearer will judge the lowly and wretched justly and protect them. But he will overthrow the oppressors with the word of justice. He is called "God is our righteousness." His justice and righteousness will bring peace; swords and spears will be beaten into tools for peaceful work. No nation will lift up weapons against another. No one will prepare for war anymore. The king of justice will obliterate all war chariots and weapons, for the earth shall be filled with the knowledge of God as the waters fill the sea.

Through the centuries, the prophets' call for justice resounds like an echo heralding the peace to come. For thousands of years peace is the direction of the prophets for the earth and humankind. This call is more distinct than the stamping and roaring of all the wars of the world. The approaching day of the prince of peace is mightier than any throughout all history. The works of humankind come to a halt! The work of God comes over humankind and over the whole torn earth in final and all-embracing peace! The work of God breaks straight in! It penetrates to the depths and spans the breadths! In the midst of collapse, Jesus, the man of peace, arises without whom no peace can be achieved.

The people of peace follow the Master whose nature is the lifeblood of their order of life. His spirit, which stands up for the mean and lowly against the great tyrants, inspires their unity. This spirit of peace opposes war. His journey of peace on the humblest beast of burden displaces cavalry, breaks the weapons of war, and inaugurates national peace. This peace bearer sets prisoners free and redeems the downtrodden. The majesty of his divine peace is framed by the princely forms of justice and well-being and gracious kindness that shines out on the poor.

No peace and disarmament without social justice! No prophet recognizes peace and disarmament or the changing of deadly weapons into tools of civilization without social renewal and reconciliation, giving back to the poor the use of all tools and products.

The prophet Moses had already proclaimed: "There shall not be any poor found among you anywhere!" Yet he knew there would be poor people in this world until every remnant of injustice had disappeared, when all hearts and all energies would be concentrated on peace, giving brotherly love unlimited authority. Because Jesus sees this approaching, he can and must say, "Blessed are the poor! Woe to the rich!"

The majesty of God comes very near to this earth! Kindness and faithfulness, righteousness and well-being kiss each other. Faithfulness springs out of the earth! Righteousness comes down from heaven! (Ps. 85:8–13). Going out from the heart, peace penetrates into all lands because it comes down from God's highest heaven like lightning. It comes as justice. It reveals its clear and simple nature as the love expressed in fairness and brotherliness. This descending ball of lightning annihilates unpeace in its blazing flames.

When peace conquers, it means the abolition of wealth as much as of armed force. Both powers wield enormous influence, but faith stands against them and conquers. Faith meets with deeper understanding among the poor than among the rich. The will to peace is strongest and most genuine where poverty of goods goes hand in hand with the hunger and thirst of spiritual poverty. The kingdom of God will bring fairness and brotherliness. It will bind in complete unity all those whose longing hearts hunger for justice and righteousness. For this reason wealth and all surfeit must be dispersed.

The prophets make inflexible demands to cut out all ostentatious extravagance in clothing, housing, and social life, root and branch. Utmost simplicity shall be established in everything. Unity demands it. The style of unity is expressed in the beauty of the simple line. Social peace can be achieved in no other way. The circle and the straight line are symbols of the love that gathers and the genuine truth that goes with it. When no one outspends another, when no one embellishes life to suit his vanity, everyone will be drawn into the community of shining clarity. When privileges and luxury are abolished, justice has broken through.

Social inequality, the result of rifts in society, destroys the sense of community and all possibility of community. It must be attacked with the sharpness of the Spirit if the cause of peace is to go forward. Luxury and greed, property and wealth are the roots of discord. So the beginning of the great prophecy of Amos mercilessly assails the unequal distribution of the joys and goods of this world. Hosea and all the other prophets follow his example with the same sharpness.

What applies to the root applies to the fruit as well. The violence of killing and warfare is and will always be the height of unpeace, the bitterest fruit of injustice. Isaiah therefore points to the law of peace: "The violent shall come to their end." But the peace of Christ's justice shall never cease. The kingdoms of this world shall all be destroyed because they are warlike kingdoms. Dominion, power, and might over all things under heaven shall be given to the holy people of the Most High. For they are the people of peace and justice. The kingdoms of this world with their predatory nature will be swept away without distinction, whether their emblem is the eagle, the lion, the bear, or other beast of prey. The Son of Man has come to destroy the works of the devil.

The hour of decision approaches: "Ask of me, and I will give you nations as your spoil and the ends of the earth as your possession." "The nations will be glad and sing for joy: for thou dost judge the people justly and govern the nations upon the earth." "Sing among the nations that the Lord is king; he will judge the people justly." "Let the heavens rejoice and let the earth be glad. The Lord is king." In the kingdom of this king, justice is loved. "He helps the weak gloriously."

The new covenant takes up this proclamation and makes it a reality, as Ezekiel had foretold: "I will make them one nation in the land...and one king shall be king over them all; and they shall be no longer two nations, and no longer divided into two kingdoms." In Christ, Isaiah's words became reality: "O thou afflicted, tossed by the tempest, I will teach thy children great peace. Violence shall no more be heard in thy land, nor destruction within thy borders." In the church of Jesus Christ, Jeremiah's word is fulfilled: "The days are coming when the city of the Lord shall be uprooted no more."

The Spirit says through Peter: "Change from the root up! Make a complete turn in your life! Your sins must be wiped out. Let the time of new life break in! It comes from the presence of the Lord of all worlds! The coming time sends the Ruler! He will be announced to you beforehand. In heavenly power, Jesus Christ waits until the time has come when everything shall be fulfilled that God has spoken by the mouth of all his holy prophets since the world began."

Jesus Christ is the goal of our history. God's prophecy with its all-commanding view proclaims the final peace of Jesus Christ. In this peace all enmity is extinguished, all war put down, and all strife brought to an end. Christ is the beginning of God-created humankind and its life-bringing end. He is the first and last of the living letters that spell out the divine plan of peace. In Jesus, the whole course of history turns toward its conclusion, when everything will be renewed. The long-awaited unity of peace, approaching at last with the coming of Jesus, will lead in the completely different and entirely new rule of God.

The kingdom of God draws near. God's will shall at last prevail. What is hidden in his heart will reveal the mystery of his name. Jesus' first and last concern, the entire content of his will to live (which was also a readiness to die) was the glory of God, that is, the glory of God's heart.

Jesus, who revealed the heart of God, knows that the future is dedicated to it. From now on, all those who believe in this future reign of God are dedicated to his perfect will of peace. For the deeply longing hearts of Jesus' inner circle, the first petitions of the Lord's Prayer show the old covenant's prophecy of peace endowed with new and final perfection.

E verything Jesus says and does makes the rule of peace foretold by the prophets a reality. It confirms the truth of all their promises. In the church of Jesus Christ, the long-prophesied community, bound by common covenant, becomes reality now, precisely as it will in the coming kingdom. The word of the prophets of old has paved the way for the messianic rule of peace. Now from all nations, the future citizens of the kingdom of peace stream together. They gather around Christ. A call to the power of perfect peace goes out from the church to the whole world.

God's people of old are and will be the starting point for the new people of unity. Yet in Jesus all national barriers have fallen and his kingdom of unity spreads unimpeded. In the presence of the uniting spirit of the future, the divisive spirit of this age is of no significance. Through the spirit radiating from the church, all national boundaries are abolished forever. The heirs of the old covenant, now consecrated in Christ, extend the work of peace over the whole earth. All land belongs to God. Jesus has burned his fiery rule of peace from the other world into this world.

In Jesus Christ, the fiery spirit of the old prophecy of peace comes to perfect expression for all time. It starts in the present: the peace foretold by the prophets penetrates into the church of Christ as love, justice, and truth, present here and now down to their last consequences. Jesus, like all the prophets, knows no reconciliation with destructive opposition. His prophetic truth knows no giving in or making of concessions. He does not work for peace by making compromises. His peace makes no covenant with unpeace. He never joins any hostile opposition. He destroys unpeace. His opposition to the roots of unpeace is inexorable.

Jesus, sparing none, hurls his sevenfold woe at the hypocritical destroyers of all true unity. Their answer is murderous. As foretold by the prophets, every government and all powers of world economics are bound to fight with the most deadly violence against the perfect expression of peace in Jesus Christ and his church. In this way, the character of unconditional peace shines out more strongly and clearly than ever and delivers up the peace bearers, unarmed, to the flaming sword of the enemy. Jesus' Sermon on the Mount, the most powerful prophecy of the kingdom of peace, stands for the will to peace with its resistance unto death – any death. Against the peace-disrupting power of the whole world it sets the passive resistance of the cross: the cross versus the sword!

The cross is the radicalism of love. The peace of the Sermon on the Mount tackles everything at the root. Out of love it gives away the last remnants of property, right down to jacket and shirt, and gives every bit of working strength to the community spirit of absolute unity. As often as love demands it, this peace sacrifices itself and goes serenely twice the distance and gives twice the working time. Without pause, the church of peace conducts an active and creative general strike against all the surrounding injustice of outward unpeace. In this break with the status quo, Jesus recognizes no claims justified by law. He does not allow his church to carry on any lawsuit or to sit in judgment in any court of law. He demands that the church should drop or interrupt its religious worship whenever brothers need to be reconciled, whenever the genuineness of brotherly unity is in question. He places the restoring and maintaining of the unity of love over and against the insincere cult of disunited piety.

In his Sermon on the Mount, Jesus gives an absolute mandate never to resist the power of evil. Only thus can evil be turned to good. Jesus' will to love prefers rather to be struck twice than to counter with even one blow. Love matters more than anything else. Love allows no other feelings to come in. In marriage too, love keeps faith and fights against any separation or divorce. Because it is forgiveness, love governs private prayer (Matt. 6:6). As complete reconciliation, this absolute and all-embracing will to love determines our attitude to society (to our enemy as well – yes, particularly to him). Love does not take the slightest part in hostilities, strife, or war, nor can it ever return curses and hate, hurt and enmity – neither in the individual nor in the community.

Love is not influenced by any hostile power. No change of circumstance can change the attitude of Jesus and his followers; he does nothing but love, make peace, wish and ask for good, and work good deeds. Where the peace of Jesus Christ dwells, war dies out, weapons are smelted down, and hostility vanishes. Love has become boundless in Jesus; it has achieved absolute sovereignty.

Here at last the justice and righteousness that was begun in the prophets becomes complete reality in Jesus Christ, which is better than that of all moralists and theologians, of all socialists, communists, and pacifists. For the sap of life flows in it for the plantation of the future, for the living community of perfect peace. Here the salt of the divine inner nature is at work in strength. Here the light of God's heart streams out as the beacon of the city church whose towers proclaim freedom, unity, and dedication. Here what each one wants is wanted and done for all. Here no one lays up possessions and no ones heart is cold with icy fear for their own existence or how to make ends meet. Here the peace of love reigns.

In this city church, all citizens are gathered with one goal in mind: God's will and God's rule, God's heart and God's nature. No one is in opposition to another here and no one is condemned. No one is coerced here; no one is despised; no one is violated. And yet love rules as truth and the nature of our inmost heart is recognized by the fruits, by deeds. Here everybody knows well that such a determined common will provokes the sharpest opposition from the surrounding world. Perfect unity, which gathers and binds, is seen as a provocation. It is regarded with enmity because it is misunderstood as an infuriating exclusiveness. It makes all

those resentful who, like most people, feel that they are neither able nor willing to accept the call to such complete
community. So a clash is inevitable. No one can escape it.

This living community of hearts, this combining of goods
and working strength, stands out in absolute contrast to the
attitude of the whole world. This is bound to cause resent-
ment, especially in others whose ideals drive them to violent
action for which they want support. For in this community
of love every hostile act is rejected, whatever the circumstances and however weighty the reasons. Any participation
in warlike action, police activity, or law proceedings is out of
the question, however justified it may seem on the grounds
of protecting the good. This community of peace has nothing in common with violent revolt, however necessary it
may seem in the name of suppressed justice. The very fact
that such a life exists, symbolizing the kingdom of peace and
love, challenges all (both right and left) who regard government by force as the primary duty of the hour.

B ecause the expectation of the coming peaceable kingdom leads to a life in full community, all those who
look upon community as impossible are affronted by it. As
long as they are determined to refuse the continuing fellowship of the wedding feast, as long as they cannot accept what
is so great and yet so intimate – the bond of peace, the common table, the unity of life, the cooperation in work, and
the church that carries responsibility – they have no other
choice than to fight it. In the end, though reluctantly, they
take measures to destroy it. So, in spite of the church's unconditional peace stand in all situations, severe struggles and
clashes are bound to result from the will to community, pre-

cisely because of its uncompromising nature. They are bound to grow in number and intensity the nearer the church of peace draws to the final kingdom of peace.

In the true church, the beginning of the coming kingdom is present in full force and challenging clarity. Before the final extension of the rule of peace, there has to be a last battle between the power of strife and discord and the strongest power, the power of peace. The severity and dreadfulness of the last battles will be more and more startling as the peace witness of the church reaches its consummation and her martyrs once more go unarmed to their death. But under no circumstances can the opposition be left in repose. For there, people will not give up their selfish separation as individuals or as national groups. People cannot or will not let the root of sin, of curse-laden unpeace, be taken away from them. They maintain it is absolutely indispensable.

People cannot trust peace, want nothing of faith, and reject the better future. They would rather trust the idols of brute force than the spirit of love and the God of peace. Property needs the protection of law and force. People want to hold on to what belongs to them, and will not accept anything from others. They demand their rights and reject grace. Under the law, sin continues and unpeace remains. The law's iron hand holds on to bloody judgment and the sword. It strikes down individuals and mows down whole nations with its ghastly weapons, which poison continents and will in the end destroy the whole earth. Sin and the law make death inevitable. Finally God himself, against the ultimate will of his heart, must assent to this judgment of wrath, which is necessary according to the justice of the law.

When the nations harden their hearts completely against the one way God wants, the way of pure love, they call down judgment on themselves. They are the origin of all those abnormal events that happen as unavoidable natural catastrophes. When they despise the creative will, God has to give people up to their degenerate, impure, and depraved love-life. When people of their own free will reject the will to peace, the raging torches of civil war will flare over them. God in his wrath brings on the judgment precipitated by self-will. The old state of affairs is repeated: God in his wrath once gave his beloved people a warlike king because his own kingship had been rejected by war-lust and greed for the status of a major power; still earlier, God's law had allowed blood vengeance and the death penalty to replace the rejected leadership of the spirit; and the flood had buried the flesh that had turned away from the spirit. So now, as antichristian strife reaches its inevitable climax, the judgment of God will let loose a fiery flood of war.

This fate is inescapable – a matter of cause and effect. War is karma, the necessary consequence of discord, unpeace, and lack of community. It is the deadly fruit of the broken fellowship with God, the inescapable judgment over the causes of war – separation from God's unity, division of life into hostile opposites, injustice and disunity. It all arises from property and selfishness. War judges itself. It is based on unpeace with God and disunity among people. War is the monstrosity born of the covetous will, the hell of disunity. War intensifies this compulsion to sin to the point of self-destruction. It drives the law, which kills, to the point of massacring nations. In war, loveless injustice surpasses itself. It becomes murderous lawlessness.

War is the insane culmination of the clash between judging law and unbridled lawlessness; its ultimate purpose is to reveal sin. The judgment of war should crash down on us, hammering and shaping us, so that at last a longing arises for the cause of death to be overcome, for community in God to become everything. To be rid of war, the roots of sin must be exposed and eradicated. Once the cause of separation is overcome, unity and community will break in – then not a hand will be lifted, not a foot will be stirred, to serve the monstrosity of hell that is called war. With sin destroyed, brothers are no longer killed. The way ahead is made free, and in the empty space, the peace of God arises. Repentance gives birth to faith; faith brings peace. Ending separation to establish unity – that is the gospel.

To sin belongs the law. To law belongs killing (1 Cor. 15:56). These three uphold each other. Jesus Christ, through the Holy Spirit and in the name of God, has conquered this triple alliance of death forever and ever. He broke the weapon of death – sin. He tore up the writ of accusation and judgment. His death unmasked the origin of all killing: he tore out its root cause. He plants resurrection and the unity of the Holy Spirit in the places where dissolution, separation, and sin are eradicated.

The law of Moses brought war, which it then had to control. The grace and truth of the gospel bring unity and the order of community (John 1:17). Because national and international laws determine the prosecution of all illegal conduct, they require war, imprisonment, and death. The sons of Christ's spirit keep peace, bring freedom, and are responsible for the forgiveness of sins. Through the mission of their spirit, they spread abroad unity of life.

Where Christ takes over the government, the rule of all other death-dealing powers is annulled. Where the spirit of grace rules, the law of governmental authority withdraws. Death's judgment retreats before the salvation and resurrection of life. Gathering replaces enmity. So it is in the church, and so it will be at the end when the first and last fruit of separation from God, death itself, is swept away. All the works of enmity will be destroyed and last of all the final enemy himself. Before then, all enmity and hostility must be given up; it leads to death. The auxiliary troops of death will be the first to be surrounded; first the tree with its roots will be torn up. Then the poisonous fruits of death will be attacked to the very last seed, till death itself is done away with.

However, evil and murder are still on the increase, gaining more and more influence. The stronger the power of love grows, the more it drives poisonous hostility to a peak. The reverse is also true. When evil has matured, it is time to clear out what has ripened in death's plantation and make room for the laying-out of God's garden. This dual development of completely opposed events forces decision. It leads to tearing-down and rebuilding. The course of all history runs up from below and down from above. From both directions it converges on a single point. Apostolic prophecy (in the book of Revelation) follows this dual line of development to the end. The point where they meet is the end: the judgment and the kingdom. Both lines are drawn by "religiously" motivated hands: "satanism" and "faith" are the mysterious forces that direct this dual line of development.

Siding with the deadly power of evil, the godlessness of a life of hypocrisy and murderous corruption mounts to the maddest heights of arrogance: with amazing pomp and splendor, it claims the highest place of all in the house of God. It is the false prophecy of a church that has fallen away from God. It hypocritically flaunts the raiment and the mien of the animal of peace, like a sacrificial lamb, while making propaganda for the dragon of war. In the form of the lamb it speaks like the dragon against the lamb. To wage war against the church of peace, it joins forces with the warring monster of worldly power, the power of all armed nations.

The church of peace sets out against this overwhelming and twofold power without the protection of murderous weapons. It refuses to worship either power and knows that the whore of Babylon will fall. Certainly, this false and faithless woman is still firmly seated on the throne of the world's ruling powers and authorities. Elated by power, she is still intoxicated with the blood of the martyrs she has sacrificed. But the breath of the coming reign of Christ sweeps her off. The twofold world power from below is broken from above. The lying dragon of unpeace is expelled and war is banned. The reign of peace comes.

The last outburst of war from humankind's major powers storms out of the night. Like every war, it bears afresh the marks of Satan's power let loose and so is bound to assault the kingdom of God once more before it is overthrown. This final war, this last world conflagration, must forever annihilate all states based on force and all major world powers. The new aeon begins by putting a final end to all the powers of war. The joyous unity of the wedding feast and the gathering of love at the common table of God's kingdom replace the horrors of war, enmity, and death.

In solitary greatness amidst a world full of enemies, the prophets of old felt compelled to make known their opposition to the priesthood of established religion and to the sovereignty of their state – all this to the same degree that these two powers expanded their double-faced rule on the lines of the great heathen powers with all their wars and magnificent pomp. In the same way, the apostolic prophets of early Christianity have had to fight with ever-increasing ardor against the bloody violence of political power and against all religion that hypocritically supports them but in truth has fallen away from God.

To the prophets, the God of Abraham is and always will be the God of the kingdom. According to the faith of the apostles, the Father of Jesus Christ does not want to be forever a God of the law. He is the same God as he was at the time of the lawgiver and prophet Moses; but the way of his heart (love) triumphs over the ways of his wrath. His peace supersedes the law. What the law could not achieve, God accomplished in Christ. Through Christ's spirit, faith in the God and Father of Jesus Christ is obedient to peace, because faith – perfected – has as its object the God of perfect love. It is the God of history who makes all the threads of history run together and come to an end in the one, single way of peace – the peace of his Christ.

We must distinguish between the innermost heart of God and his waist that is girded with judgment (Isa. 11:5). For hidden in the somber flames of judgment lives the ray of his pure love. The deadly accurate judgment of his presence is nearer to love than the cold distance of a god who hides his face. The brazen footsteps of God's wrath are dreadful. It is a

terrible thing to fall into the hands of his judgment. But se-
cretly his pulsing heart spreads out a mantle of love for all his
enemies. Beautiful are the feet of his messengers, spreading
joy as they come from the mountains and bring the message
of God's heart to the valley of judgment. Their greeting to
everyone is peace. Their message is clear: the judgment of
God is fulfilled in his heart. He himself has been met by it.
God's heart becomes king! His ambassadors wept bitterly
because peace had been lost. For them, there is no harsher
judgment than the loss of peace. But now they hand over
this sealed message: that miracle, the heart, is stronger than
all judgment.

Though mountains were to melt in volcanic eruptions
and hills laid low by appalling earthquakes, and even if the
earth itself were to totter and crack and the judgment of his
mighty wrath were to demolish great powers – still, the love
of God's heart, the rainbow of his perfection, will never wa-
ver. The sun of his heart shines upon the devastating storm-
curtain of his wrath and the rainbow of peace spans it. What
if leagues of nations and world peace itself suffer shipwreck,
what if all treaties be torn up – the seal of God's covenant
will not break. Times of judgment will come and sink into
the grave. But peace will arise and remain. That will not
change. Peace is God's final word; it is his heart. Peace is and
always will be the ultimate will of God.

We should stop looking merely at the historical instruments of judgment, at the human vessels of wrath, and with
deep discernment turn to the heart of God in all his works
throughout history. Then in spite of the murderous chaos of
war and the injustice raging around us, we have entered the
garden of peace. The historical Jesus is the heart of God. As

the coming Christ, he shows the importance of God's heart for the whole world. His command empowers us to sheath the sword and put it away forever. The heart of Jesus foresees with fearful clarity the catastrophe ahead: it will devastate all the kingdoms of this earth and the whole world economy through major international wars and bloody revolutions. He knows that because of strife and discord, the hour of wrath must precede the day of peace. The approaching fall of civilization with the final war of judgment is one of the main themes of his great prophetic speech, which John and Paul have enlarged upon so powerfully in apostolic prophecy.

The dreadful cup cannot be avoided. The plowland must be cleared; the corrupting weeds must be burned. After they have run riot for the last time, they must never again be able to spread their seeds of murder. If evil is to be uprooted, it must be exposed for what it is. Political chaos, outbursts of war and revolution, economic depressions, and frightful natural catastrophes shall once more deliver humankind to the knife of its own unpeace. But in the midst of all the hellish tumult, the paradise of peace is revealed. Those who hold out and shed no blood in spite of the mounting horrors of the final desolation, doing God's holy work in pure, brotherly love, will come through the sharpest judgment and the last catastrophe.

The old world collapses in terrible self-destruction, but the church of Jesus Christ takes no part in all this horror. The frenzied power of the world loathes the unassailable peace stand of Christ's church. In their fury, all warlike powers persecute the gathered unity of God's peace. Even in the battering storm of extreme need, the church rejects the slightest sign of militarism – the inhuman beast of prey. The power of love opposes the violence of unpeace. Just for this reason, persecution reaches the heights of its fury. The prophetic spirit of the king of peace sees through the tension between these ultimate and diametrically opposed powers of love and hate as the shaking force at work everywhere in world history and in end-history. This spirit sees that the throes of extreme need must precede the birth of world peace.

The dreadful birth-pangs of the end times are part of the curse of death, brought by the loss of our original peace. The peace of God and of the great advent cannot be born without a final judgment over frightening unpeace, bringing forth its last monstrosity. Just before the new breaks in, all that is old must be shattered by appalling need. All institutions made by human society must be overthrown. Every form of their power and slavery must be obliterated. No peace can be planted on the unchanged soil of unpeace. The plow sets to work. It breaks up the sod again. The beginning of God's rule leads to the frightening end of world history so that on its ruins, purified of all adulteration, the justice and righteousness of eternal peace will be able to rise.

Right into a world driven frantic with unpeace and injustice, Christ will let the unblemished kingdom of peace break in. But this future, coming directly from above, is already present in the spirit of Jesus Christ: in his church, the will to peace is put into practice here and now. God's world judgment annihilates the evil powers of unpeace in order to sweep through the last and greatest catastrophe in humankind's history of war. It brings in eternal peace. God's rule has to make this final step because it cannot make any alliance with the powers of injustice. Under the trampling boots of soldiers, God's heart, as Christ crucified once again, beats on in unchanging love; as the church of the risen one, it carries God's peace inviolate to meet the coming day.

The spirit of Jesus Christ lets the fresh air of the ultimate kingdom of peace blow right into this sultry, disaster-laden atmosphere. His gospel brings purity, reconciliation, and unity. His new spirit is the authentication of the kingdom of peace. Through the signet and seal of the spirit, what is decreed for the future is already entrusted to the church. The church of Jesus Christ is the body of the community of perfect peace, through which life and immortality are revealed in our time. As the bearer of the kingdom of peace, the church is freed from all killing and murdering.

When we are gathered in the church and God's love fills our hearts, we cannot be tempted by any power that belongs to force. As Jesus can never be thought of as a Roman soldier, so members of his church can never belong to the artillery, air force, or police. Neither poison, bombs, pistols, or knives, neither the executioner's sword nor the gallows can be our weapon. As the revelation of the heart of Jesus, as Christ's letter, our task is simply to pass on the image of absolute love in all its clarity (2 Cor. 3:2–3). Standing in the presence of Christ, we must represent that he has arrived; when Christ reveals himself now, we must proclaim his future coming.

What is invisible in the world of peace to come becomes visible in the church. Everyone shall see this work of God. Everyone shall honor the Father of Jesus Christ through it. This unadulterated image of Jesus is the only hope for the future. The church is his uplifted torch, the radiant city on the hill.

The stars of prophecy have shone through the night of unpeace, moving for centuries across the celestial sphere of world history. As history draws to a close, the starry heavens of prophecy will let the great gods of military power spread their twilight. When the days were fulfilled, the morning star – the king of peace – rose in the firmament of prophecy. He heralds the dawn of the coming day. The church is wedded to the sun of peace. Whoever lets the morning star rise in his heart is freed from all warlike powers of this world and belongs with every beat of his heart to the coming day of God's great peace.

The dawn of the new age lights up the invisible city of peace. The hidden land of community appears. In the Holy Spirit of the church, the new Jerusalem comes down from above. Only the perfect city without a temple has done away with cultic religion. In this city, community life is the temple of peace, the temple of the great king. The church bears the seven-armed lampstand of the Sabbath of peace, on which our own works shall rest forever because the mighty works of God have begun. The city of peace and justice and joy reveals the radiant brightness of the new creation. The old order has passed away. The new order comes into force – everything becomes new.

This is the gathering and uniting from all four ends of the earth to the ends of heaven, the unity of those still alive with those living in glory – God's kingdom of peace. Its power in the future begins in the unchangeable community of life and spirit, which in our time bears the name "church." In the peace of the city-church, the bride, the church, prepares herself to receive the bridegroom, Jesus. She will go to his wedding feast carrying the blazing torches of the spirit.

This feast day of the king of peace establishes the throne of his government; his infinite joy makes it possible for his reign to begin. The places of work for his kingdom are already there; will and deed crown his feast. When we celebrate our freedom from the hideous monster of bloody violence and from the powerful woman of seduction and unfaithfulness, a fruitful life arises with a clear authority. On the foundation of the atonement, which brings unity and enthusiasm, the reign of the priestly king begins, inaugurated by his feast. It is a feast celebrating the perfected reign of peace. The bride of the king has prepared herself for it.

This message of apostolic prophecy was entrusted to John as certain tidings of the approaching time. It is "the revelation given to Jesus Christ by God to show his servants what must very soon take place." The Christ who appears among the seven candlesticks of the church receives the book of the future from the sovereign of the world, who is surrounded by the twenty-four elders and the four radiant living creatures of the star-world. Only he who is the faith of the church is able to open it. So his present is the ultimate future of the dawning kingdom of peace. This is true in the church, so that John had to write his revelation to the seven churches as a reality in the present and a certainty for the future: what exists now is a picture of what shall be. To the seer whose eyes are open, faith's present and hope's future are one and the same. What unites them is love.

In the church of the Holy Spirit, the future kingdom of God is present with its perfect justice, its absolute peace, and its joy in love and unity. In the midst of the church, the king of peace brings here and brings now her inviolable community of peace both within and without – nothing but peace. Where there is redemption and reconciliation through Christ, even the locking-up of Satan for the thousand years of rejoicing is present reality because peace is here and now put into action. The church is the door of peace, open in the present as an entrance into the kingdom of the future. So for the believing and united church, Satan is already bound; in the church, his divisiveness and hostility have been done away with. The kingdom of peace has been won. Weapons are laid down. Christ is king, and he is king here and now as the head and the heart of the church.

From the church, Christ's spirit of love and his will to unity press outward into all the world. This fact, in the present, guarantees certainty about the future: he is the one to conquer and renew all creation, to make the whole torn cosmos into a new and living unit. In Christ the old world passes, and the new creation arises. Jesus is the new man of the church, as the son of man in the coming kingdom. In Jesus, God's rule has now become love to our brothers and to our enemies through faith. For those who have eyes of faith to see, the life in his church shall be the living parable of the unity and peace for which God wants to conquer the earth. In the church, the world of today can see the image of the city of peace. It is the signpost to the future, and everyone will see it. No corner on earth is to be left in darkness; the light, held aloft, floods into all rooms. The city of light sends out bearers of light. Community in the city on the hill and constant traveling for the sake of mission are identical.

The unity of the early Christian church and the apostle-ship of peace are one. From churches formed in brotherly love, power is sent out to all inhabitants of the earth – the power to create peace and harmony. Rays from the small sun-city light up the whole world. From apostolic times, the early Christian church has been assigned the world-embracing task that the one cause of the kingdom of God shine out in all directions with unalloyed clarity. She is to represent noth-ing else. Not only the generation immediately following the apostles makes this abundantly clear: the clear light of the original Christian truth through succeeding generations checked the slow but persistent growth of darkness till far into the third century.

The post-apostolic elders of the earliest times took apos-tolic mission as their authority. About A.D. 150, Justin also took the prophetic spirit as proclaiming a future begun with the apostles. That swords should be beaten into plowshares and lances into sickles, that nation should no longer lift up sword against nation, and that we should forget how to wage war – for him, all this had already begun. As he writes, "from Jerusalem men and women went out into the world… not mighty in speech, but sent through the power of God to the whole human race."

Justin describes Christian life around A.D. 160 in just the same way, as an expression of reverence, justice, love to all, and confident expectation of the future. Here again he testi-fies: "We also were once just as conversant with war and murder as with everything else that is evil. But all of us, wherever we happen to live in the whole wide world, have all exchanged our weapons of war: swords for plowshares, lances for farm implements."

Theophilus writes still more strongly to Autolycus around A.D. 180: "Even to watch fights that are dangerous to life is forbidden to us. We can be neither active participants nor conscious spectators of acts that lead to death. Not even our eyes or ears shall take part in any act of murder. We must avoid witnessing any death-dealing act and also listening when such deeds are glorified, even if it is only in song." Every outward but also every inner participation in war is impossible. Any kind of propaganda for the glory of shedding blood is rejected. For "in the church of Jesus Christ, justice is put into practice and faith is testified by deeds; here grace keeps watch and peace protects. Here God is king."

At the end of this early period, Origen writes in no uncertain terms about what the consequences of this attitude of faith were for the early Christians: a Christian may never use the sword against anyone; the church of Jesus has a completely different politeia. It has a completely different public responsibility from that of the military and judicial power of state authority, a completely different political task, a completely different citizenship, and a completely different form of community life.

For this reason, according to Tertullian, the holder of a government office could be regarded as a Christian only if he exercised his duty "without condemnation, without punishment, without chains and prisons and torture, without capital punishment, and without depriving anyone of civil rights." In spite of the ascendance of the institutional church, the third century still held the same view as Athenagoras in the second century, who expressed it in these sharp words: "To force people through lawsuits in which their lives are at stake is a crime against human flesh." Anyone committing this crime against Christians attacks those who are not allowed even to withdraw from blows, let alone return one.

As late as A.D. 248, Origen wrote to the anti-Christian Celsus: "Military service should not be demanded of Christians." This attitude was still as clear to post-apostolic Christians as it had been to the early Christians of the first church. After all, military service is not demanded of priests. "We do not go with the emperor to the battlefield, not even when he demands it." Christians support the governmental authorities only through their prayer, which is determined by Christ; only through prayer for peace; only through prayer for the community of the new humanity; only in the prayer that all inhabitants of the earth shall be given peace and harmony; only in the request that the governments of all nations shall exercise their authority with reverence, in peace and benevolence, and without violence; and only in the faith that the peace of a new life is brought about by the power of the resurrection from the dead.

The First Letter of Clement (written before A.D. 100, yet strictly in line with the institutional church) and also the much less ecclesiastical "Acts of Thomas," written soon after A.D. 160, express complete agreement with Origen. Justin, too, declared that all the kingdoms and powers of the world look upon Jesus with fear and yet must recognize that everywhere believers in Christ are peace bringers. Moreover, around A.D. 150 Justin wrote, "We, more than any others, are your helpers and allies for peace." Tertullian sums up the attitude of early Christianity from the time of the apostles right into the third century with the words: "Only without swords can Christians wage war. The divine and the human banner do not go together – the flag of Christ and the flag of the devil!"

War is in fact the most powerful act of violence, the work of demonic power. Under the banner of war, measures of the most murderous kind (coming from a hostility that even without war is constantly present) are carried so far that they become an unbridled storm. "World peace" is a state of war waged by other means; it is not peace. Not only war is satanic; satanic is also the root of war – unpeace in times of political "peace." Under the false name of peace, it commits demonic crimes against life everywhere. The outbreak of military hostilities in civil and international war is not by any means the only evil the peace bearers of the church must stand against. They must stand as much against the widespread damage done in private life, seen most clearly in the destruction of nascent life, which was labeled "murder" and "child-murder" by early Christianity. It calls those women "murderesses of human life" who "procure a miscarriage through medicine" or those who in tacit agreement allow it to be done to them.

Bearers of peace are familiar with all the murky sources of death-bringing division. They fight money's power to buy and rule as passionately as they fight unfaithfulness in love relationships because there they see the dangerous seat of murderous unpeace. Tertullian testifies that the Spirit

"makes everything communal with one exception – love for
women." In essence, the dragon's teeth of covetousness, in
privileged ownership and in unfaithful love relationships, is
the power at the root of the widespread state of war – latent
or active – between people who are meant to live a pure life
together in God as brothers and sisters.

Money, according to the prophetic faith of early Christianity, is a "source of godlessness and license, an inciter to
war, and an instrument for waging war. It is the hated plague
and torment that belongs to what is falsely called peace." "As
long as the earth is divided among the rich by defrauding
others, as long as the wealthy possess this earth that could
feed so many, the poor will be exploited and the downtrodden kept in oppression." Then justice can never be achieved,
and peace is a sheer impossibility. Without justice or love,
peace cannot last a moment.

According to this early Christian prophecy (which gained
widespread recognition) and according to Justin's testimony,
that power is important which proclaims the approaching
time, when people live together as brothers and sisters on the
land God has promised them. Defying death, the martyrs
declared before their prosecutors that they could recognize
no kingdom of this present world-age; that they knew only
one lord, the king of all kings, the ruler over all nations. In
the third century still, according to Hippolytus, the conditions of acceptance into the early Christian church decreed
that anyone should be rejected or excluded who was unwill-
ing to refuse all killing, even killing required by law. From all
this it is clear how state power and the church were bound to
provoke the sharpest opposition in each other.

Hermas, an exceptionally sober-minded prophet (influential in Rome in post-apostolic times – perhaps before A.D. 100 but certainly before A.D. 155), summarizes this state of affairs in the following urgent challenge:

> You know you live in a foreign country. Your own city-state is far away from the state surrounding you here. Those who acquire land, houses, perishable dwellings, and costly furnishings (as the custom is in the world state) can never expect to be at home in the quite other city-state to which they should belong. Unhappy people! Do you not realize that not one of all these things can belong to you, that with all these possessions you place yourself under a power foreign to your calling, by its very nature? Do you want to forswear the laws of the city you are called to? Will you really do this for the sake of property – fields and other things? Do you really want to live according to the laws of the city-state that rules here? Then you cannot be accepted into the other city-state you long for as your home. You have denied its laws. You have to be expelled. Let it be quite clear to you that you are living in a foreign country! Be satisfied with the bare necessities! You may not accumulate more than is enough to live on. At all times, be prepared!

Such stringent demands can be made only where people's hearts are alive with the spirit of perfect love and completely filled with the highest calling – the kingdom of God. The peace stand taken by the early Christians is possible only in the strength of the gospels. Only where the call to the church of peace takes over the whole of life can concentration on mission lead to a break with the status quo. Only where the spirit of unity establishes inmost peace can the fight be ventured upon for peace and against unpeace all over the world.

The center of life-energy that makes this stand possible is given in the church of Jesus Christ only. Peace with God makes the will to peace on earth a reality. Without this will and without the working of Christ's peace, it is impossible to stand up against all the powers of the world. Only peace of heart in the unity of the church sets people free from obviously prevailing unpeace. Where inner peace is granted, it creates outer peace.

Through the working together of all powers, the harmony of united hearts calls forth peace's maximum achievements, possible only in the church of Jesus Christ. "Without peace of heart, nothing great will be achieved." Only when the heart finds peace in the center of this gathering and uniting can it gain the impetus to go out far and wide from this one united whole. Without peace of heart, all our efforts are bound to work against each other; every good influence will be counteracted by its opposite. For this reason, no one should approach the question of nonviolence until he has truly decided to take up God's peace: the peace of the church, found in the gospel of Jesus Christ and given in the power of his Holy Spirit.

Peace means the greatest power possible, a gathering centered in God. Pestalozzi has described this basic requisite for all education with these words:

> Faith in God is the source of peace in life, peace in life is the source of inner order, inner order is the source of an undistracted use of our powers, order in the employment of our powers becomes in turn the source of the growth and development of our powers toward wisdom.

Powers grow in the harmony of working together. Peace has
a divine wisdom that gives shape to a fruitful life, ordered in
brotherly community. As long as we are still separate, we
cannot experience this harmony. Separation from God is the
cause of unpeace; it brings disaster. The hopeless opposition
it puts up consumes life: to oppose an inner calling means
death. Sin, as separation, is our ruin. In fact its very nature is
opposition to God, without whom we cannot live.

Peace of heart is founded on unity with God. There is no
peace when we are far from him. The soul must become
quiet, wanting to receive the hidden influence of God in silence. Only then can the strength of inner peace grow, ready
for deeds. Only when all our attention is concentrated on
God can warmth-giving energy come over us. Without it,
we sink into cold and darkness. Tersteegen emphasized that
an active life must be subordinated to inner quiet so that the
soul never gives out more than it takes in.* Those who lead
an active and fruitful life need time in which all they are and
do becomes silent – then God can speak and act in the
depths of the soul. It is in the very center of our spirit that
the words of peace must have an effect. Outside in the
clamor of our work, we can all too often fail to hear them.

The words of the great peace bringer, Jesus, that the
heavily laden soul shall find rest with him, with the further
counsel to pray in secret, have led many to take on the character of "those who are quiet in the land" (Ps. 35:20). Some
groups call themselves "the silent ones" or "those who have
achieved peace and quiet in this life." Yet there often creeps
in a much too human tendency to ignore the basic will of
Jesus: that inner gathering should become the source of

---

*Gerhard Tersteegen, 1697–1769.

strength for action. To sink spinelessly into a dumb stillness means being lost to the life to which Jesus has called us.

Even Augustine was not always free of the old danger of ascetic detachment and withdrawal from life.* The way to joy as he saw it was that the soul and all its powers of imagination become so silent that the soul itself is swept away and engulfed in its own oblivion.

Self-examination before God never dulls or stupefies: it brings about the liveliest concentration of all energies. It is a regenerating bath, clarifying judgment and strengthening character. God is personal and holy will. There is nothing of a gloomy, all-engulfing abyss about him. The God who redeems us is not the dark morass of our subconscious or the depths of our own soul, which is nothing but the fathomless mirror of our own self and all our experiences, good and bad. It is God, the wholly other power of the divine, who wants to illuminate this night so that like the prodigal son we awake and long for the nearness of God – the exposure of hidden darkness and the breaking in of light.

We must emerge from the tranquillity of indifference, passing through dumb despair to the holy calm of inner peace. Hildebert of Tours has expressed it in the following words:

> There is a threefold silence. The first comes from ignorance of misery, the second from despair of salvation, and the third from the feeling of life-energy rewon.
>
> Before the law came into the world, we did not recognize our sickness; therefore we were silent and did not ask for help.
>
> When the law was given, it exposed the festering wounds; the silence was broken immediately; the sick sought help in the works of the law. But all their seeking in this direction was in

*Augustine, A.D. 354–430.

vain; tired and faint, groaning and sighing, they fell silent again.

Now at long last the almighty word of the Father has broken the silence once more. Because the Father has spoken peace and promised grace, the sick come to him from all directions and urgently beg him, the physician of the soul, to save them.

Once perfect health is restored, however, they will have nothing more to ask for. Then the third, the holy silence begins, which shall know no end.*

Nevertheless the third silence of worship (as the active peace of the kingdom of God) is productive quiet, coming from creative life-energy. It leads to undreamed-of power and influence, obstructed in every way before. Whoever has gone through the depths of misery knows the cause of the sickness that takes away all strength and paralyzes activity. As David describes it: "There is no peace in my bones because of my sin!" But he is permitted to find healing. God has paved the way even for the most burdened.

Over this world of sharp inner contrasts and conflicting storms, the colorful rainbow of his peace is spanned. His mystery is that he reveals his heart as the will for love. Through this he transforms the clouds of judgment into unveiled light. Without the storms of judgment, the sun's rainbow cannot be formed. Only one can bring it, who is himself without darkness, but who has nevertheless taken the clouds of judgment upon his own life of light so that in it we may see the rainbow of peace.

Jesus is our peace. He has brought us complete reconciliation and union with God. His death is the gospel of peace,

*Hildebert of Tours, 1055–1133.

for he brings death to the sins through which we were excluded from unity. The gift of grace has set peace over and against division. Whoever receives Christ as his conciliator has peace with God. Through his cross, what had hindered us and removed us from God's influence has been swept away. Through the indwelling Christ, the heart submits to the rulership of God. It has won through to unity in the will of God. Whoever is one with God has peace. God is peace. The son of his atonement is therefore called the lord of peace; and as the king of joy, he is also called the king of peace.

When his gospel of peace reaches the heart, God in his overwhelming light exposes everything that has hindered harmony and made it impossible. Inner gathering is possible only when all sources of division have been rendered powerless. The essence of all inner division, the hindrance to peace, is separation and resistance. Sin is enmity and disbelief. Serving peace has one goal: to establish the obedience of faith so that everything trying to hinder and destroy unity with God is abolished.

How inner peace overcomes division is shown clearly in first-hand accounts. August Hermann Francke was a man whose inner peace brought forth a creative power of love effective up to the present day. At one time, in great fear, disbelief, and despair, he had called on the God he did not know. His prayer was answered so suddenly that peace flooded his heart. It was like a river inundating the land before anyone has time to realize that the dike has broken.

> In the twinkling of an eye, all my doubts were gone; I was assured in my heart of the grace of God in Christ Jesus; I could call God not only "God" but also "my father." At once all the

sadness and unrest of my heart was taken away; I was suddenly overwhelmed by such a flood of joy that I praised God with a full heart for showing me such great grace. When I got up, I was in a completely different frame of mind from when I knelt down. For I had bent my knees in great distress and doubt, but I got up in great certainty and unspeakable joy.*

Research into religious experience has confirmed that peace is inevitably preceded by turmoil and doubt. The first thing that drives the conscience toward peace is the agony of a bad conscience, a consciousness of sin that grips the soul. At the same time, the desperate longing for purity and perfection, for harmony and community with God, drives the heart on to peace, like a storm before the calm.

A burdened conscience may not always be ascribed to obvious offenses that give generally accepted morals a slap in the face. Rather it is the depressing conviction of an all-pervading disharmony and bondage to guilt that has its origin in separation from God. The whole of life today is "sinfulness;" it lacks entirely the joy of peace, the strength of justice, and the uniting works of God.

Starbuck made a collection from numerous accounts of such experiences.† He says that essentially the inner turmoil preceding the state of peace is a despairing consciousness of sin combined with the striving toward a new and better life. A crushing sense of doubt and alienation from God leads to pessimism and sadness, to deep-seated fear and helplessness. The more we give way to intellectual doubt, the more effort we make to resist the consciousness of guilt and the greater grows the agony. Fear, doubt, and a sense of sin and depres-

*August Hermann Francke, 1663–1727.
†Edwin Diller Starbuck, 1866–1947.

sion are the throes of the coming birth.

This new birth is the narrow gate to the kingdom of peace. Inner peace is seized hold of as liberation, freedom from the gloom of sin, and redemption from the curse. In this birth, we come into the new world and see the kingdom of God. The more keenly we feel the contrast between our weakness and helplessness on the one hand and the power and glory on the other as the contrast between us and God, the more powerfully does what is new show itself. God's cause takes the place of us and our misery. The peace of the coming kingdom brings with it forgiveness for division and sin, and harmony with God's power of love. All energies formerly squandered by the will are from now on directed toward God and his kingdom in a new and unknown clarity. In war we felt more the blessings of peace: so peace of heart depends on the intensity of its contrast to sin, disharmony, feebleness, and disruptedness. Life can arise only in this tension between our torn and feeble state and the energy of God's peace.

It was for this reason Paul was told: "Let my grace be enough for you, for my strength is powerful in the weak," and Luther said:

> God is a God of those who are poor, wretched, troubled, oppressed, despairing, and indeed brought low in everything. In such, God can carry out his right and proper work, which is to raise the lowly, feed the hungry, give light to the blind, comfort the poor and miserable, justify the sinners, quicken the dead, and save the damned and despairing.

It is God's nature to show his superior power just where darkness and weakness have destroyed the last hope. "Where

sin became mighty, grace became mightier by far." It is
God's will that our own strength is broken. Our strength, in
its morbid self-love and within its own narrow confines, is
bound to exhaust itself utterly. The end of all our own is the
beginning of the other: the birth of faith begins. Faith
presses on to God's love, to the future of his kingdom. From
faith, love arises as love to God and Christ put into practice:
joy in God's creation and in other people, joyful and confident expectation of God's kingdom, unity with the church
of Jesus Christ, and the life of God's new creation. Utterly
new and unexpected, this life comes over the believers as
Jesus' words being surprisingly fulfilled: to give up oneself
means to win life. A new life, God's true life, replaces the
former selfish and ungenuine life. Those who love their life
lose it; those who hate their life receive true life.

T he new life is an undivided whole – perfection that exists in God alone. The previous life let two irreconcil-
ably opposed egos exist side by side: the "I" as it is and the
"I" as it is meant to be. Through peace of heart, an undivided will dedicated to the new life, allows the holy "shall
be" to triumph over the unholy "is." "God will be born in us
only when all the bound and captive powers of our soul become entirely free, when all our plans and ideas are silenced,
and when our conscience ceases to punish us." All plans and
ideas disappear into the inner imperative of the holy "thou
shalt," and the soul experiences unity and freedom. The
peace of Christmas depends on this freedom of obedience.
The ground of obedience bears peace. Mary believed. She
obeyed. The Spirit came. Christ was born.

Mary listened to God's word and treasured it in her heart. The word given to the prophets had said, "If you had listened to my commandments, your peace would have been like a river." The flood of the spirit penetrates to the depths. The riverbed is saturated deep into hidden ground. Though the level of the water may rise or fall, in the deepest depths there is abundance. The peace of God penetrates into the depths. Without these depths, all religious exercises and Christian forms are nothing but a delusion: mists but no river. Action begins in the inmost heart and then penetrates far into all areas of life. The water Jesus gives is from a well of depth.

The inmost depths are decisive; Jesus exposes the heart. He directs his glance to what is going on there. He lays his finger on it, for he sees things as they really are. "He knew well what was in us." He made this clear: what rules in our heart gains control over our life. "A good person brings forth good from the goodness stored in the heart; a bad one brings forth evil from the evil stored in his or her heart." "What fills the heart, the mouth speaks of." As the heart, so is the deed: peace of heart brings about a life of peace. The spirit of Jesus affects the inmost depths first and foremost: "Let the peace of God reign in your hearts." "The peace of God will keep your hearts and your minds. It surpasses all understanding. It keeps and preserves you in Christ Jesus."

The word of peace penetrates to the depths. The living word brings about living peace: "What I have said, I have told you so that in me you may have peace!" Through being kept in the heart, the word becomes deed, which is the bedrock of the unity of peace. Peace exists in Jesus because through his life and deeds community with God is given. The life of Jesus leads us to the wellsprings of inner strength and shows us the way this strength is overwhelmingly at work right to the end of the world, to the final goal of all time.

Jesus hid himself from the multitudes on the secluded heath, on the lonely mountain, and in the quiet boat. He loved the peace of solitude for his communion with God. He loved to gather his strength in God's quiet. He spent whole nights talking with God. Contemplative quiet, however, was never Jesus' goal but the source of living works and strength for his heavy task. Out of this quiet he went to the people, he gathered thousands to him, and he advanced to the big city. His mission goes out into all the world. His love heals bodies and saves souls. His was a life of active love that needed the power of gathered concentration in order to reach the widest circles. In quiet before God, he gained the strength for each advance right up to the last battle – his bitter death.

The peace of Jesus is altogether different from a mood of impassive withdrawal. Without God we may try to force a false peace of soul, a placid repose. The cool tranquillity of a selfishly withdrawn life is far removed from the peace of God. God works a different peace: one that comes from having a confident spirit and, out of a full life, working for our ultimate calling – the all-embracing kingdom! A God-conscious life becomes a source of rich activity. When the heart is filled from its deepest depths, there is a well-grounded certainty that the crucified one is the one and only source of a peace that is both inmost and all-embracing. The crucified one rooted out sin, which allowed no peace to grow, and he does the work of peace in creating perfect unity.

Like fresh water flowing hour after hour in a river, the peace of God lives in the continuously renewed experience of Christ at work within us. Christ wants to remain in us so that even in the greatest need and distress we do the same works of peace as he did. Times of severe storm and violent unrest, like cloudbursts and torrents of rain that widen and deepen a riverbed, will serve to deepen and strengthen peace. Need and misery shall lead us to that final state of determination which the scriptures call repentance. Divine sadness and fruitful remorse bring forth peace, the good fruit of repentance. No sudden storm can change the character of peace. Storms merely test and confirm it. There may be waves on the surface of the water as if the current were flowing backward. But the direction of the current does not change: the main body of water goes forward unperturbed.

Peace strengthens. Courage that comes from peace is without fear. God's plan of peace for us does not anticipate suffering without the courage of joy. Peace, as community with Christ, is a fruit of the same spirit as joy and patience. The spiritual fruit of peace is a love that builds up in brotherliness. Its power is the kingdom of justice. "What is sown by peace becomes the fruit of justice." The kingdom of God, according to the church both in this age and in the ultimate future, is "justice and peace and joy in the Holy Spirit."

The kingdom of God in our hearts is the foundation of God's rulership over the whole earth, over all worlds. The peace of the church of Jesus Christ is commissioned as a forerunner of the peace of the future and of all eternity. Francis of Assisi used to begin each address and conversation with the greeting, "Peace be with you," as did the Anabaptists of Reformation times. So today too we must confront the unpeace of the whole world with the words of true brotherhood. "We must proclaim peace. We must cherish it in our own hearts. Through the life we share together with others, we must see to it that everyone is led to concord and unity – to the creative and openhearted justice of peace."

LIGHT AND FIRE

In every epoch of history there have been terrible calamities and bitter injustices. Faced with the daily suffering of masses of people, the spirit of humankind has proved throughout to be cold, indifferent, and insensitive, no matter what appalling depths the misery reaches. In times of crisis we need a new and shaking jolt to see the darkness and coldness lowering over us. There is no salvation without judgment upon injustice and unrighteousness. Such universal and persistent need as today's drives us to look for the cause. The source of help can flow freely only when the debris is cleared away.

Times of darkness call for faith in light from above. Before this light, all darkness will retreat, just as morning triumphs over every night. The ugliness and horror of darkness and its cold, murderous spirits must penetrate our consciousness. In utter helplessness, we must be on watch for the hour of redemption, for no human being can bring liberation or relief. Help must come from the other world if all life is not to sink into death's cold night. Under this crushing burden of the nightmare of darkness, we need a glimpse of the fire descending from above – the light that frees.

The light of faith must outshine darkness and all-pervading cold. Light triumphs over darkness, which is death. Death attacks life. When love grows cold, injustice escalates beyond measure. Darkness hates light, and, forced to retreat, it puts up the most violent resistance. The brightness of awakening life is terrifyingly painful to all those who have become strangers to strong light. Accustomed to the darkness all around them, they find the blazing glory of light unbearable torture. It burns in their eyes like fire. The victorious light becomes judgment. The radiant flame of life, which demands love, judges the darkness of unpeace and puts to flight the coldness of injustice.

A few days after Pascal's death, a sheet of paper was found in the lining of his suit. The great philosopher had kept it with him constantly for eight years, as a reminder of his deepest experience. On this parchment, the shaking description of an overwhelming enlightenment begins with the solitary word: fire.

Jesus brought flames of judgment and salvation. He wanted to kindle a fire, and his greatest longing was for it to burn: "How I wish it were already kindled!" (Luke 12:49) He brought glowing fire to the earth. But the fire he hands over to darkened humankind is not a sacrilegious theft, stolen by a second Prometheus from a jealous deity as in Greek mythology. Jesus is the fiery rays of a divine heart that pours out its fire constantly over all people. God is the giver here, God himself. The torch of wrath became a dispenser of life.

The flames of judgment became one with the fire of life, alive in the liberating and gathering light of love. Jesus knows what this blazing fire meant to the fearful heart from the beginning of history, what trembling and terror it brought upon erring humankind. He knows that there is no fire without consuming judgment over withered and hardened life that is on its way to death.

Flames of lightning from heaven and volcanic bursts from the earth, forest giants burning like pillars of fire and fiery

missiles erupting from mountaintops, lightning that strikes
with rolling thunder, and the lava of earthquakes setting fire
to everything in its path – they all fill the creatures of the
earth with shuddering awe and make them shake with fear at
the all-powerful might of their deadly, blazing heat.

Before fire can show radiant warmth and protecting, uniting power, the flames of its wrath must be revealed as consuming judgment. The flames of God's heart have to be
dreaded before they disclose their ultimate purpose. The
prophet could not help trembling with fear lest he lose his
sight in God's heavenly fire by looking with impure eyes at
the God of the shining hosts. God himself says, "My face
you cannot see. No one can see me and live"(Exod. 33:20).
We have fallen too deep into demonic darkness to be able to
bear the fiery light of the holy one, deadly to all the powers
of envy, all that serves death. Fire consumes. The light judges. It brings death to what is dead. Dry wood feeds the fire.
Death by fire is not caused by rays from the blazing fire but
by the nature of death and darkness – opposition to light
and enmity to life.

> When your eyes are blinded by the sun,
> Then blame your eyes,
> Blame not the sun.

Our night-cold nature makes us unable to live in consuming
fire. By challenging this cold night, fire breaks in: God's fiery
flames are the answer, also to the call of faith. God descended upon the mountain of Moses in fire. His word is
never anything else than fire; his voice flashes flames. Lightning flashes from his heart of burning fire. The Lord on his
throne of flaming fire radiates fire from within. He is

clothed entirely in flames. His servants and messengers are rays of flame – fire goes out from God. He speaks from the midst of it and his mouth pours forth fire. He sends it down from heaven: devouring fire goes before him. He comes in consuming fire: it is his very nature. He rains down lightning and brimstone. His fury flashes out as fire when his wrath begins. His spirit kindles judgment when he calls for fire. Whoever waits upon God awaits judgment and fire, in which the light of God's salvation shines out.

Jesus shines out in our darkness like the sun after the black tropical night. Jesus is the light of the world; whoever loves him hungers for his fire. Whoever knows him thirsts for his light, which outshines all suns. Angelus Silesius declared, "You may have the light of the sun; Jesus is the sun that illuminates my soul."*

It is impossible for us to visualize how far the sun is from the earth it illuminates. Ninety-three million miles are beyond earthly comprehension. What an effect this distant kingdom of fiery life has! How blinding this light is so far from the earth! Against this distant ball of light, our dazzlingly white magnesium flame appears as black as ink. How can we grasp it that the light of Rigel is five thousand times brighter than our sun, or that the rays of Capella send out in one day as much light as the sun in a year? What effect the proximity of such sun giants must have is more than we can imagine in human dimensions. In the face of their living energy our little sun dwindles to a candle. The whole universe, as we see it in the heavens, is an endless ocean of light made up of many millions of these mighty fixed star-suns. Night is

*Angelus Silesius (pseudonym for Johannes Scheffler), 1624–1677.

to be found only in the shadow made by the dark planets. If we were able to leave our planet completely behind, we would be exposed to the inconceivable power of a divine sea of light.

In Jesus, a fiery light infinitely stronger than all suns put together draws near to the earth. The footsteps of Jesus come near in burning fire. His eyes are blazing flames. His countenance is radiant with the supreme power of all suns. Seven lampstands of golden fire surround him. Seven sun-stars are in his hand. His light casts us to the ground; Paul fell at his feet as though dead. God, however, gave him the resurrecting power of radiant life: he entrusted to the apostle the glorious mystery of the church, the mystery of the kingdom. He is the rising morning star. It shall become clear to us through the nature of the sun-fire what effect the sevenfold starlight of his church has, what power breaks in with the morning light of the coming day of the sun. The spirit of unity is the light of God descending from heaven, closely kin in its inmost nature to the glory of all suns.

Therefore, if the mission of Jesus is to be understood, the nature of the sun and of fire has to be understood. Our sun is a central fire world from which our planet gets its life. The sun's force of attraction gathers and holds together all the worlds that surround it. Its heat keeps us from dying of cold. Its warmth awakens life in plants and animals. Without its light, all life would perish in darkness. The tiny fraction of light-energy our planet receives from the far distant sun is enough to engender and maintain the boundless life we know on the earth. Every manifestation of earth's power, each breath of wind, the water-vapor cycle, the movements of deep-sea fish, every beat of our heart is the work of the sun. What bracing power it gives body and soul! Without it we fall prey to death.

We could call every organism of the earth a sunbeam come to life. Light and warmth sustain all life. It is the energy of light that makes it possible for plants rooted in the earth to make food from air and earth and to maintain life. Only through light can green plant cells carry out this life-maintaining process. And no living creature, no matter how accustomed to darkness, can live without light or without the organisms belonging to the world of light. The sun is the king and heart of the deep as well as of the heights. The sun is the fire that gives life to all that lives.

It is not by chance that God's being and nature in Christ's radiant glory is compared to the sun, to light, and to fire. What Paul states as a fact – that God's invisible being has been perceptible in his works since the creation of the world – can be seen first and foremost in the light of the sun and in the blaze of fire. Here in the works of creation this eternal power and divine greatness are recognizable with particular force and clarity. From time immemorial, sun and fire have appeared to man as uniquely significant images of divine powers.

Again and again, God the creator, the spirit of the shining, blazing sun, and the controller of storms and lightning has been worshiped as an all-inclusive oneness. In Egypt the god of the great eternal light was the supreme deity, the creator of all things and the true god of heaven. The light-giving god is the one who reveals and exposes everything. The life-creating god of light is fire. It both awakens to life and consumes all that is dead and cold. In India they say of him: "Rays of light proclaim the fire-flashing sun as it rises in splendor to give light to the universe. May the much-to-be desired light of the divine sun awaken our spirit!" The eye of the sun appeared in olden times as supremely beneficent, as the perceptive, good-creating power.

An ancient Brahmin prayer says: "Protected by divine power as we gaze at the heavens above the regions of darkness, may we draw near to the deity, to the most radiant light." In his letter to the Romans, the apostle Paul quite clearly appreciated this pagan recognition of the nature of God; yet at the same time, with the prophets of the Old Testament, he emphasized the other side, that in those days this shining book of nature was never read outside the ultimate revelation of light in Christ without dangerous errors – that is, idolatrous misconstructions – being made. Sun and fire were continually being changed from clear and obvious symbols of God's nature to supposedly independent deities of sun and fire – "lords over all the planet gods" or the dispensers of life itself. The nature of the radiant God of heaven ought to be recognized through his shining creations as infinitely transcending all created things; yet erring humankind all too often exalts the light created by God and makes an idol of it as the highest deity. In this way, unhappy man brings stifling darkness toward the radiant, created light. When we consider the religious significance of sun and fire, therefore, we must keep pagan idolatry in mind just as much as the dawning intimation of God.

From the earliest times, everything burning and blazing, everything shining and radiant has been seen as divine. Indeed, in many cultures, the name for God originated from the word that stood for radiant light. In the old Nordic tongue God is called "Bright Heaven." Like the sun, the mighty spirit of the divine light of heaven appears to all as the fire of the universe, dispensing life and sustaining life with its power. Through the shining universe, a faint perception of divine unity dawned on fallen human beings. As a result, they became conscious of the light and unity that alone was to awaken and create the highest form of life. They implored light and fire to come from heaven. As the Native Americans chanted, "Great Spirit, come down! Fire and earth, smoke with me!"

From the very beginning, the human mind has associated that which is creative and life-bringing, good and noble, with warmth and light, radiance and brightness. Down through the ages, people have always been conscious that the warmth of light and love's life and vitality belong together. Light and beauty are one. But light does not shine everywhere. The sun goes down. Night follows day. Throughout the ages we have always known that the radiant, blazing brightness of the good and powerful spirit of light has an opposite – the evil, sinister spirit of cold and darkness. Everything that keeps back the awakening life of spring is death-like winter. Everything that opposes warmth is deadening cold. Everything that opposes unifying love causes disintegration and death. Death threatens life. Between light and darkness there is enmity and warfare to the end.

We are placed in a tremendous tension between life and death: we are called to burning, life-giving light, but can we overcome or conquer the freezing cold and deadly darkness? Will we survive in the struggle against this very dangerous power, which constantly besets us from within and without? The good spirit of light was revealed from the very beginning as divine, as the leader and champion of life. The evil spirit of darkness was from the very beginning the enemy, the sinister demon of night and death. Between the two stood the people God had created, struggling as it were between heaven and hell. This struggle filled their life. Full of alarm, they feared descending night as the cold threat of death and hell. Rejoicing, they greeted the dawn of shining day as the approach of glowing warmth, coming from the heavens and from life.

Light meant life and power. People saw the glorious morning sun rise to course triumphant across the heavens. In the sun, in light, and in fire, they saw nothing soft or insipid, nothing weak or servile. To them, the victorious power of light was armed with the radiant arrows of the sun and the flashing weapon of lightning. To them, the strong sun-hero of radiant morning and of bright springtime was welded to a fiery unity with the thunder-god of storms and threatening lightning. The light-god of the sun's power was for them masculine and manly, like the thunder-god of storms and lightning. Spring, when the sun is ascending, was for them a youthful, courageous war-hero, who as a triumphant conqueror overcomes the aging giant of mighty winter and leads in a new time over the earth and all its inhabitants – the sunny time, the longed-for time, the expected time! This time alone can awaken strong, prolific, and abiding life.

For humankind, light was to triumph over darkness at the end of time. The day was to dawn when the last springtime of all worlds and ages would melt and abolish forever the whole present age of wintertime – this cold, dark, dead, and numbing ice age of the world of today. In early Christian times, Hermas, a prophet of the church of Rome, wrote his book, The Shepherd, in which this age-old enlightenment is given new meaning in the early Christian sense. In the third parable he says, "The present world-age is wintertime. The coming world-age is summertime." What facts lie behind this prophetic language? It is important to get a picture of what sun and fire are and have meant in nature from time immemorial if we want to understand all the prophetic word has to say about the sun-energy of God, about the light of Christ, about the fire of the spirit, about the dawn of radiant day in the coming kingdom, and about the living church with its fire of unity and its power to shine out.

Nothing can make the powerful significance of glowing fire clearer to us than the very beginning when, cast out and still far from God, people met fire for the first time. It came as a terror to them. And yet the same fire was soon kindled as a campfire and as a sacrificial altar fire. Adam was once master over fire, and light shone in him. But what happened after this light was lost? How did the first man, cast out into the darkness, experience fire? In a flash, lightning would descend from heaven with a crack of thunder, and a forest giant would be set ablaze. Everything would take flight. Soon, however, people would gather round the felled and still burning tree, encamp there to feed the fire as their own, and so find protection for the community they craved.

Or it could be that the depths of the mountain would rumble. The foundations of the earth would quake and crack. Enormous pillars of fire would shoot up out of the smoking mountain. Volleys of stones and showers of ashes would be hurled high into the air and immediately spread far and wide over the land. Slowly a river of glowing, blood-

red substance would pour its way into the valley. Trees or
bushes would be caught by its fiery breath, and everything
would go up in flames. Gradually the surface of the red-hot
lava would grow pale. It would lie there like a gigantic snake,
covering the valley bed in a mound of heat. People would
venture to draw their camp nearer the slowly hardening lava.
The nearer they came, the warmer they would be, even in
the middle of the cold tropical night. Should a piece of dry
wood touch this dangerous glowing stream, the branch
would burst into bright flames. Then fire would be kindled,
just as when the tree was struck by lightning. And as people
put more and more wood on the fire, the warmer and
brighter the flames.

So people learned to combine their terrible fear of fire
with a reverent thankfulness, for here they encountered an
element that united the wrath of a destructive power with
the loving gift of life. In reverence they wanted to preserve it,
so they fed and tended it. They learned how to acquire and
handle it. Soon they began to carry it, glowing and glimmer-
ing, to kindle a blazing fire where they wanted it, using tiny
sticks. They carefully kept alive the glowing embers borrowed from the destructive lightning or volcano, carrying
them to where it was cold and dark. They learned to take
care of the fire.

So they revered the spark of fire as something sacred, a
truly holy possession the deity had given to the human race
alone. No animal had an active part in this possession or
took it along. No gathering of animals tended the fire as
people did. Only the frail community of people was never
without fire; only they were fire bearers. The spark was never
allowed to go out in their hands. "Fire guardian" was their

name. Their fire must never be forgotten. They passed it on from hand to hand. As fire givers and fire borrowers, true to their origin and goal, they proved to be communal beings. Fire united them in mutual help. Even the total stranger was included in this fellowship from the very beginning.

Tending the fire was basic for community. The radiation of light and warmth generated a power to gather. The campfire meant that community was formed and preserved. The most valuable heritage of the people of old was the community fire passed on from generation to generation. Everywhere, the flame remains the focal point of all cravings for community. The flame creates community as a way of life.

The first light of God's image was lost when humankind fell. A sign of the new humankind was that they fostered the flames originating from those terrors of the heavens and of the abyss. Then, after the loss of God's first peace, it dawned on them that judgment by fire meant a gift of fire, that the wrath of the highest powers bears within it new, loving grace. Service to the fire became service to God; worshiping the lost God, people wanted to keep the warm glow of fire alive through the sacrifice of wood. They did not want its light to go out at any time. Their aim was to gather the community and to keep it gathered. Food also, like life, should be preserved from decay and death. Thus the community of the tribe, of the nation, and of humankind was meant to come into being from campfire, hearth fire, and altar fire. The light of paradise had disappeared, unclouded community with God was lost. Could the new communal fire light the way back to God?

Through fire, people very slowly gained more mastery over the forces of nature – the mastery they had been called to in the lost garden. They seemed to become more and more free, especially in choosing and changing habitations. They felt increasingly independent of the outward circumstances of country and climate. In the community of the fire, they strove to press forward to the freedom and mastery they had forfeited along with God's community of light. A glowing light once more gathered them round a blazing central point. It showed them a communal way through the threatening night to freedom. It seemed to them that the brightness of the flame would set them free from the cold's deadly breath and from all the forces of nature that tried to tear them to pieces and destroy them once they had lost the peace of God.

Set free from the fear of night and enslavement to nature, if only to a small extent, people could venture slowly to take up their lost mastery over things and circumstances. So they learned to share their food in community; they learned how to keep it edible for the whole band. So they made a step forward from the campfire in the open, on the bare ground, to the protected community hearth made of two layers of stone set opposite each other, between which the holy fire was to burn uninterruptedly for all. Here it was to be kept alive for the tribe for always, an awe-inspiring mystery of the hoped-for community.

Fear and terror had once led to a common flight from the predictable fiery wrath of the deity; later, a common reverence bound people to the flame. For they had experienced what the dangerous fire gave the tribe: protection from freezing to death and from the evil powers of night, conservation of life-energies and preservation of food by seasoning with fire. But the gathering power of fire was seen more and more as its most powerful element. The gift of life and community, so much desired, was greater than the destruction caused by lightning and fire-belching mountains that had once driven people apart. What had once meant the terror of death and separation became a power for life, a power that gathered.

This is how people tried to survive the awful horror of the ice age. This is how they passed through those deadly ages that drove much mightier animal species into distant parts or completely exterminated them. Only like this could they (whose limbs were unarmed) hold their own against the countless murderous creatures of night, and withstand the spirits of darkness, feared most of all.

The fire gave protection; for this reason it was protected. As the protective gathering point of the community, it became the focal point of the human dwelling. Houses were created for the sake of the fire. People first started to build houses in an effort to protect the flame. The sacred hearth fire is not without reason the very essence of home life. In choosing a campsite, the only consideration was to protect the flame, to find a shield for the hearth, not to find or erect a sheltered hiding place. Once protected from the wind, the blazing flames frightened away all dangers that threatened, whereas no hiding place (however carefully chosen) could hold off stealthy and evil powers.

To shelter the fireplace from storms and floods, walls were set up under the cover of trees, or sometimes the fireplace was built in a protecting cave. But in each case the shelter afforded by the embryonic house was mainly for keeping the flame alive. Not the house but the fire was the protection from freezing to death in the ice-cold night and from being frightened to death by nocturnal enemies. Not the people but the fire was what they tried to protect with walls and roof. To protect it was a holy cause, the holiest obligation. The dwelling house evolved as a sacred shelter for the hearth.

The raised hearth was the token of a holy place, symbolizing the great cause that held them together. It became a holy symbol of sublime significance, an altar and a memorial. The word "altar" was used for God's holy, blazing hearth of smoking sacrifice in the temple, and the same word was used for the cooking fireplace in every secular house – this was holy too. For primitive people, the hearth of their daily dwelling was just as inviolable as the altar fire in a temple. The reason is clear. Light and warmth, as gifts of the deity, were always the power that gathered the community. Since the very first community, the hearth needed reverent care as the crystallization point of the common life.

The raised fireplace was a symbol of greatest significance not only for the living community but also for the dead. In the earliest times of communal life, communities constantly moved from place to place, and in the passage of time, the old leaders of the tribe passed away one by one. Along the path taken by the tribe, holy symbols arose as abiding memorials and permanently sacred places. Wherever the holy community fires had burned, wherever a gathering ground had been a place of sacrifice and religious union, earth and stones would be piled up to make a mound, which kept on getting higher and wider. The first memorials were marks of old fireplaces consecrated to the

eternal. They were rightly regarded as holy graves by those
who traveled by. In primitive times, a leader's tomb was
erected beside his beloved hearth – the place where he had
lived and worked in the midst of his people. The altar of a
temple and the hearth of a simple house were given the same
veneration – the tomb and the hearth also became one at
this same fire. The tomb became a place that was consecrated forever: the former fireplace, beside which the dead
had been active in life, was preserved as a holy place by enclosing the hearth and the grave within a circle of stones.
Thus arose the "hill of worship" where God and heathen
gods were worshiped, as it says in the Bible.

With the living, it was the same as with the dead. The area
around the fire was enclosed more and more until a closed
square was created, housing the living in the same way as
the stone circle housed the dead. The vital center for the living as for the dead was and always will be the hearth – the
essence of the home and of family life. The words for fence
(*Zaun* in German), town (*tun* in Old English), enclosure
(*tun* in Old Norse), and fortress (*dun* in Old Irish), with
their common Nordic root, all point to the fire and the
buildings around it. Around the fire, the permanent center,
arose the individual house, providing a roof for the hearth.
And around this hearth, the settlement grew up, its fences
and walls protecting the roofed dwellings: the fire is the secret at the heart of all communal dwellings.

The hearth fire, then, was regarded as the power uniting
the communal household settled around it, just as earlier (as
a campfire) it had gathered the nomadic tribe. And despite a
tendency in all people to limit their will to community to

their own few kin, the fire would stimulate friendship between tribes. The fire, as the basis of hospitality, would pave
the way for peace and unity between strangers; and by freely
borrowing and lending fire, even enemy tribes became
friendly. Carried from hearth to hearth and from one people
to another, fire would be given or received as a token of
peace and unity.

The service paid to the dead indicates the friendly relationships between the living. The community of food, field,
and fire among these primitive people becomes clear in their
service to the dead. The dead were provided with food and
fire in their graves, just as in life they had practiced community of food and fire with the living. Primitive people helped
each other; in fact, the fields and pastures consecrated by fire
were managed collectively by the whole tribe or village. The
dead, too, like other members of the tribe, had to be provided with earthly goods of the community. They were not
to be left cold and hungry to a dark grave. Therefore they
were given a share of the communal food or the harvest from
a piece of land that was dedicated to them.

Nothing that belonged by rights to the dead was to be
kept back for the living. From ancient times, therefore,
when anyone died, the fire shared to the last in living community was extinguished; it was to be surrendered completely as a consecrated gift. After the fire had been put out on
the deserted hearth, a new fire had to be kindled. Still today,
the Roman Catholic church extinguishes all the old fires on
Easter Saturday to commemorate Jesus' death and lights the
new flames on Easter morning so that every household can
light its fires, tapers, or Easter candles from it. When they gave

fire, primitive people testified to their faith that life continued
for the dead. Today too as the candles are relighted, the cry
rings out: "Christ is risen!"

Because of their faith in life after death, primitive people
gave to the dead what they held to be the best and the highest
also for the living. As the dead were given food and fire for a
new and different life, the living were given food and fire for
every new undertaking on earth. Fire-virgins were indispensable as an escort for every move or new beginning. Like Germanic youths, the "sacred spring" consecrated to the deity,
Roman youths selected for the founding of a new settlement
were sent out from the parent stock on the first of March. As
the consecrated "spring" of the race, they had to take the
community fire with them when they were ready to leave,
while all home fires were extinguished. The holy tending of
the fire and the kindling of the new spark were entrusted to
the fire-virgins, who were not to be hindered in this priestly
service by love or childbearing. Later, chastity was still rigorously demanded for the vestal virgins too and for the consecrated virgins who watched the holy temple fire.

The continued protection and maintenance of the tribe
settled on home ground also depended on service to the holy
fire. Continuance of the race and continuance of the fire
were regarded as one and the same thing. When the tribe
died out, the fire went out; as soon as the fire ceased to burn,
the independence of the people was lost. And should a traveling band lose its flame, they would fetch a new spark from
the old home hearth, not to be indebted to strangers: Gretti
the Strong swam through the stormy waves of the fjord and
brought the home fire back in his uplifted hand. As Homer

says in the Odyssey, "The seed of fire is fostered, that it need not be kindled afar."

Through fire, the homeland was dedicated to the tribe and its deity. Just as the flame of the land was held in holy community, so from time immemorial the land, as "common land," was common property with no individual possession – marked-out land held communally by the "commonalty." For the Norwegians, "to sanctify with fire" meant their taking over territory through their communal flame. Where their fires burned was their homeland. The home fire, like the land they had taken over, belonged to the whole community of the tribe.

Like possessing the land in common, sharing the tribe's fire was a religious matter. To be denied fire meant banishment from the homeland. Fire could be refused only to someone exiled for religious reasons, a punitive measure sanctioned by divine power – as a ban. Left to be judged by the gods, they could no longer share the necessities of life with their people; the fire needed was denied, the homeland forbidden. Therefore, to be exiled, this hardest fate that could befall anyone, was called "being deprived of the community of water and fire." As Herodotus reports about Aristodemus of Sparta, no one spoke to those who were denied fire. Similarly, according to Cornelian law, loss of Roman citizenship was pronounced by denying water and fire. Among Germanic peoples also, no one was allowed to give outlaws fire or water; they were cut off from the whole communal life of the people.

Granting or refusing fire like this had a leveling effect. With regard to women, the flame had an elevating effect too, raising them to a status of equality or even to priestly dignity. All people are equal before the fire. Women everywhere had the greatest importance in giving or withholding this holy service, as with the vestal virgins or the fire-bearing virgins of the Vikings and other Germanic races, who were consecrated to the service of sacred springtime. It was nearly always the woman who had to tend the hearth fire, guard and foster it, carry it with her, and feed it with ever-ready material.

Perhaps woman was also the first to bring fire to birth by rubbing sticks, for it was in the process of work that the way to rekindle the lost flame was discovered. In the process of making tools or cutting wood to feed the fire, a new spark would fall into the pile of wood dust and blaze up into a precious flame, the result of heat and friction and the collection of fine particles of wood. Work with fire-making materials was a holy function – a priestly service. Fire was generated by rapidly twirling two sticks (called the fire-father and fire-mother), so that, as the Edda says, "it could be allowed to grow and immediately send messages far and wide."* This kindling of fire practiced by men or women was from the very beginning a sacred service. Among the American Indians, the priest was called the "fire maker" just as the priestesses of Rome were called the "fire-virgins."

The swastika (symbolizing both a wheel of fire and the turning wheel of the sun) points to this kindling of flame, which from remotest times was held to be holy. The swastika is an ancient symbol of fire sticks laid at right angles. The hooks at the ends of the sticks suggest quick motion like a whirling wheel, showing the quick rotation that causes ignition. The spark is the result of the motion. Thus in the Far East the swastika, as the fire-cross denoting kindling in

---

*The Edda – a collection of old Icelandic poems.

primitive times, became the symbol for cause and effect. Rotary friction was recognized as the cause and fire as the effect.

The fact that we find this fire-cross of two hooked sticks as early as the new stone age proves that it had universal significance. As a symbol of life and community, the kindling of fire by the twirling of sticks is the common property of all peoples. As a symbol of fire-kindling and of the sun-wheel, the swastika belongs to primeval people. All descendants, without distinction of race or blood, have a right to it. So it is not surprising that all the Aryan tribes as well as the Phoenicians of Canaan preserved this sign of the life-giving power of sunlight and fire-kindling. Fire, the kindling of fire, and the community of fire belong also to the Jewish inhabitants of Canaan.

Among all peoples, the holy service of guarding and kindling the consuming fire led to sacrifice by fire on the holy altar. So the people of Israel worshiped Jahweh-Jehovah every morning and evening through the ascending smoke of the incense offering and the rising flames of the burnt offering. Offerings on the incense altar become in the new covenant the fiery offering of intercession: Jesus Christ, the High Priest, interceding for his people. At the same time (through the pleading of Jesus and the Holy Spirit), they are the fiery prayers rising from his saints, and as such are also described as daily offerings (Rev. 5:8).

The burnt offering on the fire altar was not only the most frequent but also the most common and comprehensive sacrifice, the complete sacrifice. Abraham for instance, the patriarch of Israel, showed an unlimited readiness to sacrifice when he was prepared to give the only son of the promise as a sacrifice by fire. And even before the patriarchs, Noah, saved from the annihilating flood, sent up to heaven and to God's rainbow of peace a burnt offering of a whole animal, a symbol of complete dedication. For this reason, Paul spoke of the death of Jesus as the fire offering of the new covenant, of his cross-gallows as the altar of burnt offering (Heb. 13:10–12). But John saw and heard those who had witnessed to Christ with their blood – saw them under the altar, like the spirits of the ancients under the hearth that was their grave and their memorial (Rev. 6:9–11). In this baptism of blood, Jesus' question was answered: "Can you be baptized with the same fire that comes over me?" The blood baptism of the crucified one and the church's martyrdom by death afterwards point to the complete sacrifice, as if on the hearth of a burnt offering.

Among the people of Israel also, the flame of a sacrifice pointing to the ultimate like this could be kindled only at the holy altar fire. No "alien" fire was allowed on the altar. As among the most ancient peoples, the fire blazing on Israel's table of burnt offering was never to die out. As eternal fire, it was sanctified to God. The stone hearth or stone table (which even at this time was occasionally built up with earth and turf) was later at the time of the prophets called "God's mountain" or "God's hearth" (Ezek. 43:12–15). As the table for the fire, it was the altar of God.

In accordance with age-old custom, this altar, the place of sacrifice and fire, was built of undressed stone even as late as the second temple of Israel. Moses (like the earliest man) made a fire altar of earth and surrounded it with twelve piles of stone as the Israelites' court of sanctuary; Joshua (like later primitive men) made one of undressed stone and surrounded it with the stones of the law. In the new covenant, commitment unto death must be offered, as it were, on just such an ancient burnt-offering altar as Abel's, without the artificial embellishment of human skill and its sham riches, in the primal simplicity of humanity at its poorest and simplest. When the apostle of Jesus proclaims him who was baptized by fire and executed on a crude cross, his words have effect only if they have no rhetorical skill or lofty wisdom (1 Cor. 1:17). Sacrifice by fire demands utmost simplicity – the original genuineness.

To sum up, it was by that simple fire-altar in the temple court that the prophet Isaiah recognized the full significance of the fire of God: "God has a hearth in Jerusalem." "Jahweh has a fire in Zion." "Jehovah will kindle a light-giving fire over all the dwellings on his mountain so that in burning it may shine through the dark night." "The light of Israel will be fire." "His spirit will judge and will kindle a fire."

Like lightning from heaven, the fire of the Lord comes down to strike where it will. When Elijah, the only remaining prophet of Jehovah, confronted hundreds of false prophets who represented the sun-god Baal and the moon-and-Venus goddess Astarte, he ordered two altars to be prepared, one for the idols and the other for Jahweh, the God of Abraham, Isaac, and Israel. He built his of twelve stones because it stood like Moses' for the hearth of the twelve tribes, Jehovah's people. He poured water over it; for on both altars, wood and a beast of sacrifice were to be laid, but no fire of human making. The priests of Baal and Astarte were to call on their gods, and Elijah was to call on his God to send lightning and kindle fire: "The god who answers with fire, he is God!" Here the battle between the fire-gods and the fire coming from God was settled. The frantic calling of the priests of sun and moon got no response. When Elijah called, however, the fire of Jehovah fell from heaven upon his altar and devoured burnt offering, wood, stone, earth, and even water, the enemy of fire; the flash of lightning proved that "Jehovah is God. Jahweh is God. The Lord is God!"

Fire that descends from heaven is the blazing sign in which the God of the covenant draws near. For he is the creative spirit of the central fire. He created heaven and earth, sun, light, glowing heat, and all life. Consuming fire proclaims God's approach. When Abraham, the patriarch of divine faith, asked for a sign of the covenant to put all his doubts aside, it was God's flame of fire that came between the pieces of the sacrifice at the right and the left, just as people making a covenant used to stride between the parts of the divided animal to strengthen their vow. God makes his covenant with fire; this covenant we must follow.

When the dwelling place of the covenant – the tabernacle – was set up in the wilderness, a shining flame and a cloud of smoke settled over it because it was the house of God's fire. When this fire of God would not move ahead, the people stayed at their camping place and waited, even for months at a time. When the flame went ahead with a cloud of smoke, however, the whole company, pledged to the fire, made its departure. They saw the guiding light of the fire as God's call, God's breath, and God's word. God the sender of fire was himself their fire bearer, and it was impossible to make any move unless he went ahead.

Again, to give the prophet Moses his commission, God appeared to him as flames of fire in a burning bush. God's word was a burning fire also to Jeremiah; it glowed in his heart and became a blazing flame in his mouth. This is also said of Elijah; he burst forth with his prophecy like a burning fire. Fire and smoke are signs from God, breaking in like flaming words to proclaim his glory – both as the fire of wrath and judgment and as the fire of love and unity.

The fire of God's light never appears without judgment, consuming what is old, withered, and dried up, what is lifeless, disunited, and unjust – all that has fallen prey to death. We should never forget that fire from heaven and from the abyss came in lightning and in volcanic eruption. Bringing fear and terror, it strikes into the cold darkness of night and unpeace. It floods the dead and withered landscape with a fiery sea of horror. It reveals and consumes the darkness of evil, death, and separation. Always, the fire of judgment must burn the felled tree and the useless chaff.

God calls down this fire as a final judgment over the darkened universe, just as he let it fall on impure and degenerate Sodom and Gomorrah, on the tyrannical injustice of Egypt with its slavery, and on the divisive and rebellious company of Korah and other subversive Israelites in the wilderness (Num. 16:1–35). It will consume heaven and earth. Like jewels to be tried by fire, they are destined for a sea of flame, kindled on the day of the last judgment. It destroys all that is disunited, separated from God. In this judgment, a grim, dark fire will be kindled, sending out jets of torturing smoke without the blessing of justifying flames.

The hellish fire of expulsion and banishment is the last mystery of judgment. It is separated from all community of life, from all the protecting and liberating power of the camp or hearth fire. It burns with lurid flames and belongs to the

nocturnal powers of darkness. In the Sermon on the Mount
Jesus declares that whoever destroys the community of love
and despises brothers and sisters and denies them dignity,
whoever leaves the hungry and thirsty without food and drink
or the homeless and naked without shelter and clothes, whoever ignores the sick and imprisoned deserves this final fire of
judgment because he or she has forgotten God and love.

Cold hearts that shut out the misery of others, that are
callous to injustice, and that resist community in their hard-
heartedness call down judgment upon themselves – they are
cast out into the consuming darkness of complete absence of
community because their whole nature has the characteristics of darkness. Jesus declares this very severe judgment inescapable: divisive, destructive, and disintegrating unpeace
must be exposed and judged. There is no other way of approaching this unpeace. Yet Jesus, in proclaiming impending
judgment, wants to bring salvation. His fire judges evil by
showing the way out of the dominion of darkness into the
kingdom of light. In his hand, the torch of wrath becomes
the dispenser of gathering and sustaining life. Jesus is God's
fire bringer.

The early Christians preserved this memorable saying of
Jesus: "He who is near me is near the fire; but he who is far
from me is far from the kingdom." Jesus glows like fire and
sun; he brings the judgment of the spirit of fire; through the
approach of his kingdom of light, he lays the foundation of
the community of fire in his church household. With him
comes God's kingdom, God's rulership; God himself is the
shining sun, putting all created suns in the shade forever. In
the light and unity of Jesus Christ, God's heart of glowing,
blazing love has achieved the fulfillment of his eternal will.

The Son is the sun hero, who needs no created suns when he brings in the victory of the coming age of light. His radiance is consuming fire and life-creating light. "Just as the sun fills everything that absorbs its strength, so the voice of God echoes through everyone – but also as a voice of wrath. If a plant has no sap, the sun's rays burn it; but if it does have sap, the sun's rays warm it and make it grow."* If we are not ready for God's fire of love, for Jesus Christ's victory of light, we succumb to the fury of the all-consuming judgment by fire.

I n the burning love of Christ's approach, the blazing wrath of judgment by fire comes to an end. Annihilation ceases in his glowing warmth; life begins in his spirit of light. His followers know that, unlike Elijah, they cannot intervene and call down destructive fire on the enemies of the cause, or actually spew it out themselves. They know how loving is the spirit whose children they are. As when Elijah ascended, their fire, coming from God's radiant heart, is seen in the sun chariot and the horses of fire that carry the liberated spirits of all nations into God's unifying kingdom of light. The burning fire of Christ's followers shows itself in their fiery mission of love, in the glowing light of their joyful message. Their nature is that of messengers sent out by God: through their service the light of the heavenly world is brought to those who are to inherit the salvation of the final kingdom.

The mission of Jesus Christ brings the Holy Spirit – the radiant, burning spirit of perfect love. The fire of this mission, originating in the coming world of light, consumes all that is unholy and fans to radiant brightness all that is of God. Jesus came to kindle a sea of fire on the earth. His

---

*The German mystic Jakob Böhme, 1575–1624, is the source of this and other unidentified quotes throughout this chapter.

whole longing is for it to burn. He is the last of the men of old, one who has never fallen. As the bearer of the spirit of fire, he is the only possible bearer of the light, guardian of the embers, and kindler of the fire. The flame of this spirit offers the last chance of becoming true people, uniting with God, and gathering together in community.

The first Adam forfeited the privileges of his holy calling – the old nature spurned the possibility of the life of light once granted it. But God did not want us to lose forever our destiny of light as his images. He sent to earth the divine flame and loving fire of the last Adam, and in him the burning light of God breaks in again. In its white-hot glow lives the strength to awaken life, the light- and life-bestowing energy of the new creation.

Through the blazing flame of the spirit of Jesus Christ, people once enslaved by fear of death are set free from all bestial and infernal powers of night. From now on they can assume lordship of spirit over the aging powers of nature and also over body and soul, both creatures of the first creation. Only the power of the spirit of Jesus Christ can bring about kingly freedom. For only he who is more powerful than any other spirit is able to bring the authority and lordship of the father of Jesus Christ to victory over the enslaving powers of death.

The power to gather and protect, coming from the flame of his spirit, drives away the murderous spirits of night; it supplants the ice age of the prevailing world-spirit that makes everything grow cold; but not only that – its blazing protection brings the one thing that is decisive for our world and age: the church gathered round the altar fire of the crucified one, the communal household of God with its missionary bands sent out into all the world.

The focal point of this new people is the new fireplace of the new church; around it the central communal dwelling arises once more. Around the radiant fire of the Holy Spirit, the spiritual temple is built up as a tangible house of God: the city on the hill, whose light streams out over all lands. Her place of worship is on fire with the Spirit; she shines forth in the truth. The fire of the Holy Spirit brings the church above – the glorified ones who have witnessed with their blood – down to the band of believers gathered round Christ's throne of fire. In this flame there is living unity between those who have gone before and those who remain on earth. The unanimity of the people gathered to full community in the house of God is the unity of the church above. It dwells in perfect light, inaccessible to the mortal life of our darkened earth.

From the city above, the fire of love descends and takes the leadership. Coming from the spirit of perfect unity, it leads the body of believers in all its weakness not only to community of goods – food, land, and everything else – and to community of work: it leads them to pass on this flame through hospitality and fiery mission, serving as messengers to all people on earth. From the kingdom of light, the unity of the church becomes a message of peace for the whole world.

For this fire-carrying service, the holy flame of the church's pure spirit must be kept unadulterated. The church of fire can maintain permanence only because she fosters and reveres the holy flame to the end. Those united in faith and love in the church protect not themselves but the flame of the spirit, the only surety of true life. What they try to preserve is not their own life but that of the holy fire, to which they have surrendered their own nature. Only in this way do they gain real life, which shall become fullness of life for everyone. Their hearth burns for the whole world without assimilating the unholy fires of other elements from the world. Nothing of our own nature, no alien fire from other altars, no other spirit may approach. The church's altar of light is holy; her works of love are of a different nature.

Yet as soon as her radiant fire is mixed with the fuel of alien flames, it dies out. When such a church community forgets the light of unadulterated love and denies her first works, which were free from everything alien to love, her lampstand is knocked over, her light goes out. As soon as the inviolable fire of the Holy Spirit is taken from such a community, it loses its commission and its freedom. The dying hearth ceases to be an altar; robbed of the fire of God's love, it is nothing but worthless ashes. Without light, the house of this people is no longer a temple of God. Unity and community are extinguished with the loss of fire; they have become impossible. The church can never gather without the focal point of holy light and fire. Only when the Holy Spirit is called down from its homeland in the church above can such a lost people be set free again from the dominion of slavery and lack of community.

Without the fire of the Holy Spirit, community dies. It peters out in slavery to alien peoples where other flames burn – unholy fires of our own works and the emotional enthusiasm of blood, which is demonic. The land once consecrated to common use through the divine fire of the spirit now belongs once again (with all the work done on it and with all it produces) to self-interest or group egoism, whereas in the church it had at long, long last belonged to God. In the church of Christ was realized in a small, hidden way what will appear in greatness at the end of time: "The earth is the Lord's." It belongs to God. No inch of its land may be claimed as the property of an individual. Where the spirit of the last and eternal king rules, the land belongs to the light and fire of his church and his kingdom. Where God's flame goes out, God is robbed of his land, and it falls back to private property. The life of community is dead.

Yet the message of the gospel is resurrection from the dead. From his resurrection on, Christ shows himself as the Son of God in the coming-down of the Holy Spirit again and again. When the old flame has gone out – when the living, as slaves to death, drift apart and turn away from the hearth that once gathered them and leave it to those of old (now dead and gone) who were faithful to their altar – then the spirit of the risen one wants to kindle new fire to set up community of life again with the watchword: "Light your lamps; the Lord is truly risen!"

Inspired by the Easter message and the Pentecostal flame of the Holy Spirit, young people – "the holy springtime" – set out to consecrate new land to the church of the risen one. Again and again, bands of awakened young people have set out. A hundred years after the first full community in Jerusalem, a new outpouring of the spirit of fire created the church again in Asia Minor. In total community, this church awaited the Jerusalem that was to come down from God, the image of God's city-state, the work of God alone. With mutual hospitality, they waited for this city with its holy order of divine justice. In the suspense of this expectation, virgins carrying fire appeared before the gathering of believers and wept in repentance, as if bewailing the dead, and lamented over the life people were leading, estranged from God. As a result of the gospel, proclaimed like this with power characteristic of the future, a life took shape that corresponded to the coming kingdom. The serving church was to learn how to direct the holy life in such a way that the purifying fire of God's future brings the all-embracing harmony of true community.

More than a hundred years after that, Methodius the Martyr sang of the fire-virgins of the expectant church:

From on high, O virgins,
Rang out the voice that quickeneth the dead:
Go out in haste to meet the bridegroom,
Robed in white and bearing lamps,
Before the morning dawns.
    Awake,
Before the Lord doth vanish through the door!
    I consecrate myself to thee,
And bearing lamps that shed forth light,
    I go to meet thee, bridegroom.
O Christ, thou art the prince of life.
All hail, thou light that never settest!
    Hear our cry!
The choir of virgins calleth to thee,
Thou flower of life, thou love itself,
Joy, understanding, wisdom, everlasting word!
    I consecrate myself to thee,
And bearing lamps that shed forth light,
    I go to meet thee, bridegroom.

No longer are we robbed of paradise,
For thou dost give once more by thy decree

The land we lost
Through guile of cunning serpent,
O immortal, unshakable, blessed one!
I consecrate myself to thee,
And bearing lamps that shed forth light,
I go to meet thee, bridegroom.

Characteristic of the readiness for martyrdom in this movement of the Spirit (and of Methodius himself, who was to die a martyr's death in A.D. 311) is the cry of these fire-bearing virgins:

Fleeing the cunning serpent's
Thousandfold flatteries,
I endure the firebrand's flame
And the dread onslaught of wild beasts,
To await thy coming from heaven.

To expect Christ is to be ready for the fire, in the strength of the flaming spirit. Jesus baptizes with the Holy Spirit and with fire. Whoever expects God's kingdom prepares in spirit for the fire-baptism of martyrdom. With the spiritual flame of his fire of judgment and light of love, Jesus brings to earth the fire of the burnt offering, a fire of purification through utmost suffering. As the bitter Christ, he brings the salting fire of extreme need. Making ready for the burnt offering, his fire seasons. Defying persecution and death by fire, the blazing torch of his mission calls for the ultimate sacrifice.

"Everyone, everyone must be salted with fire" (Mark 9:49). "You must not be surprised at the burning fire. It burns for your purification." "The time has come for judgment to begin with the household of God" (1 Pet. 4:17). Faith, like gold, must pass the final test by fire. God tests hearts through need and suffering as fire tests silver. The coming day will disclose what each one has been building (1 Cor. 3:12–13). God's day is revealed in a fire that melts everything. All that the nations have labored over comes into the burning fire. God will pick out the gold and the silver in the smelting flame. His burning is like a goldsmith's fire.

The purifying effect of fire and its power to ward off all animals and nocturnal spirits have been obvious from time immemorial. The fire-beacons at springtime and Easter, like the fires at the midsummer and midwinter solstices, were meant to cleanse the land and the springs of water and set them free from all powers of evil. The fire-baptism of the spirit of Jesus Christ, the cleansing fire that banishes everything unclean and malevolent, brings purification through need and suffering and, above all, through the fire of judgment in church discipline.

In the light of the believing church – the light of the spirit – everything destructive, everything belonging to humankind, is continually sorted out by the fire and rejected. Everything that cannot stand before the purity of the holy flame is thrown out and swept away. The mystery of the church is Christ shining in her. The pure fire of the Holy Spirit is proof of Christ's presence. His clear light tolerates no defilement. The mystery of the church is the purified expectation of God's coming glory and majesty. The light world of the coming kingdom tolerates no darkening of the waiting church. The pure light of God allows no darkness to approach his lampstands.

Believers in Israel already testified: "The Lord is my light." They called to God, "May thy countenance shine upon us!"

They knew about living in the sight of God's shining eyes.
They let themselves be guided by his light and his truth. They
came to the recognition: "In thy light do we see light." The
light knows nothing but light and refuses to let its purity be
impaired. The prophet proclaims: what the light shines upon
shall become light. "Arise! Shine, for thy light has come; the
radiant glory of Jehovah has risen upon thee." Where there is
light, everything shines. Light wishes to be light and remain
light without any darkening.

Yet the believers of the old covenant lacked the secret that
was entrusted to Paul: that radiance alive in the church, the
radiance of glory to come, which in its inner aspect is in fact
the light of the "Christ within you." The innermost becomes
one with the outermost and with the ultimate. The light
burning on the lampstand of the church proclaims the death
of Christ, his second coming, and the future world. It proclaims the burnt offering of the present time as well as the
universal conflagration of the last day.

The prayer of the apostle is that Christ should dwell in
our hearts through faith. Jesus Christ, the resplendent reflection of God's radiant majesty, gives light for God's kingdom.
He is the true light, which enlightens everyone and shines
into their darkness. He brings each one to the crucial decision whether he or she loves darkness more than light and
wants to turn from darkness to light. When this happens, a
sudden and wonderful change takes place in those about to
be born anew. It shows the stark contrast: formerly, in and of
themselves, they had been "darkness"; now, in Christ, they
become "light" (Eph. 5:8). They come to the light of the
world. They see the light. They are saved from the ruling
powers of darkness so that from then on the fire of unity, as

the light of peace, rules in them. Out of this rulership of inner light, a life of light takes shape that includes everything, transforming all previous confusion into clarity. It excludes the works of darkness. It leads to the works of burning light: self-consuming deeds of love sending out rays far and wide.

Even Meister Eckhart recognized the dynamic effect of light when he said, "In this birth, God pours himself into the soul with so much light that in its ground and nature there is an abundance of light. As a result, it bursts out and overflows into all energies and into the physical." Light is clarity and effective action. As the mystery of the "Christ within you" at work in the enlightened heart, the inner light brings clarity about Christ and his work, about a person's inner being, about evil the world over, and about how to conduct life in both attitude and deed in accordance with the source of light.

Light is clarity; it never wishes to bring gloomy uncertainty with it. A witness to light must be clear and definite. Mechthild of Magdeburg often spoke of the "streaming light of the divinity," yet even her words suffer from a certain cloudiness.* She speaks more of the broadened stream than of the generously flowing source. The light of the moon does not prevent us from recognizing very clearly all its hills and mountains and the whole of the surface turned toward us. The moon withdraws from our view only as far as it sinks into darkness. When we study the sun, we can look into its depths in spite of all its radiant brightness. To the eye searching in these depths, the sun reveals its heart whenever it opens up before us in whirling solar storms. Every light radiates from a source, the giver of its energy. True enlighten-

*Mechthild of Magdeburg, 1212–1299.

ment must reach the final goal of grasping the Light Bearer himself. It is the nature of light to reveal itself directly and without intermediary. The more refractions and reflections the light has gone through, the more noticeably is it changed and weakened when we receive it. We must dare to look the shining sphere straight in the face. We must receive it into ourselves as it is.

The mystic's concept of submerging into darkness and unconsciousness is poles apart from the apostolic enlighten-ment given to Paul, who is able to recognize who God is and what his heart is. The inner light of the spirit penetrates to the very depths of the Godhead. It reveals to our spirit what no eye has seen and no ear has heard – what has never en-tered our hearts. Only light sees light. "We cannot grasp even the smallest spark of light unless the burning spirit of God himself enters our soul like a fire." "There would be nothing to catch the sun's brightness if in the depths there were not the same nature as the sun." Only the pure light of divine power gives us sight. "There has to be something present to catch the light of the sun. It is the star in your eyes." Christ, the morning star of our hearts, sees within us the sun of the future. We ourselves do not have the power of vision. The inner light can see deep into eternity only be-cause it is more than reason, more than human ability, more even than the deepest depths of the human conscience. It is in very truth the spirit of the Son of Man in the believer, the spirit far superior to our reasoning, who recognizes the spirit of God.

He alone sees. He is the light in the eye, the seeing pupil of the eye. He proclaimed himself as the light that illumi-nates. The light kindles life in the one who sees. To the inner eye, Jesus Christ shines as the ultimate reality of God's new creation. As God's creative, illuminating clarity – as ultimate decisiveness – he penetrates into the perceptive heart. As the shining tree of life and knowledge, he spreads his roots into the depths and his branches afar. The root is the spirit of joy that leaps up when life is kindled. "When the soul is kindled by the Holy Spirit, it triumphs in the body, and a great fire of new life flares up in the soul."

The origin of this illuminating light is the pure clarity of its source, of its bearer. Recognizing it always depends on the inconceivable contrast between this light and the darkness of human life. The meaning of darkness can be detected only in the light. Darkness is shown up only when it is dispelled by light, and without a dispelling of darkness there is no knowledge of the source of light. When light is accepted, it brings liberation and redemption. Forgiveness is the removal of the darkening powers of night. When the land is flooded with radiant brightness, the landscape of human life is purified from the works and creatures of darkness. Then land and life enter into the community of light. Darkness is banned. Creation, redeemed, shines resplendent in the worship of God's holy mountain, pouring out light because the heart of God's light dwells there. Through the light of this holy mountain, everything that used to live in darkness will be led back into the bright community of God's heart.

We experience the Lord through the light that streams out from him. Whoever sees him in the light, sees him as he is. In the coming world of light, all works, all life, will be transformed by the inner vision into his nature – light. "Then the sun and the stars will pass away; for the heart will shine as the light of God and fill everything. When God's heart triumphs, everything will rejoice." Until this transformation takes place, the believing church of today must be led onward step by step from her present imperfect recognition to the ultimate vision. She must be led more and more deeply into the mystery of God's heart. In Jesus she must learn how to distinguish between the footsteps of God, which show his judgment making the history of nations, and the inmost heart of God.

The early Anabaptists of Reformation Europe distinguished between the ultimate depths of light in God's heart and the mighty consequences of his flaming wrath. Along with their leader Peter Rideman, a Silesian shoemaker, they gave clear testimony in this regard, particularly in their so-called "articles" and confessions of faith. There they maintained that whereas the rod of his wrath must punish profligate nations still today, God's wrath has long come to an end in Christ. In Christ has begun the quite other kingdom of blessings, the quite other rule of love and kindness. "Wherever blessing comes, or has already come, wrath comes to an end."*

Whoever is unaware of this difference will not be able to come to an understanding of God's light. In Christ alone is the whole blessing of God's heart revealed. Therefore what is still ordained under the curse of wrath, under the mercilessness of fierce judgment, has no place whatsoever in Christ. And vice versa: the child of blessing and love can never be the servant of wrath and vengeance. What the Father has ordained in Christ will remain in Christ and will never be changed. It is love, peace, unity, and community. What God has appointed outside his Christ, however, is death, wrath,

*See Peter Rideman, *Rechenschaft*, (1541).

mercilessness, curse, and vengeance – all this cannot continue, as the prophet Hosea declared so sternly about the
power of governmental authority: "I have given you a king
in my anger, and I have taken him away again in my wrath."

C hrist stands in opposition to every worldly ruler. His
kingdom is not of this world. Therefore he said: "The
princes and powers of this world lord it over the people, but
you should not." A Christian, therefore, is not a ruler, and a
ruler is not a Christian. A ruler must exercise judgment with
the sword. In the church of Christ there is an end of war and
violence, lawsuits and legal action. Christ does not repay evil
with evil. His followers show his nature in all their doings.
They act as he did: they do not resist evil, and they give their
back to the smiters and their cheek to those that pluck off
the hair. Their task is to reveal the kingdom of love. Legal
authorities are appointed to shed blood in judgment; the
church of Christ, however, has the task of preserving life and
soul. The law courts of the state must bring evil to account;
the church of Jesus Christ must repay evil with good. The
authorities that sit in judgment must hate and persecute the
enemies of their order; the church of Christ must love them.

With the instrument of governmental authority, God's
wrath punishes the wicked. Through the authorities, he
compels nations that are estranged from him to protect
themselves from the worst harm so that the whole land does
not become guilty of bloodshed, the whole earth does not
have to be destroyed. Christ gives his church a completely
different task. She must confront the forcible execution of
justice in the world state with the peace of unity and the joy
of love, with brotherly justice. She builds up and maintains

her unity with no other tools than those of love and the spirit. In the faith of the church, death and the law come to an end. The freedom of the kingdom of God begins in the church.

Those who are grafted into Christ demonstrate the mind and the spirit of Christ as unchangeable love. They do what is good and do not need to fear the forcible execution of punishment over evil, nor do they need to exercise it. Punishment, which belongs to power and judgment, is quite alien to Christ and his church, like all the evil that calls for this punishment. In Christ, the inmost heart of God's love frees itself from the historically necessary wrath and world judgment, in which he has to assert the holiness of his will through the force of the law.

A hundred years after this had been put into words by Peter Rideman, Jakob Böhme tried to grasp the depths of this far-reaching recognition. He saw it as the difference between God's fire of wrath and his heart of light: God is love and wrath, light and fire, yet he calls himself God according to the light of his love alone, not according to his wrath. Whatever does not belong to his love belongs to his wrath. Yet God is not called God according to his whole nature but according to the light; he dwells in himself with light alone.

Those who live among the thorns of God's wrath live outward lives. The love of God, as light, dwells in itself. The darkness does not comprehend it, nor does it know anything about it. The eternal rulership of God according to love and wrath, light and fire, is to be revealed in the lives that stand in this conflict. In the darkness, God is a God of wrath and a devouring fire: darkness calls for fire. If it were possible for darkness to be lit from the light directly, the light would have no root; if it were not possible to produce fire, there would be no light either. For this reason, the kingdom of fury has to be; wrath is the cause of the fire world as judgment over darkness. It lives in darkness. It is not called God but the wrath of God.

The devil kindled the wrath of God. He wanted to have his own will; he wanted to be his own god in order to rule as he wished in and over everyone with the mighty power of fire. The nature of his fire is choleric; it produces daring boldness, furious wrath, and mounting pride; it always wants to rule, which is typical of power. Severity, harshness, fear, torment, and unpeace are part of it. This fire-will brings fear. Without this fear, fire would not exist. It was in God's wrath that the devil forfeited love. In the fire-will, the devil and God meet face to face. The powers of wrath, of judgment, and of the sword are pagan. They remain far from the heart of God. They can never be Christian. And yet they have been appointed by God, for God's holy majesty would not exist if his wrath did not exist. It salts and seasons the darkness so that it is transformed into fire.

As war and violence, this wrath burning between God and the devil consumes all that is godless. Every soldier is a rod of God's wrath. God's judgment in its fury punishes through him. The soldier belongs to the order of fury through which God's wrath sets up and tears down countries and kingdoms. Tinder calls for fire. God's wrath has always existed, just as fire lies hidden in wood. As soon as the wood dried out – as soon as the people turned from God – the burning had to begin.

Yet God wanted a supreme light of love to be born out of the consuming blaze of murderous fire. That other majesty of God – the utter sublimity of his heart – was to be revealed in this light. The somber fire of wrath is not God but a hellish fire. Yet if there were no fire, no light would be given. God's fire of wrath becomes the root of his compassionate love, that is, of the light in his heart. In the critical times of his judgment, his love shall become manifest. In the fullness of God's time, the last judgment will become the wedding feast of his kingdom of love. The fire is overpowered by the light. Out of the burning torment, a sublime kingdom of joy shall arise. As soon as a burning fire blazes up, light shines out. The light takes on all the vital characteristics of fire: it awakens life, it draws people together so that they find each other, and it leads to the God-given community of the circle, the encampment, and the consecrated house.

In short, it is a question of deciding between love in light and blazing wrath in darkness. In light, God is a merciful and loving God; only in the strength of light is he called God. The light world, which is God himself, has no craving for destruction. There is no spark in God's heart that could desire evil, even as punishment! In God a great joy of love surges out of the wellspring of his heart. Then the fight arises. God's heart wants us because we are meant to be God's image and likeness; the kingdom of wrath wants us too because we now belong to the very nature of darkness.

Souls once left the paradise of love for the fiery life of wrath. So these souls died to God's light, perishing in selfhood, in possessions. They died to God and lived in utter fear of his stern wrath. Yet the ray of light came once more to the soul and said:

> Acquire the love of God in your heart so that out of the heart of God you will be born again in the center of your life. The light of his heart shall send light into your life! You shall become one with him! You had willfully broken away from my love and fallen into the fiery clutches of wrath. Now I will shed my rays of love with bright light into your fear-ridden life of fire. As love, I will transform the fire of your fear into the open flame of my joy. As the essence of light, I will impart my rays of love into your life and work, renewing them with light.

So from the heart of God the life of light, full of joy, shines with power into all powers and sets them on fire for the work of love. The will is gathered to give birth to light. Lit by God's light, the inner vision breaks swiftly through, keen as a flash of lightning; it soars up from the heart and catches fire in the will to love; it is no longer furious lightning but a power of great joy.

Christ is this joy. What has arisen in the enlightened heart is the joyous light of the Son of God as the fire of love. From now on, the life that gives outward expression to such a heart should reveal the inmost spirit of the light world in all it does; the essence of this light is the kingdom of God. From the most inward and tender love of Christ arises the kingdom of joy.

True faith in the kingdom of God is the power, spirit, and life of a shining light, welling up from the heart of God. It is the supreme power of God, real and living, the flaming love that shines out of his heart. The work is accomplished by this love. The essential part of faith, burning in the believing Christian as strength that also loves, is Christ himself, who is the life and light of the renewed soul. The love of the church is faith in the heart of God, who pours his sea of light into all lands.

Christ is the joyful urge to love, coming from a flood of light that gains dominion over wrath's urge for fire. After the soul forfeited light, God spoke the name "Jesus." In him, God's wrath is extinguished. Christ is the heart of God, triumphing over all the consequences of God's wrath and hastening to all lands met by it. Christ sends his light into all the world; it rises over all nations, shining on them without partiality. Even to the most godless, gripped in consuming fire by the violent wrath of God, the gates of birth into light stand open.

Through the death of Christ, Christians die to wrath and its fierce decrees: they die with Christ to all the elements of wrath. In Christ's spirit, in the love of God's heart, those who live in that other justice of loving forbearance have been newborn. Where once wrath burned in darkness, love is burning now, radiating from the shining heart of God. The fire of wrath and the light of love are as alien as day and night. Neither understands the other; neither sees the other.

Yet from the very beginning, every human being has both within. It is just as if the right hand wants to enter into the majesty of light, and the left hand wants to stay in its original state – fire. Whichever of these two attributes is being awakened burns in people: the soul can burn with the light of love or with the fire of wrath. If it surrenders to wrath, wrath spreads like a cancer and subjects everything to the laws it makes, an avenging fury. But if it surrenders to the heart in God, it learns that the spirit of Jesus Christ dwelling there knows no wrath, wages no war, and administers no violent punishment – he only loves and gives.

The wisdom of God's heart has no desire for death or war. The children of God's heart may not kill or go to war. They need no murderous weapons. No one who is a Christian can go to war. Whoever does, does it as a heathen within the order of wrath, never as a Christian within the order of love. Countries and cities are laid waste in war only where the relentless cycle of guilt and vengeance, of offense and retaliation, strangles and murders and kills. In Christ, the vicious circle of cause and effect is abolished. Mars grows pale and vanishes as soon as the sun rises. Lightning storms retreat before a sunlit sky. The heart of God disperses the clouds of his wrath: even in the midst of judgment, his heart triumphs over his wrath. Led by this heart, the church of Jesus Christ passes through history's fires of wrath without being in contact with them. She is dead to the world of wrath's elements; they can do nothing to harm her; she stands quite apart from them. Because they are all rooted in darkness, the church of light keeps her back turned on all their characteristics.

The church has died to greed for property (the ultimate root of all evil) and the pride and respect that go with it. She has left behind her all fear and insincerity, unfaithfulness and covetousness, those ugly, monstrous offsprings of the fires of hell. She abominates the heart and will of mammon who rules the world, the great Antigod who uses war and strife to build up societies and classes, kingdoms and countries, in order to shatter them again. The church discerns the spirits. She knows what she is waiting for, what she loves, and what she believes in. She knows what she has left behind and can never take up again. The church stands in the dawn of the coming day. Therefore it cannot take part in the works of nocturnal darkness that rule the world, nor can it take part in the blazing wrath of fiery judgment on the world of today. It is in Christ that it lives, and it dwells in God's heart. It does the work of love; it believes in and waits for the reign of light. Its members are weak, but the spirit that dwells in it is the shining fire of God's heart. True, the plant cannot say, "I am the sun" because the sun is at work in it. And quite certainly, the believing member of the church cannot say "I am Christ," because Christ dwells within and is at work there. But the believing church shall be transformed into the image of his radiant beauty insofar as it looks with unveiled face upon his being. The vision given to faith, like the transformation to come, is an enlightenment that springs from the heart of God. Christ, the future lord of the eternal light world, reveals himself in his wonderful light as the spirit of his church.

Christ dwells at one and the same time in the shining throne of God's heart and in the spirit-filled body of his church. God himself, who let light shine out of darkness in his son, has "caused a bright light to shine in our hearts to give the light of the knowledge of God's glory as we see it in the face of Jesus Christ" (2 Cor. 4:6). In the quickening spirit of his church, we can see his bright radiance face to face. The image of his love is bound to grow dim where dogmas, however good, are merely learned by heart; where the Bible is read only literally; and where all obedience remains outward obedience only. As the inner eye of the community of believers becomes brighter and livelier, it becomes more and more open to enlightenment in the uniting spirit of Jesus Christ and increasingly able to grasp the exuberant greatness of his

radiant power. For the most faithful in Ephesus, Paul prays
for the enlightened eyes of understanding. Only those who
have Jesus himself in their hearts as an illuminating light can
gain strength and clarity from God, who reveals the infinite
life and power of light in the church of Jesus Christ.

The ground of inner enlightenment is where the Lord of
light himself is revealed to us. It is inextricably bound
up with growing clarity about the true way, which leads in
the full light of truth to God's final objective. "Awake, O
sleeper, and arise from the dead, and Christ shall give you
light" (Eph. 5:14). This rousing call of the spirit goes with an
urgent challenge to lead the life given only to children of
light. It is a matter of the new life and growth of the church,
which must itself be described "as a light" for it lives in unity
with Christ: "You are the light of the world, for the Christ of
the final kingdom is your lord." He is the light of the whole
world here and now in his church.

This light tolerates no community with the barren works
of darkness. Both in the innermost recesses of the heart and
in the outer aspects of life, it exposes everything that is secret
or shameful or that has a bad effect. "Everything will be visible
when it is censured by light." The action of light discloses
and transforms everything. "For everything that becomes
visible is light." Light is clarity. Therefore what believers of
old experienced is renewed in the light of Jesus Christ:
"Thou hast set our iniquities before thee, our secret sins in
the light of thy countenance." Light unlocks the doors of
night. It encourages honest open-mindedness, the only state
in which we can become convicted of sin. God brings about
an open-heartedness that leads to absolute decisiveness: in

order to be renewed in the light of Jesus Christ for the life of his church, we have to give room to light, do away with all that is dark as something to be hated, and recognize and leave behind the depressing feelings of guilt that shackle us.

Light does not work like dynamite, yet it is stronger. The weapons of light fight without any murderous force against the works of darkness. Love does no evil to its neighbor. And nevertheless at the eleventh hour before the coming day, it puts an end to the waxing powers of night and their violent works. Anyone who wants to put a dark cover over hostile actions can pile up as many layers of dark, hateful thoughts and deeds as possible: we know that there are rays that in all quietness penetrate even the thickest walls of the strongest fortresses. When the working of the spirit's light is perfect, it has latent in it a power to remove and overcome, stronger than all the forces of destruction.

One of the most remarkable discoveries is that of the impetus of light. Every perpendicular ray of light exercises a pressure that is quiet, gentle, and firm, in keeping with the nature of light. This is how astronomers explain why the tail of a comet turns away from the sun. When the dark and distant comet nears the sun, clouds begin to form out of its head, through the action of solar heat. The sun's radiation pressure blows these vapors away from the head, producing the long tail. The light of the sun repels the expanding vapor. It destroys nothing. But when another body approaches, the light quietly and almost imperceptibly drives anything it cannot tolerate in its vicinity out of the center of that body. Unless we turn to the sun of the universe, we remain in the dark. "If the light that is in you is darkness, how great is the darkness then?" Unless we hasten with open eyes toward the divine light, we remain blind. Just as those who are blind from birth can never find a substitute for their eyesight through their intellect, so we can never be led to inner light through our powers of reasoning. Only when the power of the sun opens our inner eye, can we see the light that shines down upon us from the distant presence of God.

Faith is a light from God that surpasses all human understanding. The light of faith is God himself drawing near and intervening. Those in the sun have no lack of light. Everything becomes clear and bright as soon as the inner eye is enlightened and sound, focused on the Ruler of the central fire. It is given to the eye of faith to see and understand the perfect light. If the eye were not in its nature like the sun, it could never see the sun. "Therefore see to it that the light that is in you is not darkened. When your body has no single particle of darkness left in it, it will be completely light, as if you were illuminated by a bright flash of lightning."

God's enlightenment draws near with elemental force. Unforgettable are those moments in which a bright flash of lightning lays bare the deep-black mantle of night. It exposes every hiding place, bringing to light all the vermin of darkness – those predators of the night that would flee from every ray of light. "He who does evil hates the light. He does not want to come to the light lest his works be punished." Yet greater than lightning at night is the sight of the rising sun, especially where the contrast between night and day is not veiled by our northern twilight. Life awakens with the light. Birds of daylight sing, flowers of the light open, and the whole land is radiant with the glory of the morning. This is what happens when the morning star heralds the sunrise of life. Whoever longs for light is open to it. Whoever loves light hastens toward it. "Those who live by the truth come to the light so that their works may be clearly seen, for they have been done in God."

The light is the exposer, the liberator, the leader. The inner light begins to lead the whole of life where a life in God begins, where the inner and outer life go to meet Christ's shining countenance, where his power dispels darkness. The believing church finds the way that leads to the kingdom of light. It lies clearly in front of her. "If a man walks in the daytime, he does not stumble, for he sees the light that lights the world. If a man walks at night, however, he stumbles because he has no light." The way has to be well lit if we are to find it. The light wishes to bring our entire way of life into one single, very clearly defined direction. It wishes to lead our whole life on the one way that is the only way into the kingdom of God.

Words of eternal truth testify to this influence on the direction our life and work takes: we must work while it is day. No one can work in dark night. Therefore Jesus says:

> As long as I am in the world, I am the daylight: I am the light of the world. He who follows me will not walk in darkness; he will have the light of life. Walk while you have the light; the darkness shall not overtake you! He who walks in darkness does not know where he is going. Trust in the light while you have it. You shall be children of light (John 12:35–36).

Even the people of the old covenant knew that "the path of the righteous is like the glorious light of morning that grows brighter and brighter until it is broad daylight. The way of the lawless is like darkness; they do not know what makes them stumble and fall." To be divinely led by this guiding light is to be protected from the deceptive bypaths and will-o'-the-wisps of night. From his wellspring of light, God has given clear vision to steer the right course. With this vision the way cannot be missed. For those nights when the sky is overcast, a bright lantern is put into the traveler's hand: the word of God, which lights the dark way ahead until the day dawns and the morning star rises.

Jesus reveals himself as the guiding light to the people of the new covenant. He is the fulfillment of the words of old: "The commandments of the Lord shine clear and give light to the eyes." "Thy word is a lamp to my feet and a light on my path." Guidance through the inner light of the spirit of Jesus Christ is accomplished through the lamp of the word. Nevertheless his truth bears a new criterion, decisive for this present age, one that proves the purity and unity of the guiding light: the unanimity of the church throughout all ages. In this church, God lets his thoughts of light be known without deflection. The church is the city of light: its foundation is community through the mystery shining in her.

In Reformation times, the body that was once the church of old set up the lamp of her unifying light again in the midst of severe persecution. Peter Rideman writes:

> The church of Christ is the foundation and bedrock of truth. It is a lantern, a light-star, and a lamp of righteousness. In it, the light of grace is brought to the whole world and held aloft so that the world's darkness, unbelief, and blindness may be made light and clear through it; also so that people may learn to see and know the way of life. For this reason, the church of Christ is first of all illuminated through and through by Christ, as a lantern is completely illuminated by the light that shines

through it; so that, secondly, the light may shine through her to others.

Just as Christ's lantern has become bright, clear, and illuminated with the light of divine knowledge, this brightness and radiance reaches out into the distance to shine for others still walking in darkness, as Christ himself has commanded: "You must shed light among your fellows, so that when they see the good you do, they may give praise to your Father in heaven." Yet this can never happen except through the power of the spirit of Christ working in us. Natural light, in accordance with its nature, sends out rays to give light; in the same way, divine light sends out divine rays wherever this light is kindled, and its nature is true and divine righteousness, holiness, and truth. It shines out from the light-star or lamp – that is, from the church of Christ – to give light to all more clearly and brightly than the sun.*

This task was given to the apostle Paul, as he himself testified: to bring light to all people regarding the mystery of the church, which is inseparably bound up with the mystery of the coming Christ. The inner light of Jesus Christ reveals the oneness between his nature and the unity of the church with its future destiny. Enlightenment through the Holy Spirit has the unmistakable characteristic of leading to complete unanimity, to undisturbed harmony and agreement between all the members of the church of light.

The light of God's heart reveals the mystery of the church: it is the radiant body of Jesus Christ. This body cannot be dark – its eye is clear and bright. Focused on the center of its field of vision, its eye receives the light. Christ himself in all his radiance, and nothing else, dwells in this body. He is the faith of the church. His future is what she awaits. She is filled

*Peter Rideman, *Rechenschaft*, (1541).

here and now with the future rays of his majesty. The hope of her life is to extol his glory.

Those who confess Christ, like those who receive their mission, can experience rebirth only through the living church of love and light. The people of light are gathered by the torch of the Master in order that he may establish his sun-kingdom with them. Only the lamps of the church can show the light of the future to earth's darkness. The spirit of Jesus Christ, as the light that from now on determines everything, rests on these seven lamps. From these lamps goes out the transforming power of God's approaching future.

The gift of inwardness is a two-edged sword. Some people are serious about wanting to fathom not only God and his truth, but just as much Satan and his abyss: we can see this from literature. Which do you want – God or the devil? A decision has to be made. God is good, and he is spirit. The realm of the evil spirit is the demonic. Do you want to submerge yourself into both at the same time? You can recognize a spiritual being only by becoming one with it: there is no other way of comprehending spirit than by uniting with its essence, its innermost nature. Here you are, a living person: which spirit do you want to unite with? After long years of indecision on this question, Augustine made up his mind: "God and my soul are what I want to understand. Nothing else? No, nothing else!"

The human soul is dominated by flesh and blood. With one hand it grasps at life, with the other it grasps at death. As Friedrich Nietzsche said, "Woe to those who have no ground under their feet! Woe to those who have no support! This is the danger I slip into: my vision soars up to the heights while my hand wants to keep hold of the depths and find support there." We have started out on a dangerous journey because the life-giving spirit of the heights and the life-hating spirits of the abyss are fighting a hard battle over us. On this journey, human nature in its own strength is incapable of lifting itself above the level of flesh and blood. Our soul may turn its gaze inward as much as it likes; our head may be turned by great visions, plans, or ideals, but without the spirit of God we will remain on the all-too-human lowlands of limited mortal sight.

Because our spirit is so closely bound up with our psycho-physical makeup, it comes under the same judgment as our body: "What is born of the flesh is flesh." Flesh is bound to decay. The horrors of our time have shown what harvest is reaped when the seed of life is cast upon the soil of unchanged human nature. Only the harvest blown upon by the wind of the life-giving spirit will be good. Without the Holy Spirit, human nature remains dull and feeble. Without the wind of his spirit, the tilled field of human nature remains barren. Cut off from the fountainhead and drying up in its independence, the life of human nature is doomed to destruction. Our nature is debased – we ought to know how degenerate and desecrated it is.

Our mortal nature longs for a superior power to free enslaved humankind from all powers hostile to life. Only the spirit of perfect life has this power to overcome death. Without this divine spirit who overcame all deadening and evil spirits, we are lost. God and his spirit alone are life. The spirit of the Son redeems from bondage and fear of death; only he can give full and abiding life. Those of us who are unable to discriminate between him and the voice of the blood condemn ourselves to remain sensual; enslaved beings, we remain in bondage to our corrupting nature and its murderous powers.

Those who lay decisive value on the sensual impulses of their blood are described by Paul as carnal, even if they are able to probe the depths of inwardness or rise to the loftiest ideals of nation or humanity. The soul by itself, like the blood, is always limited to the mortal life of the individual and the nation, conditioned by the body and subject to demons. And yet the soul knows that deep down it has a disposition created for higher and purer spheres. The conscience continually bears witness:

> A human being! Yes, but only he is worthy of the name
> Who lifts his spirits high above the human plane.

Without Jesus Christ, we can never be more than living souls. This enfeebled life leads of its own accord toward death. Nations who let themselves be led by nothing but their racial community fall under the law of hate, which paves the way for death and for belonging to the kingdom of death. From humankind in general – as such – no help is to be expected. Only the one Son of Man is a life-giving spirit. His life is everlasting and overcomes all death. His strength is the boundless power of unchangeable love; it releases an inextinguishable vitality such as the immortal Spirit alone can give. It leads mortals to eternal life. The spirit of Jesus Christ is stronger than all other spirits; he alone unites the believing heart with the living center of all creative life.

In this center, the Spirit creates the sublime unity of all freed spirits, a unity that can be achieved neither by nations nor by humankind. The Holy Spirit is this unity in Christ – he brings about a united life in God. He alone guarantees one people and one kingdom – that is, God's people and God's kingdom – as an eternal inheritance. Only the spirit of the great Liberator can give that eternal reality to our spirit in which the children of all peoples are children of the one God. God's people come into being in the Holy Spirit. Only in him does true humankind come into existence. In the power of this life-giving Spirit, God's firstborn was shown to be his son. As the risen Christ, he grants his people the spirit of his sonship. In him alone is the power of a renewed and unified life. The king of the kingdom is himself the life of God's people, the life in the kingdom of God. Only he whose life was without any inconsistency or hint of darkness brings the harmony of the kingdom of God, without which all people and all nations remain in the power of death and destruction, the power of the devil.

Christ alone is God's crowned one. Only he was so completely inundated and penetrated by the Spirit that no spark of his life was separated from the living flame of love. This fiery life of the spirit of Jesus Christ is the love in the coming kingdom: his final kingdom is love as justice. For this reason the life of Jesus, in holy fire, belonged to the poor and wretched. Jesus is the only one to whom the prophetic word of Isaiah applies completely, and with it Jesus proclaimed his messianic mission: "The spirit of the Lord is upon me. He has anointed me king of the kingdom; he has sent me to bring the poor a decisive message"(Isa. 61:1).

This anointing of Jesus is his coronation as ruler of the kingdom, the imparting of the Spirit as the sovereign power of love, which alone brings true freedom. His gospel is the joyful tidings of the coming one, who leads to freedom all the oppressed and enslaved – freedom for God's kingdom! In Jesus, the king anointed by the Holy Spirit, the kingdom of God has come to forsaken people in a world growing cold. As perfect love it has come to drained and empty hearts, in which the flame of love was trampled to the ground by cold and sinister powers. The spirit of hate had extinguished human love. In Jesus, the spirit of divine love overcomes the demonic spirit of servitude. Jesus Christ is the one, the only one, who has driven out the murderous spirit of this world and all his subordinate spirits through the spirit of perfect love. Where the ruler of God's kingdom intervenes, their rule comes to an end. Those held captive by emotions and their own blood, however, perceive nothing of this decisive action of the victorious spirit. Only the Holy Spirit himself recognizes the Holy Spirit. Without the spirit of God, no one can acknowledge the liberating rule of Jesus Christ or see how he has already taken it up for all time. Outside the Holy Spirit, the rule of Jesus Christ and the power of love in it are not given recognition. Only the Spirit reveals the divine king and the freedom under his rulership; only in the church of the Spirit is his kingdom at work on earth today.

Only through the Holy Spirit, only in the spirit of the church, can Christ be called upon as lord and king. In their uniting with the church, all those who want truly to acknowledge Christ as their lord must have received the spirit of the church, must be immersed in the strength and reality of the spirit that creates the church. They must prove themselves free children of the one pure Spirit in their common action. Only in the unity of the Spirit can they call upon the holy name in communal prayer.

The Holy Spirit establishes his work as God's work. Only believers can grasp this. They should accept and act upon it as God at work; they should bear it serenely as God's doing. In the strength of another world working in them, they acknowledge Christ as their only lord. In this spirit, the voice from the eternal throne answers them, "You call me Master and Lord; and you say so rightly, for so I am." This recognition can come to those estranged from God only when they accept the Holy Spirit – God's spirit. The church covenant of this king and his kingdom can be established, strengthened, or sealed in no other way than through the Holy Spirit, in a life lived in God. From God, through Christ as the ruling Lord of God's kingdom, he comes to a believing church. Only in this way will enslaved humankind become free once and for all from any self-glorification. There is freedom where the spirit of the King is. His covenant separates the sons of freedom from servile slaves. This difference is there for all eternity. Those who are prompted by God's spirit have become God's free children; those who are not do not belong to God.

There are no slaves in God's church; all those who live there are children of equal birth. The covenant of sonship is established. All the unchildlikeness of human greatness or degrading servitude is banned from this covenant. All its members are promised an amazing perception, granted only to trusting children by virtue of the childlike spirit. It remains closed to those who are great and wise in their own estimation or enslaved by servile fear. God's spirit bears witness to and does what God has in mind for everything free and childlike. When this covenant is made, the superficiality and darkness of our own nature has to disappear, whether domineering or servile. In the freedom of Jesus Christ their authority has been broken forever.

The light shows the way to childlike freedom in the power of its spirit. The slaves freed by Christ now become his free property. Nothing that is or might become theirs can belong to them or to any other, only to him. In life and in death they belong to their master. As freed people who would have remained in ignoble servitude without his intervention, they take their place with a freed will in his household. They belong forever to the spirit of his house, with a right to his gifts as free children. They honor their liberator as the only sovereign of the only kingdom they may serve. The Holy Spirit is the pledge of a future inheritance, given by their royal liberator. With the covenant of the spirit in their hands, they have a passport to the people's community of God's kingdom. The spirit of the church is a free pass and certificate of citizenship for the kingdom of God. When they show his seal, the gates of the final kingdom are opened.

All members of the church seek the Spirit with their whole life. They live for the king of God's kingdom. They strive for his freeing and uniting justice and righteousness. In the spirit of Jesus Christ, they represent the perfect justice of the future. The Holy Spirit seals their faith in the king he has crowned. This king has come in advance of his kingdom; in him they have accepted its coming. As strength arising from absolute freedom and unity, his justice and righteousness are the ultimate reality of their lives. In the dynamic presence of the spirit, they taste the powers of a future world, of a different being ruling their lives here on earth.

The seal of the Holy Spirit is the presence of God, his future, as it can be experienced in the church of Christ. The spirit of Christ is certainty of God. The power stemming from faith in the future makes the church firm and steadfast in all the storms of the present day. In this spirit she is certain that in his own good time God will redeem the firm promise he gave in Christ. Faith is as certain of this promise as if it is already fulfilled. In the reality of the spirit, it is.

Through the imparting of the Holy Spirit this faith is sealed, as if in the safest of documents, in each who lets himself be informed of the truth through God's word and believes in the kingdom of God. The spirit of Jesus Christ is the only certainty of the kingdom of God: this is the meaning of the saying of Jesus that no one can enter the kingdom without being born anew from above through the Holy Spirit.

It is the Spirit who makes alive; through him, we are engrafted into the divine nature. That applies to all who belong to God's covenant and are to inherit his kingdom. God's word becomes true through them. All the promises of the living God find their yes and amen in him. The Holy Spirit accomplishes all that God wills in those who receive him with joy and delight. From him comes the joy that seeks out and loves all that is God's word, and God's work. The believing church finds God at work in her in power and in truth, purifying hearts and whole lives for his will. The Spirit implants what is true and good, what is just and holy. Under his protection it shall take root, grow, and bear fruit. For this reason, everything in our nature that prevents his plantation from growing must be suppressed and killed like weeds, rooted out by the Spirit. He not only abolishes evildoing; he takes away any desire for it.

Under the influence of the Holy Spirit, the old person dies, and the new starts to live in its place. The law of the spirit, the law of life, annuls the law of sin and death. Only through baptism by the spirit can this be done. The spirit himself does these works; everything is inspired by him, prompted by him, and urged on to new life by him. A new creation has arisen – a new plantation, a new birth!

This re-creation and purification, this rebirth and renewal, take place as baptism in the stream of the Spirit, poured out in Jesus Christ over the church. The covenant of the Holy Spirit is a promise of the freedom of sonship. By virtue of this birth and impelled by the spirit of God, we live in the covenant of sonship. Only the spirit creates children of God. His impelling power is proof of sonship and its freedom.

Flesh and blood have nothing in common with birth through the spirit. The Holy Spirit has an abhorrence of all unfaithful idolatry and false appearances. He withdraws in the face of the demonic lack of discernment in all religious mishmash. He disappears where our own greatness takes over, where sin gains authority in opposition to God. With this, every possibility of sonship, of being a Christian, is blotted out. Whoever lacks the spirit of Christ does not belong to him. The nature of humankind and God's nature are opposed to each other. Where flesh and blood are allowed to dominate, God must keep his spirit apart and refuse to recognize any sonship.

God's pure breath reveals the genuineness of all God's children. He never allows children to be passed off onto him. He acknowledges no bastards. Only the lordship of the Spirit reveals the image of God. It alone is genuine. Everything else is deception. The nature and character of God is revealed in his children by the purity of their spirit. Only God's spirit has this purity. Where the truthful and genuine nature of a child of God is found, it governs the whole of life and gives it shape according to the image of God. Genuine truth is God himself; his sons and daughters bear his image and display it as their light as long as they allow themselves to be ruled and led in all things by his spirit. They are his heirs in the spirit alone – God never denies his own nature. The divine nature becomes truly and effectively rooted in those born a second time, replacing the old carnal nature of their soul and blood. As a result, with this divine spirit, the completely different and entirely new life of the kingdom of God is given them. The Holy Spirit is the first witness to the last kingdom. It is he who establishes living community with God and causes it to begin in truth and deed. It is he who brings the divine nature of the kingdom of God into the believing church. It is this spirit who assures the church of Jesus Christ that her members are God's heirs. Like a royal anointing in the final kingdom, the pouring-out of the Holy Spirit belongs to baptism in the name of the coming king.

The so-called baptism of those who have not perceived anything of this spirit can have no validity for Christ even if it pointed toward him, as baptism by John the Baptist did. On the other hand, Peter held baptism in the name of Jesus Christ in readiness for all those prepared for a change of spirit in their hearts and lives, making them ready for the kingdom of God. He promised they would receive the gift of the Holy Spirit at baptism. What had happened? The king crowned with the Spirit had been killed and had risen from his grave. After these earth-shaking events, the reality of the outpouring of God's spirit heralded the breaking-in of God's kingdom as promised by the prophets. This was the content of the Pentecostal address: the one who has arisen and been glorified has received the Holy Spirit from the Father. Now he has poured it out: you can see it! You can hear it! The Jesus you have executed is the Messiah of God's kingdom. Now at last he pours the spirit of his kingdom over all flesh. The spirit is there; the kingdom breaks in!

The world-shaking question of the believers at Pentecost – what they should do in the face of this overwhelming fact – led to Christ and his kingdom. The forgiveness of sins that prepares the way for the kingdom culminates in a longing for the Holy Spirit, that through him it would be possible to lead a life worthy of God's kingdom. Longing for Jesus Christ and the kingdom of God created the readiness for the Holy Spirit. Jesus Christ can never be separated from his spirit. The early Christian gospel of the forgiveness of sins cannot be separated from an apostolic life in the Holy Spirit. The church of Jesus Christ cannot be severed from the kingdom of God.

The king of God's kingdom, as the spirit of holy unity, is the sap of life that brings unity to the living organism called the church. From Christ as its root, the Holy Spirit rises into its branches and vines and makes of the believing church a single, undivided plant in God's kingdom, an integrated growth that is one with the crowned king. Christ is God's vine; the believers are his branches. The spirit, as the sap, rises from the roots and fills the branches; he makes them fruitful and keeps them alive for the kingdom of God.

At the first Pentecost, from the one who had died and risen again, the life of the spirit broke in as the coming of the kingdom. The open tomb proves that God rules. He does this through the spirit of the risen one. Jakob Böhme bears witness to it in his own imagery:

As a candle is consumed by fire and, out of that very dying, light and strength go forth as powerful life, so should and must the eternal, divine sun rise out of Christ's dying, out of his death. When Christ arises, when the sun comes up, night is swallowed up by day and there is no night anymore. So it is with the forgiveness of sins.

Out of the wellspring of Jesus Christ, out of the power of his resurrection, the forgiving spirit of the crucified one flooded over the people at Pentecost. The word broke forth. All divine spirits and powers were set on fire:

As the breath determines the word and gives it shape and sound, so the breath, wind, and spirit of God makes the word become active and alive in us and leads us into all truth; the power of God does, works, and accomplishes everything, strengthens everything, and welds everything together. It assures us through God's works that we are children of God.

What Peter Rideman attested about the unity of the Father and the Son in the Holy Spirit became a fact at Pentecost:

Just as in speaking we exhale and let our breath out with words so that a living breath of wind blows from both the speaker and the spoken word and a voice comes out and makes a sound, so the Holy Spirit comes from the Father and the Son or from the truth and the word. But just as the Son, or word, proceeds from the Father and yet remains in him, so the Holy Spirit proceeds from them both and yet remains in both for all eternity.

And as fire, heat, and light do not separate or part from each other (for where one is, there are all three, and where one is lacking, all are lacking), so it is with the Father, the Son and the Holy Spirit too: where one of them is, there they are all three; but if we lack one of them, we lack them all; for just as little as heat and light can be taken away from fire and yet leave it a fire, just so little and even less can the Son and the Holy Spirit be taken away from the Father.

So the great movement toward brotherhood throughout all centuries, a continually renewed Pentecost, has witnessed vigorously to unity in God. God is unity. Only those who remain in unity remain in God and God in them. Böhme goes on:

> The eternal Father is revealed in fire in its entirety; the Son in the light of fire; and the Holy Spirit in the power of life and movement in the light of the kingdom of joy, as the power streaming forth from the flame of love. Imagine then that the Father is the fire of the celestial bodies; that the Son is his heart as the sun, which bathes them all in blissful light; and that the Holy Spirit is the breath of life, without which there could be no sun and no stars.

Perfect unity in God is the spiritual reality of his love within himself. It can be comprehended only in the very center of his heart. Only by the central fire of his love can God in his unity be known. He cannot be recognized by the nature of the first creation, nor by its wrathful fire of judgment, nor by its laws (necessary in the coercive rule of governments). The central light of God's heart has been revealed in Jesus. The Son, as an independent person, yet in the Father, is the inmost depths of the Father's heart. Jesus Christ is the loving center of the heart of God. From there proceed the all-compelling powers of the Holy Spirit.

In the spirit of Jesus Christ, the Father's heart as the joy of perfect love comes down to a love-impoverished earth shaking in the judgment of God's wrath. In Christ, God's heart comes as spirit, the Holy Spirit, to those who had become estranged from God's love. In this spirit the church is created, whose unity is God's unity. The king of the kingdom of God is the spirit of the church. His church knows no other commission than peace and unity. She is charged with the commission of love and justice, the heart of God's kingdom. At work in her is the eternal power of love in its radiant glory, coming from Christ.

He who has gone out from the heart of God has been exalted to become the ruler of God's kingdom. At the same time, he is the spirit of the church. Here he brings about the transformation of believers into light. Now they have the task of representing the coming kingdom in the power of this spirit of love. Where the heart of God's love prevails, the spirit of Jesus Christ rules. But where the thoughts and deeds of hot-blooded people have broken with the heart of God in anger (however justified), where they have broken with Christ's nature of love, his Holy Spirit retreats, filled with indignation and aversion. It was the same when the law with its bloody sentences was first introduced and when human monarchy first arose in Israel. The spirit calls for God. The spirit of Jesus Christ flees from human greatness and power. He seeks the humble, those with a childlike spirit. In them he glorifies the inmost heart of God.

Only in Christ, in the perfect love of God's heart, only in the way that leads to the cross, does God show his unity. He does this through the Holy Spirit. Without Christ and his way, without apostolic poverty in absolute simplicity and dedication, without a love that has nothing to do with rights or violence, people will always be far from the kingdom of God and far from the workings of his spirit in the church. Only those who abide in God and God in them live in the unity of a love that sacrifices everything. Ulrich Stadler, a contemporary of Peter Rideman, witnessed to this truth with these authoritative words:

> Whoever does not follow Christ on his way and walk in his footsteps, whoever is unwilling to carry his cross, does not have or know the son; and whoever does not have the son does not know the Father; nor can he be enlightened through the loving-kindness of the Holy Spirit. It is into Christ, who dwells in us, that we must be incorporated in order to become partakers of the one Trinity through the solemn justice of the cross of Christ. Through this we become incorporated in the body of Christ, of which Christ is the head.

The church of his Holy Spirit, as the body of Christ, is the only place where the unity of God is revealed in Christ, that is, in the Holy Spirit. The nature of God is shown so clearly and unitedly here that his one will is done on earth. His kingdom comes as the unity of the church. Here the way of Jesus is followed to the end – death on the cross in the name of love. Here we receive the Holy Spirit as community with God in Christ:

> God cannot forsake those who are spiritually poor, who hunger and thirst after righteousness; he will feed them through the spirit with his body of unity. They must thereby be trans-formed into the community of Christ's body. To such shall be revealed the third part in God: the loving-kindness and mercy of the Holy Spirit. Such people do not live for themselves, however, but for Christ in them, and they are therefore glad and joyful in the Holy Spirit, through whom they truly know the Father, the Son, and the Holy Spirit.
>
> What then do they actually see through the Holy Spirit? The Father in the power of his omnipotence, by whom they were created; they see and know the Son in whom they are

tested, purified, justified, and circumcised, in whom they have
truly become children of God. Therefore they have free access
to the Father and are now one with Christ and all their fellow
members: they are all one church and one body in Christ. They
are in the kingdom of God and have Christ as their Lord. In
this unity, everything is held in common; nothing is privately
owned. Here it comes to pass that the Lord pours out his spirit
over all flesh, and all are taught by God to live to all eternity
according to his will, filled with all good things.

The sixteenth-century Anabaptists bore witness with Ulrich
Stadler that the indivisible unity of the church was first created in Jerusalem in the outpouring of the Holy Spirit. As a
revelation of this spirit, her life and work show the perfect
unity of the eternal will of God – and his coming rulership –
with the way of Jesus Christ. That God is in himself indivis-
ibly united (as the Father with the Son and the Spirit) is
revealed today in the complete unity of the church, and here
alone – until at the end of time the kingdom of God will
spread the rule of his unity over the whole world.

T he pentecostal spring of the first Christian church contrasts sharply with the icy rigidity of our Christianity
today. Everyone senses that at that time a fresher wind blew
and purer water flowed, a stronger power and a more fiery
warmth ruled than today among all those who call themselves Christians. We all know that in spite of the different
churches, in spite of all the various religious alliances and
societies for moral edification, the community life of faith
and love represented by the early church is almost not to be
found today. What has Christianity in general lost? What
was the all-important event that took place in Jerusalem?

The word of Jesus, and even more, his life and deeds from
the manger to the cross, were alive and present in that first
circle of the Christ-movement. What the apostles had to say
and do was drawn directly from the same reality that comes
to meet us today in the four gospels. This community of
faith and community of life in the first love was marked by
the presence of Christ – the Christ who had said, "I am with
you always."

Jesus devoted himself to people's outer need just as much
as to their inner need. It was the same in the early church. It
is not true that Jesus' Christianity is exclusively concerned
with souls, despising the body as our lot in life, a purely outward matter. When Jesus cast out all demonic spirits through
the spirit of God, the kingdom of God came to people.
When John sent someone to ask Jesus whether it was he who
would bring in the future state of justice, or whether they
should wait for another, he answered by referring to his
deeds: "The blind see again, the lame walk; lepers are healed
and the dead are brought to life again. Tidings of joy are
brought to the poor."

In Jesus' presence, the invisible kingdom of God had
become visible reality. The word had taken shape, love had become real. Jesus showed what love meant. His word and life
had proved that love knows no bounds. Love halts at no barrier. It can never be silenced, no matter what circumstances
make it seem impossible to practice it. Nothing is impossible
for the faith that springs from love. For this reason, the call
of Jesus does not stop at property. When he felt a love for the
young man who was rich in possessions, he looked into his
heart and said the word of perfect love, "One thing is still

lacking: sell everything you have; give it to the poor and come, go with me."

Yet what gave his friends strength to put into practice the will to love, as he had given it to them, was the experience of the spirit. When this spirit was given by the risen one to the new church-to-be, he overturned everything and set it on fire. Then they were able to become a life-sharing community, and only then did their love as unity in the Holy Spirit overflow. They were all on fire with the same burning love, which drew them irresistibly and for always together. Love had become in them a holy "thou must." Just as Jesus had always wanted round him his nearest friends and pupils, whom we call disciples, so his spirit drew the early Christians close to one another. Together they felt compelled to live the life of Jesus, and together, in complete community, they had to do the same as he had done. Because they felt this absolute inner must, all questions concerned with living together found an answer that accorded completely with the perfect unity and purity of love.

Jesus challenged each individual to leave everything and be with him wherever he went. He traveled from village to village with the band he had called together, and they shared their daily experiences. What their leader had asked for was kept – a common purse. Yet his mission was never meant to be limited to a narrow circle. The band of itinerant followers of Jesus became his embassy. The twelve apostles expected and represented his kingdom of justice as the approaching brotherhood in God. The resurrection confirmed the power of this mission. As soon as the spirit of Jesus flooded so unhindered over his first church, its first outward form was bound to take shape according to the way of Jesus and the commission entrusted to his embassy. The early Christians held absolutely everything in common. Whoever had possessions was filled with the urge to share them. No one had anything that did not belong to the community. Through the Holy Spirit, a steadily growing circle found unity and commitment in Christ.

This could never be an exclusive unity: all living things grow. Life begets life and spreads. Perfect love is never exclusive. Open doors and open hearts were significant characteristics of the early Christians. Therefore they had access to everyone and gained the love of whole peoples. They were a light that shone for all. The fiery spirit that filled them wanted to pour itself out over all flesh as God's will for his empire: the spirit of God's kingdom wants to be victorious over all peoples to draw them together as one. In this spirit, the early church was burning and alive, all heart and all soul; only in this could so many become one heart and one soul. No hard light of cold intellectual knowledge was to be found here, but the illuminating spirit who sets the heart aglow and quickens the soul with burning, fiery love.

Only in this way could isolation and its ice-cold existence be overcome. Communal life with its white-hot love began. In its heat, property was melted away to the very foundations. The icy substructures of age-old glaciers melt before God's sun. The only way to abolish private property and personal assets is through the radiant power of the life-creating spirit. All ownership feeds on stifling self-interest. When deadly selfishness is killed by love, and only then, ownership comes to an end. Yet it was so in the early church: under the

influence of the spirit of community, people did not think
their goods were their own. Private property was an impossibility; here the spirit of love and unity ruled.

L ove overlooks no need or suffering. In such a life-sharing
community no one could suffer a lack of clothing,
food, or any other necessity of life. Those who want to keep
goods and valuables for themselves in spite of the need
around them must have done violence to their own hearts.
God's heart is never limited in its sphere of action. Those
who held their goods in common at Jerusalem gave generous
hospitality to thousands of pilgrims. Through the outpouring of the Holy Spirit poured out upon them, they were able
to care wisely for many, for very many, with the slenderest
means; soon the early church itself experienced the support
of her apostolic daughter churches in this enormous service.

The early church had an immeasurable effect far and
wide. It shook whole worlds. It established a completely different and undreamed-of new world. But the spirit burning
with love is more delicate than the hard edifices of calculating reason or its coldly organizing social structure. It is more
delicate also than the powers of the soul and the blood,
which so many extended families and national communities
try to use as a foundation. Because the Holy Spirit is supremely noble and supremely divine, he is free from all
bondage to other elements. He drives them all away; or he
withdraws before they can offend him.

The Spirit alone is inviolable, the most delicate element
of all, never forcing himself on crude, earthy matter. On
earth what lasts longest belongs to the realm of the crudest.
The finer the organs, the more endangered is their life. The

kingdom Jesus brought, which has to do with the pure spirit, is not of this gross world. Unless this world is smelted and remolded, his spirit cannot touch it. The spirit of Jesus broke into a world grown alien to him. He overcame all other powers as the mightier one, who is and always will be inviolably pure. He cannot deny his nature. He never becomes part of any mixture. He cannot and will not let himself be changed by anything alien to him.

The Spirit is alive as the power of love at work without violence, as an inner voice of the utmost delicacy. He is perceived with the inner eye of pure faith alone. He retreats when the inner vision is not concentrated on him alone, when other spirits are given room beside him. He would rather see a spirit-filled witness murdered than allow alien and violent spirits to gain room beside him. What if this earthly life is taken from those who confess him? What does it matter? He himself cannot be killed. He is invincible. He rules forever. But he does not impose his rule on any opponent. He seems to flee from a gross and violent world. His church must suffer the same fate as Christ on the cross.

It almost seemed as if the form of life brought about by the Spirit at Pentecost fled forever from this world with its extermination at the second destruction of Jerusalem. Yet throughout the centuries, we see the same perfect form given by the same spirit again and again like a very rare gift of God. In fact it never has fled from this earth. But each individual filled with the Spirit has only a limited span of life in this time-bound world. So also the pure form in which the church took shape has been wiped out again and again by violent enemies. Individual churches were brought to a bloody end. Witnesses were slain. Yet the Spirit remained alive. Just as Jesus had to die and the apostles were murdered, the early church and the subsequent churches of the Reformation were also allotted a very limited time on this blood-drenched earth.

Yet new children are continually being born to the Spirit. The gaps made by death are filled by newly engendered life. As more are murdered, more follow on. The blood of martyrs is always the seed of the church. The living seed is always the mystery of the church and the kingdom. It would be entirely wrong to force an imitation of the form of life this mystery takes; such efforts can only lead to a lifeless caricature without the one essential element: the freely moving spirit, the life born of God! One thing alone matters: to become open to the living God, to the life-giving spirit of Jesus Christ, so that he – and he alone – can bring into being the same life he gave the early Christians. Then new life-units will constantly arise, in which the love that comes to expression in full community encompasses and penetrates everything. Full community is a question of rebirth and resurrection.

It has been given even in our times by the spirit of Jesus Christ, in the power of eternal birth and continual resurrection. The one decisive thing is the spirit which that unique circle, the early church, lived in – the quickening spirit that alone decided everything. It is a matter of recognizing the working of that spirit and how strong and pure it is. Spirit! Who is he? And what does he do?

The essence of the Spirit is unity. His love is born of that joy which pours out of the heart of God. Where people have to be disciplined, even forced, the spirit of love retreats, taking with him the unity of life he brings. Unity cannot be "made." Joy and love cannot be forced. It was the free and living spirit of joy that filled those people with the urge to be together daily and for always in love, in the bright radiance of community in God. This spirit of unity, love, and joy made community of goods and work inevitable.

There was no class hatred there; no sinister ferocity coming from a joyless, demanding power; no hint of bitterness, the result of disappointed claims; no talk of demanding human rights whereby, even as people look after others, they want to look after themselves and their own. The free impulse to give away wealth was alive there: all wanted to give themselves to the cause with all they had and all they could do. The mystery of this early church is revealed in the fact that here the spirit of Jesus Christ has disclosed God's heart. The most profound heart of all gives itself. In the church is revealed the creative spirit of a love that never fails.

In the name and reality of Jesus, a believing circle had gathered around the heart of God, a church that made God's perfect love clear and recognizable by her complete unity. God had formed an organism and the apostle was given a significant metaphor for it: "the body of Christ." It is the second and new embodiment of love and the word. The word goes forth from the heart of the Father through his life-giving and uniting spirit. Christ is the word. It takes new shape. When believing people live in full community, the word becomes the church.

The Holy Spirit can reveal himself only as the spirit he is: the spirit of unity. All members of the one body are filled with the same spirit streaming through them. That is how they know they are united as one organism. The life of the believing church is unity and community in the Holy Spirit, characteristic of the church endowed with his gifts. She proves it through the organic working together of all her diverse powers. When these powers of the unifying spirit work together creatively, the constructive peace of the church and of the coming kingdom comes into being and forms a firm bond.

We can talk about the church only when her structure corresponds to the glad tidings – the glad tidings of the all-embracing kingdom. As one heart and one soul, she must stand united for the inviolability of God's peace. In the brotherliness of the uniting spirit, she has to fight for God's justice to conquer the whole world. Because she is united and God is her strength, the church is able to hold out until this last battle. She unites all her members in the same love for the same task.

In the authority of the Holy Spirit, the whole church is of one heart and one mind. She is united in faith and common expectation for God's whole universe. Her unfeigned love and boundless faith long to put everything to the service of God. She wants to summon all the nations of the world to partake in God's kingdom. Where God gives the courage of faith, where Christ's mission lives as community, the love that comes from God's spirit proves to be power. It subjects everything to the rulership of God.

In the power of the Holy Spirit, joy in the kingdom of God will show itself in every situation. It will show absolute certainty. It will never draw back in dismay from any ruling power, however widely recognized. The supreme justice of God's constructive peace should alone prevail! Love arises from it and out of love arise joy and faith as fruits of the Spirit. What grows out of the Holy Spirit has divine strength and knows no limits. A courageous assurance of victory fills the whole church with militancy. With exultant joy in the Holy Spirit, she takes up what is humanly impossible – the word of omnipotent authority. This affects everything and applies to everybody. So does the overwhelming certainty of the believing church about the future.

Equipped with the courage of the Holy Spirit, the church dares to do spiritual battle with all powers that withstand her love. All resistance of the present age is insignificant in her eyes. The Spirit, who guides and instructs her, is himself the utmost encouragement. He sends out a summons to take up the cause, the cause that matters more than anything else. As its appointed representative, he is the administrator and advocate, interceding everywhere for the church. He leads her in battle. He tells her what to say. He fills her with courage to represent his mission resolutely in the most dangerous situations. The members of the church become his organs, for he pours the love of God into their hearts. He uses the church in word and in work as the instrument of his inmost will.

The church receives a royal promise especially meant for the dangers of persecution: the spirit of the all-commanding Father will go with his sons and daughters to speak to his enemies through them. He will instruct them at every decisive moment. Under his leadership, they will be masters of any situation until the last hour comes. He puts into their hearts what they have to do and suffer, what they have to say and be responsible for. They are filled with the Holy Spirit, ardently longing for the final revelation. In the face of death, they proclaim and represent the eternal truth as it is given to them by the Holy Spirit, who prompts them, moves them, and impels them. So to their last breath they give witness to

Jesus, that he is the messiah-king of the long-promised kingdom.

Through the Spirit, everything the prophets attested about the kingdom of God is brought to everyone by the long-suffering church. Those holy prophets, as people of God, acted in all they did according to the promptings of the Holy Spirit. In the same way, the commission and authority of the kingdom is now entrusted to those sent out by the church. When they speak, they utter his word. The apostolic spirit is the prophetic spirit: his word brings his kingdom. The apostolic mission is a matter of the prophetic embassy of God, which brings the future kingdom to everyone here and now. As prophecy, the apostleship of the church embraces the whole truth of Jesus and his future.

The Holy Spirit determines where those on this mission should go and what they should say: speaking within them, it tells them which people they should speak to, which land they should go to or avoid. The Spirit's guidance gives final certainty. Under his leadership, no matter what it points to, fear is unknown. Often he leads into the midst of the plain of death (Ezek. 37:1), making the downfall of humankind horribly clear; at decisive moments in his history, he leads us into extreme danger in the wilderness, where we are tempted by the devil. Yet everywhere he demonstrates the triumphant reality of the resurrection: victory over the temptations of hell.

To venture anything with the Spirit is more serious than death, more powerful than when all the hosts of God draw near, overwhelming in their power. He descends on people like lightning. He falls upon the weak as the strong one. Those who receive him are thrown to the ground and put on their feet again, new people. The strong one stays and dwells in them. The weak body becomes the dwelling of the strong spirit: for the church, as the body of Christ, is the temple of the Holy Spirit. All those who receive her spirit belong to her. All believers are living members of the church, pervaded by the spirit, which fills her whole body. Like Gideon, the church wears the armor of the spirit over her whole body.

From the very beginning, the Holy Spirit has filled everything that belonged to the church or was to prepare the way for it. The last prophet of olden times, who preceded the coming Christ, was filled with him while still in his mother's womb; his father and mother had become full of the Holy Spirit for him. Before Jesus' life began, Mary received the spirit; so, from the time the apostolic church began to follow Jesus Christ, it was filled with the Holy Spirit. "When they had prayed, the place where they were gathered was shaken, and they were all filled with the Holy Spirit and spoke the word of God with joyful courage."

Whoever came within the church's domain had to receive the Holy Spirit – the "servants of temporal needs" (those responsible for administering economic and social justice), just as much as the servants of the word, or pastoral leaders. Their work, as a concern of the church, was to be filled with the Spirit's divine wisdom, as testified of Stephen (the first to do this service) who until the last moment of his martyrdom was filled with the Holy Spirit. What was true of him was true of all: even Paul, the late-comer among the apostles, like all the other serving members of the church, was filled with the Holy Spirit as soon as the blindness inflicted by its initial lightning was taken away from him.

God gives the Holy Spirit to the whole church; he fills her entirely. In her body he lets the complete image of Jesus Christ shine out. He penetrates every area of her life with certain knowledge of what sin, justice, and judgment are; what faith and love are; and what work it is that Christ has accomplished and how it can be done through him alone. The spirit of Jesus Christ wants to reach and convict each member of the church, teaching and educating.

The Spirit is given to all believers – it is imparted by God to every member united with his church. He wants to make all of us people with faith. Their united action makes the justice of Jesus a reality. It is God who is called upon by the whole church, God who does everything connected with Christ's cause. God's works are done when the unity of the believers calls for them to be done. God is the one who acts. He acts through the Holy Spirit by virtue of the apostolic gospel of Jesus Christ.

The church's unity of action springs from its community with the Father of Jesus Christ. It is founded on the teaching of the apostles, on their spirit, word, and life. It is alive in prayer to God in the name of Jesus Christ. Without the apostolic spirit and without his teaching and community, no Christian can draw near to God, there is no Christian prayer. Only in the authority of this spirit can God be called upon: God shall intervene. His unity shall shine out, and his kingdom shall draw near. His will shall be done, and his nature shall be revealed. His forgiveness shall take effect, and his omnipotence shall break the power of evil. He shall give bread and life. He shall be victorious over the hour of temptation every time it comes over the earth. It is God who wills and accomplishes everything, but it can happen only through the call of the apostolic spirit of Jesus Christ, who is the spirit of God.

When in our human weakness we are at a loss to know how to stand before God in his omnipotence, when we cannot see how our pleading is to count for anything before Christ and his rulership, it is the Spirit alone who comes to the aid of our weakness. We of ourselves do not know what to pray for. Our manner of praying does not in the least correspond to what is fitting before God; but the Spirit himself represents the believers powerfully with cries that soar up, cries we are unable to utter. The one who searches hearts knows what the Spirit has in mind: therefore it wants and does what God wants and does. He is one with God. He sanctifies the unholy and represents them as holy in those things that please God.

Only through the Spirit does God want to be honored. The church, gathered in silence, waits for the Spirit's prompting; if we want to learn from him, we must be able to listen. It is those who listen, whom he wants to teach. He is their master. He wants them to call upon God in such a way that the listener becomes the speaker and the speaker, the listener. Thus God listens to believers; because he listens, they will receive the Spirit, and the Spirit's cause will be theirs, just as they have requested. This is the only way of speaking with God. All other so-called prayer is an abomination to God. Whoever turns his ear away so that he cannot hear God's voice prays in vain: God rejects his prayer. Whoever wants to combine other plans with what God has in mind fails to meet God. Whoever gets diverted loses the way.

Whoever is divided remains far from God. Whoever wants to appear in God's presence with a double heart will not gain anything Christ-like from him.

The Holy Spirit is a spirit of reverence. The holiest things, such as calling on God in the name of Jesus Christ, can be dared only through the prompting of the one Holy Spirit and only when all human wishes are completely silenced. Christians remain men and women – they do not become gods. Their own and other spirits never stop harassing and oppressing the new life given them. For this reason they are in continual need of the unchangeable Spirit. They must pray daily for him to move and fill their hearts again and again. God listens to them. This is quite certain: he gives his Holy Spirit to all who call upon him in dedicated reverence and expectant faith.

God gives his spirit wholly. God cannot mete out his greatest gift with weights and measures – it is not a substance that can be divided. The Spirit is the living God himself, as the Father and the Son are. The three are one, they are God. The indivisible God gives himself in all his fullness to those ready to obey him. Where he can act and work as he wills, he gives himself wholly and remains the one he was and always will be. He never contradicts himself: he says the same to all believers. He wants to lead all of them into the complete truth without withholding anything: he has no intention of giving them half-truths. He is the whole truth of God, as the Father has revealed it for all time in Christ.

It is God's will, through the power of his spirit, to fulfill every word spoken by Jesus. It is God's purpose, through the church of his spirit, to accomplish once more the perfect works of Jesus Christ. He lays the fullness of the Spirit on the whole church of Jesus Christ; with her, he wants to make his history among us: the history of his heart as the history of Jesus Christ. The history of the church is the history of God. The history of the last times, of his kingdom, is present reality in the church. Whoever despises the representatives of the church despises not people but God, who has entrusted to the church of his spirit the task of representing his holy cause. God's administrator, the representative of Jesus Christ, is the advocate of the church.

The Holy Spirit is the sign of the church, and shows that it belongs to the kingdom of God. By the Spirit she knows she remains in Christ. God, as the spirit of his kingdom, is in the church of Jesus Christ: the Spirit is unmistakable. He is the spirit of the Father! His heart of perfect love is a present reality. He is the spirit of the Son! The unmistakable word and nature of Jesus Christ, his perfect act of sacrifice, and his future are revealed in the Spirit.

This spirit is one of counsel and wisdom. Through the life of Jesus, he makes God's will known in all that happens, in every situation. God and his wisdom, Jesus and his counsel never become reality outside the province of the Spirit. In work and in life it becomes clear that without the spirit of new life and new works we can know neither the Father nor the Son, however wisely we talk or write about the highest things with our human knowledge. The work of the Spirit honors no one but God. Everything he does contrasts the greatness of God with the smallness of men and women and proves everywhere that God's kingdom is completely different from our world. God's heart is greater than our heart. God's spirit is absolutely different from our spirit. The divine power of the Holy Spirit can be recognized in contrast to human weakness. Like rain on parched land, the Spirit comes down to ignorant and feeble creatures. From God's free heights it pours itself out over them.

The Spirit reveals God's cause as an undeserved gift, as a grace descending directly from above, the actual fact of a direct pouring-in. God's spirit is the grace of Jesus Christ. Nothing in those who receive the Holy Spirit could possibly justify a claim that it belongs by rights to them. The Spirit comes to the undeserving and unworthy; it is a grace given to those who are humble.

The spirit of God never grows out of our zeitgeist. In all the human aberrations of today, he proves that his divine character belongs to the ultimate future. God's spirit never grows out of our works. He comes from another world. Like a heavenly dove, he comes from above to those who are below. He is the spirit of a kingdom ruling in God's heavens, and from here alone he comes to the earth. As the spirit of prophetic speech, he turns all eyes to the last things, to all things that through God shall be brought to pass at the end of days.

In contrast to the zeitgeist of any human epoch, this spirit is always untimely, pointing ultimately to the world peace of the future. He sees beyond all contemporary history. He belongs to no earthly kingdom. Every state and every nation looks upon him as an alien. Everywhere, he is the different spirit. He reveals a divine justice that can be expected only from afar. His rule comes from a world outside our space. His truth is not to be grasped by human thinking. God's light from the world beyond gives an insight that infinitely surpasses all our knowledge and experience of time and space.

Jesus brought us the spirit of the creator. Only the spirit who created all things can understand this. Only he sees into all things. He who is still at work today is and always will be above everything that happens and unfolds in creation. Only the creative spirit manifests the power that is unending and eternal. Only he knows the depths of the Godhead, for he alone is the living bond that unites the first creation with the new future, the final creation. He grants superlative clarity and power from beyond to the feeblest of creatures: in spite of a hostile and murderous age and the narrow confines of space, despite our weakness, he helps us live in keeping with the kingdom of heaven and its holy future.

Whoever accepts the spirit of the new creation receives the eternal powers of the one God who formed the first creation in the same spirit. Wherever the end that will transform everything is expected, God's future is alive now – the spirit of strength in an aging universe. The new day has already dawned. All shall see it: a new creation is arising! Its gospel is there for every creature. The groaning of the old creation meets the children of the new world.

The power of heaven, as the authority of the Holy Spirit, is at work in a church of the new creation. It lives in her as a promise of the sunny days to come over an earth growing cold. In the midst of an aging world, the church, impregnated with eternity and filled with the future, gains strength for God and his kingdom through the Spirit. The church receives eternal and infinite majesty as a first beam of light from the future. Going forth from the throne of God's rule, the Lord of light fills the church eternally.

The Holy Spirit descends from the throne of God to a small and weak band gathered in expectant faith to receive him. Faith in the Spirit is faith in the church of light around God's almighty throne. Here the old has passed away. All creatures can see the new creation! Whoever believes in the Holy Spirit has faith in the one Christian church of the kingdom of heaven, which is united and common to all believers. And he has faith in the church of God, which as the community of saints has the authority to forgive sins and believes in the resurrection of the body. This faith in the church lives in the realm of the eternal.

The sin and death of the old creation must retreat. New life arises. The church shows the newborn creation. The Holy Spirit and the mother church giving birth to eternal life are one. From the city church of the Jerusalem above, spirit and church come down as one. This oneness is new in the approaching day of creation. The spirit of the church carries the gospel to all creation. In new birth, he lets his children see the light of day – God's new day.

The church in heaven is the source of all faith. Like Mary the virgin, the church is, through the Holy Spirit, the eternal mother. Without her there are no children. Not just any gathering of contemporaries gives birth to life out of its circle. As far as life is there, it comes from union with a higher unity through birth in the Spirit. The church takes shape only where the Holy Spirit has brought about a life and faith completely at one with the whole glorified band of martyrs and witnesses, with the apostolic mother church of all centuries.

The church is built from above. This unity of the spiritual church around the throne of God is brought down to the earth by the Holy Spirit. In no other way or place can church life come into existence, or the structure of the church be built. The unanimity of the believing church is in the perfect unity between her members living now and the one truly united church of all time. The unity comes from the Holy Spirit. God's upper world becomes one with the church on earth. The secret of the city on the hill is the Spirit. There is no city below except through the Spirit's one way of unity with the city above. Apart from this there is no church. God's city-church lives only in the mountain air of her eternal hill. Her citizenship and her politics are in heaven. She expects everything from heaven and is governed from there.

Through the spirit of the city of God, worship of God begins. Only in the one city of God does true worship begin. It begins in Christ. All other ways of honoring God have come to an end. Their places of worship fall into ruins, and their towers are laid low. The houses of God built with stone are done away with – the Spirit is there instead. God does not recognize any church – or congregation or Christian community – unless it is pervaded by the one church, established and gathered by the one spirit sent by God. The wind of the Spirit blows down from above. Thus only in those who open themselves to it – who let themselves be swept clean by it – can the Spirit work.

As a house of the Holy Spirit, built by God, the church of Christ is free of belfries and all architectural show. In all the houses of religious worship we build, the spirits are mixed. In the house of God there are never many spirits: only one is acknowledged there. No person can stay in this house who does not receive in his own heart the one spirit who fills the whole house. God himself has built this church. It stands there without towers made by human hands as the simplest house of God. His church bears the lowly and childlike spirit that alone is of God. It is with Mary in the stable. It comes into being by the side of Christ on the cross. It goes the way of apostolic poverty. With one heart and one mind, it glorifies no one but God in Christ Jesus.

Through this united spirit, all the members of this church prove they are Christ's disciples. Their perfect unity of heart and mind shows the true character of Jesus Christ. He stripped himself of all greatness and laid aside all privileges; so does the church. He refused to hold on to anything that might seem to be his as a special right; so does the church. It seemed to him like robbery to own anything that did not also belong to those he loved from his heart; to the church also it seems like this. He took the lowliest place of a hanged slave; so does his church. All her members deny themselves as he denied himself. They bear his cross.

They are his friends, for they do what he commands. His spirit has called them to his way, to discipleship; he keeps them on it and holds them to it. In unity with the life of Jesus, they are led in the fight by the Spirit. With the authoritative word of his absolute rule, the spirit of Jesus Christ regulates everything that takes place among them. On the way of Jesus Christ no person rules but only the Holy Spirit, through the power of Christ's sacrificial love. Unity lives in the readiness for death that comes from utmost freedom. Here the miracle of a dictatorship of love comes into being; prompted and guided by the Spirit, it is a supreme freewillingness, a freedom whose deepest longing is to sacrifice everything.

There is no other church of Jesus Christ than the one completely free of human authority, built and directed by the spirit of Christ's sacrifice. She remains at one in the Holy Spirit, the one foundation of truth, the very soul of readiness for the cross. In the church, the truth of God proves itself to be the perfect love that comes from the Spirit. The Holy Spirit continually confirms, fortifies, and purifies the church, this perfect work of God and of Jesus Christ's love, completed on the cross. Those who willingly suffer a renewal of this work in the church and surrender to it patiently and serenely, those who are prepared to lose their life for God's cause as Jesus lost his, are members of his body. But whoever does not find the courage and endurance to accept this work does not belong to the church of Jesus Christ.

Only through the spirit of the crucified one can this church with her courage to face death be gathered and held together. This spirit is her joy in life and her inspiration in death. His blazing fire kindles an enthusiasm for the ultimate sacrifice – all members of the church are ready for it. In a special way, those called upon to be ready for death in mission must be invested with a spirit of utmost sacrifice: they must bear the sword of the Spirit, drive out devils, proclaim a break with the status quo, spread the victorious light of God, and scatter the biting salt of truth. They must call to repentance and faith, represent the embassy of the city on the hill, and reveal the image of God. The sign by which they are known is the community of the cross. The working of the Holy Spirit for the good is to be so clearly recognizable in these members of the church that no one but God can be glorified in everything they say and do. This mission can be given only through the power and action of the

Spirit – not of men and women but of God. Christ commanded his disciples not to leave until they were endued with power from on high.

They were not allowed to gather people until they had received the gift of the Holy Spirit. They had to wait for it. Without it, the disciples could never become apostles. Without Christ, who is the Spirit, no apostolic deeds can be done, and no works can stand before God. The holiest work of all is the service of apostolic mission. It may never be undertaken in self-delusion or human presumption. Only according to the instructions and guidance of the Spirit can the truth be spread around, the word of mission ventured. That same spirit filled Jesus before he was sent by his Father. How much more does he long that his messengers never go out on mission except in the power of this same spirit! How could they possibly do what he did or represent his word with authority, if they lacked the spirit with which their master was sent out! How could they ever gather people with Christ if they had not received the spirit of his unity with God!

Jesus gathers. He says clearly: "Whoever does not gather with me scatters." With motherly protection, he wants to gather the sons of his people in the arms of his spirit. His church, like Jesus himself, resembles the mother hen who unites her children under her wings. Whoever wants to gather with Jesus must be of his nature, of his mind, and of his spirit. It is at the same time the will and the commission of Jesus Christ to gather and unite. Just this is possible through the Holy Spirit alone.

This commission for unity can be understood only in the Spirit. Only the spirit of Christ can lead disunited people to the united church. No man or woman can do it – no one is allowed to do it. It must begin in the Spirit and be completed in the Spirit. No arm of flesh and blood receives this authority. Only the spirit of the city above can bring the church together. Only he binds. No human strength is able to do it – no one may even try to do it. Where the Spirit is building, no other power is allowed entrance. His building is his work exclusively: "Though men watch, it naught availeth, God must watch, his arm prevaileth." He does it through the Spirit. Only under his protection is his house built.

Every building begins with the work of clearing-up – there must be an empty plot for the house to stand on. When everything is cleared away, the building begins. No foundation can be laid without the work of digging and excavating. Every house must be protected from undermining waters: its load has to be tested and fire precautions taken. In times of danger or threat, a watch is needed to prevent fire and housebreaking. The good spirit keeps evil spirits away. The house requires protection.

The house of the church is protected through the most watchful spirit of all. The best possible protection is the elimination of all dangerous powers. Only the Holy Spirit can clear away everything that tries to undermine, suppress, or destroy the church. He drives out all evil spirits. But burdens of the past, both old and recent, threaten all believers in the present. Powers fought long ago make their old claims again: they raise their heads in the present, calling to mind past evils!

The present has its roots in the past. The only way to cope with the present is tackle the roots. Without the forgiveness of sin, there is no elimination of evil. The new life cannot begin if the old is not done away with. The only way the lame can be healed is by having the cause of illness removed.

Christ destroys the works of the devil with his mission. He takes the ground from under them. The church receives the power and authority to forgive sins through the power of his liberation. Jesus himself imparted it to her: "Receive the Holy Spirit! If you forgive someone, he or she is forgiven. If you do not forgive, he or she is not forgiven." If you take away sins on earth, they shall stay away in heaven; but if you leave them unchanged here on earth, they shall stay a burden in heaven too. They will keep people in their clutches with overmastering power. What takes place in the church is valid in the kingdom of heaven; what is left undone in her is left undone in God's eyes. No one enters the kingdom of God without forgiveness of sins, and without the sacrament of forgiveness there is no community anywhere. Without constantly renewed purification, it is not possible to have community with God or among people. The church must be pure; otherwise she does not live up to what she should profess. There is no community other than that of the unblemished Spirit. This alone is the church. In the authority of forgiveness, the spirit of Jesus Christ stands by the church as his new creation.

The church is the memorial of the Christ-life, honoring the inmost character of God. The Spirit acknowledges her as the image of God. With conclusive authority it confirms that she is the rock of truth. Through her foundation in the apostles and prophets, it has entrusted her with everything she needs for her building-up. On the basis of the truth, it commands her to exclude and avoid everything that should be kept out of a consecrated building. This building, this church, is guided with a sure hand. It bears the pure image of God. It has foundations. As the rock of truth, it is built on the cornerstone, Jesus Christ.

At the end of the early Christian period, the Roman prophet Hermas saw this living monument in a vision and described it in his ninth parable:

> The Holy Spirit in the form of the church showed him a great white rock big enough for the whole world. Its gate shone brighter than the sun, and around it stood virgins clad in white. Stones that had been cleaned and dressed passed through their hands, and with these stones the holiest of buildings was to be built on the white rock. The new gate in the old rock leads into the kingdom of God and to the building that is his church. The master builder of this rock temple is the Son of God himself. Only through him is there access to his building. The pure virgins represent the powers of the Holy Spirit: through their work, the building becomes one stone with the firm rock, and through the touch of their hands, all the stones are filled with the Holy Spirit, who is still building his temple. Whoever loves peace, whoever has a childlike spirit, let him come! They shall be fitted into the building. Whoever wants to free all human beings from their distress, whoever hastens to do good to all, must be in the temple of the rock before it is completed.

In his first confession, written in an Austrian prison around 1530, Peter Rideman testifies to the same building of the Holy Spirit, who as power of the Most High brings about all that is good in his living stones:

> Through manifesting and communicating his gift, he brings the church together and unites it as the house of God; in it, her members receive forgiveness of sins; in the bond of love they

are united with him into one body. All this takes place
through the Holy Spirit, who brings it all about.

In this spirit, it becomes clear how we should build the house
of God, and what the house of God is. Then we can joyfully
begin to build on the foundation of all the apostles, with
Jesus Christ as the cornerstone.

This house is the church of God. Its stability is in God.
The first pillar that supports this house is reverence for God,
which overcomes all fear of people. The second pillar is the
pure wisdom of God, which is eternally at war with all human wisdom. The third pillar is divine understanding; on
this pillar the folly of human understanding comes to grief.
The fourth pillar is the counsel of God, which is bound to
contradict all human counsel forever; the fifth is the strength
of God in contrast to human force; the sixth is the skill of
God as against the skill of humankind. The seventh and last
pillar is the loving-kindness and friendship of God; against
this pillar break the destructive waters that come with love of
possessions and a life of pomp and splendor. As in olden
times the pillars of the old sanctuary were given symbolic
names such as "He lays firm foundations" and "in him is
strength" (1 Kings 7:21–22), so now the building of the church
is in truth founded on the steadfastness and strength of the
spirit of God. Like the pillars of the old temple that stood on
silver feet, the pedestals of the seven pillars of the church
shine out in the purity of the Holy Spirit.

All that the dark shadows of the old temple were meant to
signify has been fulfilled in the radiant spirit of Jesus Christ.
The house of the old covenant was meant to represent the
dwelling of God in the midst of his people. "They shall
make me a sanctuary in which I will dwell among them." To

this people, who regarded the old dwelling as the inviolable holy of holies, Jesus made a very daring claim: "Here is something greater than the temple." The Holy Spirit dwelt in Jesus as the Godhead embodied in his whole fullness. Jesus placed the true dwelling of God in the midst of people, who despite their old temple were without God in the world.

Jesus did this in all their hostile unbelief. When his body was about to be broken, he promised to restore the demolished temple in three days. And indeed, he who had risen alive from the dead on the third day sent his Holy Spirit. He gave the new temple to the believing church: "The temple of God is holy; you are that temple." In the quickening wind, Christ and the Father want to come to believing people. In the Son of Man, God's dwelling has come out of its concealing shadows. In the words and life of Jesus, in his deeds and works, God dwells on earth, visible to all.

Because of his works, even if nothing else made them believe, people had to recognize this established fact: in Jesus Christ the work of God is disclosed by the spirit of revelation. His work is his house, the place where he dwells; he acts from within it. The spirit of God wants to enlighten the eyes of all hearts to see the greatness of his power as it establishes his work in Jesus Christ. For this reason he sets up a throne room in the house of the church for the ruler of the kingdom of God. From here he directs the embassy sent out by his government. In the church, the spirit of God makes Christ, raised to the majesty of the king of the kingdom, ruler over all things. In the Spirit, the church can recognize everything given into her hands from God's kingdom.

The old temple was the tent sanctuary where people used to gather. In the same way, the church of the Holy Spirit is where everyone gathers who wants to glorify the heart of God and his dwelling among people. Just as God wanted to receive the sincere sacrifices and prayers of his people in the old tabernacle, he accepts the thank-offering of his church in the new temple of the Spirit. Her house is full of jubilation. Her spirit exults to God. Her festivals honor the king. She is filled with such an exuberant joy of the Holy Spirit that out of the fullness of her heart she brings praise and thanks to God, she sings him fervent songs overflowing with the Spirit, and in her whole life and work she honors what his love decrees. The Holy Spirit is the never-failing source of a joy that wells up unceasingly from the innermost depths of the sanctuary and pours out over all lands.

The old temple was divided into the holy of holies, the holy place, and the forecourts. The most important of all was the center of the innermost place: the further from the interior, the more each part of the tabernacle pointed back to the deepest and innermost center and away from itself. God had his dwelling in the innermost place; therefore even this inner covering in the tabernacle was called the dwelling of God (Exod. 25:17–22). It surrounded the throne that commanded the whole. In the holy of holies, the mighty angel-princes testified most powerfully of all to the presence of the Lord who reigned over them. The princely spiritual beings surrounding the throne of God give it honor and glory. The throne remains decisive. The death of Jesus Christ has rent the curtain that divided the holy of holies from the holy place. From now on, God from his innermost throne wants to govern and have mastery over all the forces of the church, commission them and equip them The eternal light of the holy of holies shines out far amd wide. Rulership from God's dwelling flows out far beyond the boundaries of inwardness. It becomes outwardly visible. The place of worship remains in the inner recesses of the house, but the perfect life of the spirit of Jesus Christ will not be limited and hidden any longer. Certainly it will still be true to its starting point in the deepest spirit of the holy of holies – faith; certainly it will still keep a certain reserve about its inmost prayers and its dedicated works; yet its aim is to allow the lordship of God's spirit to grow and expand unhindered. Starting from the holy of holies, the spirit of Jesus strives to gain mastery over all the forecourts.

Thus the whole body becomes the temple of the Holy Spirit. The whole world becomes the parish of his church. Christ dwells in overflowing hearts through faith, and the faith that stems from his love floods over all worlds. As in the holy of holies of the old covenant, all the vessels, all the walls, and all the coverings were radiant with gold, the color of faith, so the innermost sanctuary of the temple of the Spirit is filled with faith's golden light, radiating far and wide. The faith of Jesus Christ will conquer the whole world. The light of his kingdom will have command over all the ends of the earth. Wherever God takes up his dwelling, the throne from which Christ rules is recognized to be the center of all life.

From the throne of God in the Old Testament holy of holies, all people were to be ruled. For this reason, the forgiveness of sins was proclaimed from it. From the throne of the new government forgiveness is made a reality. This throne has been established where a different sacrifice took place, valid for all time. An ultimate sacrifice was needed; there was no other way to break the opposing regime of the sinister prince of this world. God's new government succeeds: faith in this sacrifice of the Lord of light – a sacrifice unto death that overturns everything. Then the new certificate of citizenship is freely given, promising community between God and his people forever.

The spirit of the new throne generates a power, founded on faith in the sacrificed king alone. It sweeps away everything else. In the all-decisive battle – his death – he has taken possession of his throne. His first act as ruler was to declare an amnesty for all time, promising his enemies absolute forgiveness as soon as they are ready to acknowledge his sovereignty without hesitation. Perfect love flows out of this faith in the kingly deeds of forgiveness and the sacrifice unto death. It is poured out through the Holy Spirit into the hearts of the whole people; the spirit of the King grants to his people the heart that has his own kingly attitude. Like their divine king himself, they are able in him to love – to love God – with all their heart and soul and mind and with all their thoughts! Like their sacrificed king, they are able in him to love their neighbors and all their enemies just as they love themselves! After all, they were only recently enemies themselves! What love they have received! They are filled with its glow.

In everything, the new temple proves to be a fulfillment of the old prototype. In the old covenant the congregation used to gather in prayer in the forecourt whenever the high priest bore incense into the holy of holies. So now the central fire of the loving church urges the hearts of all believers to gather as one before God. Through enlightenment in Christ, the light with the seven branches is renewed in the seven candlesticks of the church. Christ's fiery love permeates the new life so completely that the bread always offered in ancient Judaism has become, in the new covenant, the surrender of all the means of existence to God's cause. The spirit of the dwelling penetrates the life of the new house so completely that all it possesses in the way of food or clothing belongs to the Holy Spirit and his love. The whole house and all that is in it belongs to him.

The new church is filled with the Holy Spirit. Going out from the innermost sanctuary, the whole temple is opened to the Spirit. He rules over everything right down to the utmost use of all the gifts and faculties of every believer in the new covenant. The whole body has become a holy temple. The self-control that makes for the spirit's harmonious mastery of the whole person, right down to all physical urges, is a conclusive fruit of the Spirit. No fruitless branches remain on the tree of the Holy Spirit. From all his living branches, love, joy, and peace can be harvested. Unfaithfulness and all impure acts, hostility and murderous hate, discord in the form of bickering and envy, and dissension caused by anger and quarrelsomeness must be kept away from his house just as much as the idolizing of luxury and possessions. The fruit of the Spirit will not share the same bowl with any dish prepared by the flesh. It has profound significance that Jesus drove out the bankers with their money tables and middleman's profits. He did not tolerate them in God's house, not even in the outermost forecourt. Jesus used his sharpest measures against them to win back the outlying forecourt for the house of worship. Like all the outer chambers and rooms in the old forecourt, the whole life of the new church, including the management of all its economic affairs, becomes a holy temple of God. Once and for all, the power of mammon and all the dealing in money that accompanies private property have been vehemently driven out of the house of God by Jesus.

Our souls and bodies, like our spirits, must be kept as a holy temple until the day of Jesus Christ. From the depths of faith, the spirit of Jesus Christ requisitions all functions and achievements, even of a life generally stamped as profane. In the forecourt open to the profane, not only the priests and prophets of old but also Jesus and all the apostles of the new covenant represented the truth of the sanctuary. The Holy Spirit wants to spread God's dwelling over all that is earthly and temporal.

The earth is God's. All its gifts and powers are to be brought under the rule of his spirit. To do this, the church of the Holy Spirit was erected in the midst of this world; her forecourts, dedicated to God, are to expand over the whole earth. The curtain is rent. Streams of living water go out from the innermost sanctuary into all lands. Mighty works of the Holy Spirit reveal for the whole earth the power and lordship of the holy throne of God. The spirit of Jesus Christ has given the new temple of God to the whole earth.

The church believes in the victory of the Holy Spirit; she surrenders to his rulership so that God may be acknowledged throughout the world. She calls to the spirit of God to bring the kingdom of Jesus Christ to all people.

THE LIVING WORD

Every call to a more centered life is a challenge to fight for greater clarity, for certainty about the ultimate demands of our highest calling. Yet only God can bring about an inner awakening, only his will is clear. Only God gives us the one, pure light that can cope with all that a dark future might bring. Nothing in our own nature can help us to find real clarity out of our deep confusion. All those "inner voices" that speak from the depths of our own emotional hearts can be dangerous – will-o'-the-wisps, flickering up out of swampy ground and leading the traveler astray.

As heirs of fallen humankind we show our old nature again and again. On our own we can never achieve anything – only unclarity. There is only one hope: the sun must rise and cast its radiance on the swampy lowlands. Only in the light of day does false light grow dim. Jesus brings in the day. He ends night. He is the morning star of the dawning day. He brings the old humankind to an end. He is the last Adam, the founder of a new race that lights up the new humanity. As the creative word he brings into being the new people of creation's new day. He is the enlightening and life-begetting word, whose mystery can be revealed only in the unity of the creator with Christ and his spirit.

In the tumultuous period of spiritual seeking that marked Reformation times, Ulrich Stadler wrote on the power of the Holy Spirit and argued that like God himself, God's word

could be understood only in the unity of the Father with the
Son and the Spirit.

First of all, God is recognized as God through his omnipotence – he is the Father of all creation. Next, God is recognized
through the earnestness and righteousness of the Son; and
thirdly, through the loving-kindness and compassion of the
Holy Spirit. All rational minds recognize the creator of heaven
and earth through the works of nature. They see in creation
unmistakable proofs of God's omnipotence as the power of the
Father. All God's works indicate that there is a God. Yet we still
lack something decisive when giving honor and glory to God:
the hallowing of God's name. It arises out of the second article
of faith, out of the strict justice and righteousness that the Father fulfills in Jesus Christ and in the corporate body of all his
members, the church. There the third and last article is revealed: the infinite loving-kindness and compassion of the
Holy Spirit! Nowhere else, and in no other ways, can the word
of God be recognized and grasped.

If we are to gain knowledge of the living Son, we must expect God to do in us what was done to Christ. We must carry
the cross of Christ and follow in his footsteps if Christ's word is
to become alive in us. The word must become true in deed and
in reality. The works of Jesus Christ, the truth and righteousness of the crucified Son of God, are the means by which the
word is revealed. If we are to recognize the highest good, we
must submit to all three articles of faith in our own person.
The word as a whole must be received, living, into our hearts –
it does not bestow itself in part. It must become flesh and live
in pure and open hearts through the Holy Spirit. But this does
not happen without great fear and trembling, as with Mary
when the angel told her of God's will. The word must be born
in us too, and it can come about in no other way than through
pain, poverty, and misery – within and without.

New birth brings new life. When the word is born, when it has become flesh in us, we live for love itself and for the fruits of love: we live for God alone. So our hearts are at peace. As the church of Jesus Christ, we become mothers, brothers, and sisters of God.

Then the third article of faith will be revealed: the loving-kindness and compassion of the Holy Spirit. No one can come to him save through the deep waters of need and distress. Through the bath of rebirth, we are born anew. We become children of God, brothers and sisters of Jesus Christ. We are awakened from the dead, led out of hell, and made alive in Christ. Through the cross we have received Christ; now we can confess that Christ has come into the flesh, for Christ lives in us. All those who have experienced this are ruled by the Holy Spirit. Through the word of God, the third article of faith appears in them. The Holy Spirit rejects everything of the world in them. He lives in them as the living word of eternal truth.

The true light – Christ – shines in all who are given an understanding of the living word through suffering and the cross. Then they all see the loving-kindness and compassion of God. No one can really see or recognize God's love as long as his or her heart is wrapped up in worldly pleasures. But through the Holy Spirit, the living word can in truth be seen, for he brings the crucified Christ into our life; in his light the whole of scripture, with all the words and sayings of God and Christ, is encompassed in the unity of the Trinity. In this unity the scripture speaks of the true, godly life; and in the Spirit we have to see how to achieve it. The living word will place it before our eyes even though it may not be written on the pages of the Bible in front of us; for those who have the spirit of God are able to discern all things through this one spirit.

The Holy Spirit plants the living word into the heart of the believing church. Through him, Christ is the living word in the church of believers. He is in perfect accord with every line written by his apostles and prophets, who were filled with the same inner word. For it is they who in truth give witness to him as the giver of life. The word comes to life in the heart of every believer. It is essential to grasp in the innermost way the eternal, the living Christ, as the life-giving word. Christ himself is the word coming to life, the morning star and sun of the believing heart.

Only through the light of Christ can our darkened inner life be freed from all unclarity. The word of God falls into the hearts of erring mortals to flood them through and through with the divine spirit. From within, the living word has to transform everything. As soon as dying humanity follows the call from their hearts: "Turn your hearts to all the words I testify to you this day," they will experience the living word themselves. God has called his people with this deeply challenging word through all ages.

The only way to help our failing life become healthy is to prepare our hearts for the living word. A doctor's visit can help only when the sick take to heart the advice given, disregarding no instructions or medicines. Above all, the foolish patients must stop trying to cure themselves with their own ideas or with neighborly advice. Our hearts can be healed only if we accept all the words of him who said: "I am the Lord, your physician." "The medicine must be taken internally. Outside us it does no good." The inner word brings the helpful physician, who is himself the healing medicine. The best physician is the one who brings healing by the mere fact of his living presence. When in an inner way we eat and drink the life-giving word, it means that the healer and his healing have been accepted.

This points to the mystery that drove so many of Jesus' friends away from him: "Unless you eat the flesh of the Son of Man, unless you drink his blood, you have no life in you!" This stark way of expressing the innermost union with Jesus himself was bound to turn all those away who were not resolved, cost what it may, to win through to final unity with him. Only those who, like Peter, had experienced the power of his living word could say: "Lord, where shall we go? You have words of eternal life."

We must take the words of Jesus to heart, take in the Savior himself, if we are not to give ourselves up for lost. If his word is to heal, we must have it close to our heart and let it burn in our soul. The word lies before us like an open book of glowing truth on a table. There we can read and work with heart and soul. Every letter shall become living fire in our hearts. Only through the heart do we receive the word like the tasting of the tongue and the searing heat of flame.

And yet ultimately, it is not through any activity of the human heart that the inner content – the intrinsic value – of the word becomes alive. True, when the word penetrates our heart it awakens our innermost being. That is the first stage of inner growth. For how could we believe in the living one if we had not heard of him? We do hear him with the awakening ear of the heart, and slowly faith arises! But the decisive hour is when we come to the faith that only God can give. Faith in God means awakening from the dead. Like

Mary, faith holds on to the living seed of the Holy Spirit, the word of God at work within us. In every living word, God and God alone is at work.

Through the example of the Virgin Mary, Peter Rideman shows how the word becomes alive in the heart of a believer:

> Mary was sealed with the Holy Spirit as soon as she believed… The Holy Spirit worked together with her faith. So the word, being believed, took on our human nature from her…The word was conceived when the Holy Spirit and faith came together. So the word became flesh.
>
> Mary believed the word spoken to her; through faith she received the Holy Spirit. This is how she conceived Christ, this is how he was born of her. Whoever wants to be reborn a Christian must first hear the word, like Mary, and then believe it.

Whoever wants to be born of God must keep in mind how Christ's birth took place: it was brought about by the working of the Holy Spirit in faith. Every birth from God happens in the same way. When the word is heard and then believed, faith is sealed with the Holy Spirit; the Holy Spirit renews us and makes us new creatures in the life of God's justice. We are formed in God's image. Where his word is believed, God makes it alive through the gift of the childlike spirit. Through the living word, we will live from now on in the holy, divine life of the kingdom of God.

Faith arises from proclamation, but proclamation comes from the word of God. The life-creating word is there first. Faith comes second, decisive for each one personally. It is an awakening from the dead when we receive the word of God into our hearts. Then the word must come to life. Faith holds firmly to the word, as Mary did. Like a germinating seed it must remain in the heart and yet blossom in life.

From its roots in the depths of the soul, the word must spread far and wide. From deep within, the word stimulates all that faith does and furthers all the deeds of faith. The life-giving word is plainly to be seen in what grows out of it.

The Holy Spirit gives life to the word; through it, he produces the works of his love. He is not forced by the dead law. He is the living finger of God himself, writing his loving word on the pages of the heart. The word of the Spirit is the living word at work, for it pierces soul and spirit. It destroys the works of the devil and consummates the work of God. All who want to inherit the promised kingdom must be born through the living word. Through the Spirit, the word is planted in the innermost members of living people. All those in whom the word is active through the Holy Spirit, from the smallest to the greatest, know the living God and the kingdom where he is at work.

Through the word of the Spirit, what the dead law demanded in vain is spiritually alive and given its highest meaning (Rom. 8:3). In the Spirit's divine order of life, everything is accomplished in the living power of God. The written law, in so far as it is bound to the letter, is annulled through Christ; for he has given his spirit, who has nothing dead about him. The letter is dead and spreads death. If the Spirit does not accompany it, the scripture can never achieve the righteousness that counts before God. Through the spirit of freely given and newly created life, we become free forever from the law and from all dead works belonging to it. Once we live in the Spirit, we are no longer under the law.

We cannot have the freedom given by community in God without the word alive within us. Its power frees us from slavery to the letter of the law. It leads to a life of living faith in action. The righteousness born of faith knows the source of its life. "The word is near you, very near; it is on your lips and in your heart." When the word becomes very dear to our heart, it is free and living.

It has decisive significance whether we only look up the "word of God" and consider it, only hear and read it, only understand it and think about it, only approve of it and acknowledge it, or whether we receive it and cherish it in the innermost depths of our heart as a living seed of God. What use is it to contemplate the source, if we do not drink from it? What use is the word if we know it only by rote and the all-too-familiar letter stays outside us? The roots of a living flower absorb the water and hold on to it. Out of the depths, the water must bring life to every fiber. The living word has the same effect as living water: its life wells up and flows into every branch.

Therefore Jesus said, "I give living water. No matter who drinks of the water I give him, he will never thirst in all eternity: the water I give him will become in him a spring pouring out into life, into eternal life." The living word of the Spirit is the source of life. It is in the heart of each believer. Christ is at work in each heart as the living word. In Christ the word bears within it the powers of divine life. In the rebirth that takes place through the word of the spirit, the life of eternity begins, never to be repressed again.

The hidden seed of the word is stronger than anything else. It roots up all poison. It cuts until it separates soul and spirit. It divides life from death. It warns against all destruction and awakens all that the divine life demands. It judges all thoughts and feelings, shedding light on ourselves. It is radiant with the light of him who is himself life. The inner word is the inner light. It saves us from everything that darkens. It is the word that brings healing and salvation. It transplants us to God's kingdom of light. Planted in our innermost heart, it blossoms as the shining tree of life.

The garden of truth grows within us as the love of God, replacing our own ego's rank growth. We ourselves are the field of the living seed. Here, God's will becomes reality in the word of life. God's plantation is the divine word. His seed springs from his heart of light and fights against the seeds of darkness. As the living word within grows and bears fruit, it tolerates no weed of other works. The inner word, becoming deed, fills every corner of the heart. It takes over the whole of life until everything harmful to God's plantation is crowded out.

Only the new seed is fruitful. Everything that does not grow out of the seed of the new planting belongs to the soil that still contains many other seeds of the old field with all its weeds. What happens there is a miracle – the new seed grows, though the rest of the field remains barren. The living word, which goes out from God, is different from the inadequate words of men and women. The living seed of God's kingdom wants to spread over the whole world like a mighty tree. The word of truth is God's living heart. It is the creative God himself, the Christ who rules over all.

Through the eyes of the one who is alive and at work as the new word, the chaos of the old, corrupt existence is revealed. As the spirit of Jesus Christ, the living word hovers over the deep and formless void. His glance reveals the creative might of God's love, completely restoring all true life.

The light of the new creation shines out from the eyes of

the living one. Jesus is God speaking. Christ is the living word of God's heart. The new fire of his word is the love of God. An indescribable joy in the Holy Spirit, in God, and in his new creation arises when the word of Christ is received and accepted by his loving church. The church lives in this joy and exultation that comes from the creative word of the Spirit, giving glory to Christ in God.

The unmistakable sign that Jesus is alive in any heart is the working of the creative word. The word is Christ. It shapes the whole of life to accord with the mind and spirit of Jesus Christ. He who is truth at work embraces all truths of the divine life. The word of truth in all its facets represents the whole Christ. Jesus Christ is the living content of the word. A mysterious unity binds the living power of the inner word with the presence of Jesus Christ himself.

The word of God was already alive before the first pages of the Bible were written. It lived in the very beginning. It revealed the creative and loving nature of the one who spoke it. It was divine nature before the very beginning and will remain one with God beyond the end of all things. It became flesh and dwelt among people in Jesus Christ.

Even now after the last page of the Bible has been written, the word remains the living, creative word, as it was in the beginning and shall be after the end of all things. The word, in all its creative working, is one with the living God and his eternal love. Wherever new life takes shape, it comes from him. As God's free gift, it takes on shape and form. It brings the kingdom of God. It fills the church and builds it up. It dwells in the heart of God's temple and fills all the envoys of the city of God with spirit and life.

The word reveals the truth in love and the love in truth. It speaks directly from the heart of God to the heart of the believer. It speaks in the Spirit. What it gives and what it demands has absolute authority, for the word of Christ is spirit and truth. Its absolute "thou shalt" is no law, bound to the letter, but an ardent longing of the heart – in the holy "thou must" felt by all those in whom it has kindled love. It is not a dry precept but a living urge. It is not a sinister threat but the radiant light of inmost liberation. It is not the letter, it is life: it is the Spirit, it is Christ, it is God.

Ulrich Stadler testifies:

> The word became flesh so that this flesh might be ruled by the Holy Spirit in the word. Where that takes place, this apostolic witness is made: Now, not I live, but Christ lives in me; the world is crucified to me; I am dead to the world. Everyone who can confess Christ like this can boast of the living word. He can witness to the truth. All others who come without such a confession, however, go on clamoring with outward noise; all those who do not live in him come with dead words without Christ.

Without the Holy Spirit and his living word, without the annihilation of our old life, our own life, without the reality of a new life in Christ, no one should dare to preach the word of God. In his Confession of Faith, Peter Rideman summarizes this statement of the truth very clearly as the confession of all the brothers:

> Those who cannot wait upon God cannot expect that the gift of the Spirit will be imparted to them. Those who want to go before it is time, before they have received this grace, go in their own strength. To such this word applies: "They go in haste, yet I did not send them; they preach, yet I did not command them." Therefore their preaching is fruitless.

Because they lack the Spirit, they do not have Christ's teaching. If the word is to be a message and bear fruit, then it must come about through the Holy Spirit. Christ's teaching and mission must never be mixed with the human will but represented through the Holy Spirit alone. The holy people of the old covenant spoke as they were prompted by the Holy Spirit. All the more now, the members of the church must speak and teach in the way the Holy Spirit prompts them. They have to do what he brings about through them and neither do nor say anything of themselves. Christ puts it in these words: "It will not be you that speak, but my Father's Spirit will speak through you."

In this and no other way can the word be living and bear fruit. This truth applies to everything that is word, to everything said or sung before the people and before God in the church of the Spirit. Like the word that is taught and the word of mission, like prayer and worship, so the word is alive and powerful in song only when the songs of the church are composed through the spirit of God, through his prompting. Songs other than those of the Spirit do not belong in the church. Those created by the impulse of the Spirit may be sung only through the movement of the same Spirit from which they came.

All those who belong to the Spirit think about what is of the Spirit. Whoever speaks, or prays, or sings in this alert Spirit considers every word – what it leads to and how far it goes. In such members, the Spirit himself is concerned and watchful to see that everything serves to build up the one work that is the Spirit's cause alone. The Holy Spirit makes the word live by bringing Christ and the clarity of his all-embracing witness into the heart, by revealing the whole future of his kingdom – the kingdom that encompasses all worlds. The spirit of truth reveals the teaching of Jesus as light and clarity illuminating all things. Everything God wants to say and bring to people is put in the right order within the context of the whole by the word of the Spirit. The Spirit shows to each and every one where they belong according to the will of God.

The word touches each one in the right place; it strikes where God wants to strike. Without God's spirit there is no two-edged sword of the word. The living word that is Christ cuts through the heart. The sword of the Spirit knows how deep it cuts and what it is doing. Unless this sword does its work of separating, knowledge and life itself stay hopelessly confused. The spirit of Christ alone leads to the right order in the teaching of truth and in the wisdom of life. Without clarification through the Spirit, the word of God, like the heart, remains sunk in confusion and darkness. If the whole of scripture were to be put before our eyes at once, it would still bring neither fruit nor improvement unless it were done according to the directions of the Spirit who alone knows the truth. Only those who demonstrate the character and order of the Spirit in all their words as well as in all their works are its servants.

Whoever wants to be a child of the Spirit and a servant of his truth must let the power and works of the Spirit be seen in all words spoken and above all in life. Whoever presumes to preach the gospel in any other way is a thief, offering stolen goods, which have become worthless. Those who run in haste without the power of the Spirit, before Christ has seized hold of them, are murderers. They bring people to mortal ruin. Their word, devoid of the Spirit, is deadly. It reeks of decay, it stuns, it kills life.

Christ's truth does not belong to the letter, which kills, but to the Spirit, who gives life. That is why we may never let it pass our lips unless we have the spirit of God. But whoever receives the Spirit must proclaim the word. This Spirit must make it known to those who wait for the Spirit. It is the Spirit in the depths of the heart – and only the Spirit – who grants again and again the divine power of the living word. He comes to the aid of the sound and letter of the spoken and written testimony. These symbols of the word are spoken and written down; then the same living, creative power from which they sprang in the first place gives witness to itself again as their real, living essence.

Peter Rideman testifies clearly that the word of truth can be living, powerful, and fruitful only through the Holy Spirit of Jesus Christ. Therefore only those may use and witness to this holy word who bring the life-giving spirit that belongs to it with them. To Ulrich Stadler, too, signs of the living word are to him signs of the living God – in the Spirit, in Jesus Christ the crucified. Everything the Holy Spirit imparts is brought about by God through this justice of the cross, with which his word is concerned. Those who receive the Spirit in faith submit and give practical expression to God's justice, on the way of the cross.

It is a question of faith. Paul says to the Romans: "Faith comes from hearing what is preached, but hearing comes through the word of God." The right preaching and writing are not themselves God's word; rather, God's word precedes them and brings them into being. It is those filled with the spirit of God and the power of the word (outwardly invisible

and inaudible) who write and speak what the eye can read
and the ear can hear. But faith and the word itself – the word
that is believed – are of the invisible God. The outward eye
does not see God or his word; the outward ear does not hear
God himself or his voice. Before we can preach in the right
way, we must be overcome by the true word of God in the
very depths of our soul, where it is possible to see and hear
what God puts there himself. Christ alone is the word of God.
A servant of the word must have become really one with
Christ through the suffering on the cross if he wants to give
an account of the word, whose mystery is the cross of Christ.

The word preached by people is a token of the true word
that God alone can speak. God speaks this word in Christ.
The eternal word is not written, spoken, or preached by any
person, today or ever. The scripture written by the hand of
the apostles and prophets and the word spoken by the
mouth of true preachers all belong to God's well-made creation, meant to proclaim its creator. This creation is not
Christ, not itself the living word, which belongs to the creator alone. Whoever wants to use scripture according to its
true worth has to make the sharpest distinction between the
spoken word and the inner word in the believing heart.

The direct and living word is always of first importance. It
is there whenever God himself speaks to the heart. It lives in
the spirit of Jesus Christ. The spoken and written word of
the disciples comes second. It presupposes the first and proceeds from it. First of all we must be taught by God himself.
Only when scripture and outer word go together with the
power of the Holy Spirit does the inner word penetrate.
God himself teaches his word, and he does so through his
Holy Spirit.

Christ expressly commanded his apostles to proclaim the word: "Preach the gospel to all creatures." It is these apostles who have witnessed most clearly to the vast difference between the inner and the outer word. They point out that everything we hear from human beings, everything we see in creation or read in books, can never be the living word of God itself. We should not confuse an account and the retelling of it with the event of which it tells! To be an apostle of Jesus Christ means to be an ambassador of his kingdom, giving an account of it and spreading the news of its written commission. Whoever believes the message receives the same commission from Christ himself. The king reserves the right to give his commission and equip his ambassadors.

Like the water of baptism, like bread and wine at the Lord's Supper, the sound and the letter of the Bible are always only an image, a token of what is really alive and important. The token points away from itself to what it stands for. It is not the thing itself, for whose sake it exists. The eternal inner word – the living word of God is witnessed to by the outer and ephemeral word, coming from those who are filled with the living word. We grasp this witness wherever and whenever, in the Holy Spirit, we perceive the cause to which it bears testimony. It is like an inn sign announcing with truth that there is wine in the cellar: the sign is not the wine itself.

It is in keeping with God's order that everywhere in his first creation, and also in his new creation, the physical precedes the spiritual. On the other hand everything physical at the beginning and at the end of God's way proceeds from the spiritual: God's spirit is alive before he begins to work.

However, in our world the physical witness of writing and speaking and the faith that comes from hearing precede the Spirit's work of inner justification or forgiveness of sin. Only the forgiving and renewing Christ can achieve God's work. That is how, in the Holy Spirit, he brings the living word with God's authority to our hearts.

In this justification, which is Christ himself, the seed of God germinates and grows as faith that proves itself powerfully before God and before all creation in times of storm. Through the Holy Spirit, God himself confirms the living word of Christ in the heart of the believer. In the very depths of soul and heart, the believer receives the righteousness of God, justification through Christ. Through the Spirit, it is written by the living finger of God. Thus he lives in the obedience born of faith according to the directions given by this living spirit, according to the whole word of God and Jesus Christ. The heart is gripped by Christ. It is filled with his spirit. Now what is physical and material is given shape and form according to his demands.

Through the power of faith, the new commandment brings new life. True life is never old. The childlike life of the Spirit cannot help being new again and again. It is the new life of love. If the new word lives in us, if it rules in us and leads to rebirth, if our whole heart and mind are filled with it, as God demands of us, then the witness of Moses and David, the prophets and the apostles will become a living word in us: the word will be a new person in Jesus Christ. That is why the life-bringing spirit is called the living word: the new covenant, the New Testament.

That is what the writings of the prophets of God and the apostles of Jesus Christ testify – everyone must find the everlasting word within themselves if they really and truly want to seek nothing but the kingdom of God. It helps no one to know everything written in the scriptures. Each one has to suffer the work of justification (forgiveness of sin) in their own person. Christ wants to bring it into their hearts and lives as the living word. If that does not happen, they remain dead in the same way as all worldly people are dead. Were they to know the whole Bible by heart, without the living work of God in them, their confession (however loud and high-flown) is nothing but delusion. It is not the slightest use to them or others.

But those who in Christ renounce the whole world and give themselves to God as living sacrifices hear the word of the Spirit in their hearts. They believe the word and take it in. To those who are not justified through the indwelling Christ, whose faith is not confirmed by the living word within, who are not proven in Christ's suffering and cannot bear the test of his cross – to such the word will be a dead sound, a dead letter, wherever they go. Beside the living word of him who is the truth, the ever imperfect witness of the outward word is like a lifeless portrait beside the living person.

However loudly we try to persuade people that the confession we preach, the witness we hear, or the print we read are God's word, such teaching leaves them empty and dissatisfied. Left on its own, the outward word brings no improvement. The living word of the Spirit must join it, otherwise everything remains as it was. Word and word belong together. The inner word is the true and essential one. It is God's eternal and almighty power. No human being can change it; no interpretation can alter it. In the believer, it has the same nature and form as God, for it is God. As God himself, it comes to believers. It can accomplish all things. It opens up what is new. For this reason, John says about the new commandment: "It is in him and in you!"

The word-become-flesh never teaches anything – never is anything – but the living Christ. Therefore the church of Jesus Christ and her mission must challenge everyone through the outer word to surrender to this inner teacher. People must never be allowed to keep to the outer word, otherwise scripture, preaching, and all the words used in them become idols. Words should never become idols. They are all nothing but tools or images. They must, they will disappear when the word that never passes away finds its ultimate fulfillment. Until then they remain what they are: a picture of the true word in created things. However, what it represents and portrays is meant to be glorified in this picture.

In this respect, the New Testament is no different from the Old, taken according to the letter. Both remain a token or a testimony. It must be preached or listened to, written or read. People can use it. But if the living master of the inner word does not bring the power of the new covenant and pierce the heart and take command, the Old Testament remains the old commandment, the old law. Without the inner Christ and his new commandment – without the love of his living heart, without the implantation of his cross and the new life it brings – all writing and preaching are still dead letters and empty noise.

As the sixteenth-century Anabaptist Hans Denck writes:

On my own I can understand nothing of the scriptures: the Day, the Day itself, the everlasting Light has to break in: Christ has to rise in my heart if the word is to become alive. Whoever does not stand completely with God, whoever is not penetrated through and through by God's spirit, cannot understand the scriptures. If such people honor the Bible, they cannot help making an idol of it.

The scriptures are holy, they are good. But as long as we have a wrong attitude, we cannot use them as they are meant to be used. The scriptures witness to Christ, but only Christ himself can give us his life. It is love that in Christ commanded what was to be written and continues to command what could be written still. In the Jesus of the gospels, in the Christ witnessed to in the whole of scripture, the love of God is deed and reality. Through the same Christ, God's love wants to become deed and reality afresh in us! We must wait for love if we want the truth. Whoever will not wait for a revelation from God within his breast but presumes himself to undertake the work which belongs alone to the spirit of God and Jesus Christ, will quite certainly make the mystery of God in the scriptures into a horror and abomination in his sight.

Therefore, it is for the Holy Spirit alone to interpret the scriptures; they came from him, for he existed first. Our own interpretations and the false faith that results, the absolutely wrong and human ways of understanding the scriptures, will give way to true faith and to interpretation in the Holy Spirit only when we long for this pure faith from God himself.

Therefore Hans Denck cries out to God: "Lord, I wish to have faith. Help me to come to faith!"

He saw what can bring faith and the word of God into our hearts: only the rising of Christ, the sun of righteousness. Only then will the darkness of unbelief in our hearts be overcome. The almighty word of God can be grasped in no other way than when it comes in Christ directly from God above and pierces the heart. Human ways and means can never lead us to an understanding of the holy scriptures. For it is the scriptures that testify to the wonder of God, which no human being can understand.

Like Ulrich Stadler and Sebastian Franck, Hans Denck points out that often two texts in the Bible contradict each other in such a way that understanding either of them seems difficult. When this is the case, he says:

> Both passages must be true, for God deceives no one. This would be obvious if we paid heed to the one and only teacher, the Holy Spirit, for he reveals in our innermost hearts the truth that is completely united in itself. Whoever leaves two passages contradicting each other, unable to unite their truths in God's irrefutable truth, lacks the chief thing – the ground of truth, Christ in God.

The Bible is closed to the intellectual approach. The Master alone has the key to this book, which contains all the treasures of wisdom. He is the truth. Everything in this book comes from him, the word, which from the beginning was with God and in recent times became flesh. Denck goes on:

> I testify to the future coming of Jesus Christ our Lord, and pray all of you who hear the truth of God, see it, or otherwise perceive it, that you might receive it in the truth of Christ. That means you shall receive it in the one way and in the one form taught and established by Jesus Christ. The means to all knowledge and all life is Christ, whom no one can know in truth unless he follows him with his life.

There is only one testimony to the truth. That is in Christ. It is life surging directly into us. The word living in our hearts through Christ should never be denied. We should earnestly and diligently listen to what God wants to speak in us through Christ. At the same time of course we should not absolutely reject all outer witness; we should rather hear and test everything, making comparisons in the reverence born of the Spirit. If we do that, our understanding of the truth will grow purer from day to day until at last we hear God himself without human words; we hear no one but God speaking to us, God alone, "God absolutely unconcealed." Only then shall we be certain what his will and nature is.

Only those who have the living law of truth written in their hearts through the Holy Spirit have received the new covenant, the living covenant of God. Only such are truly just, for righteousness belongs alone to God, to the living one. It neither belongs to people nor comes to us through people. All righteousness of our own collapses. To quote Denck again: "Those who presume to think they can walk straight up to heaven in their own strength will fall and plunge in the opposite direction. But if I walk in the strength of truth, my walking will not be in vain." God himself makes it possible to walk the way of his righteousness. He does it through the free will of his believers. God alone can make us want his word and the works of his righteousness, and he alone can bring their fulfillment.

To believe means to be obedient to the word of God – come life, come death. Whoever believes follows God with the utmost confidence that everything his Spirit prompts in us will lead to the best.

Those who have been sent by God know God; their word is one with God's word. They realize there is no contradiction in God. They are able to grasp that the living word in believing hearts is in complete agreement with all the prophets and with all the apostolic scriptures. That is the goal – the unity of the truth.

All who have received the Holy Spirit are one with Christ in God. They are so united among themselves in the unity of his word that what concerns one concerns all. What Christ did they also do. In their unity they have Christ as their one Lord and master.

The truth has always been revealed in God's heart. He showed the truth to his prophets at all times. But through Jesus Christ it was revealed again to everyone in all its fullness. He became man and took a sacrificial death on himself for this reason, that from now on, through the Spirit, all people everywhere would have the one united witness of the truth. God has been good from the very beginning. In Christ, though, he lets his loving-kindness be known to all. Wherever trust in the loving-kindness of God's heart arises and grows through the living word of God amongst us worldly people, truth as love and justice looks down from heaven on us all. Christ reveals the heart of God.

As soon as we have experienced the righteousness of God in Christ, we realize that not we but rather the spirit of God, dwelling in us and at work in us, has given back to the Father what we had stolen from him. Then there is peace – as unity with God, unity with his apostles and prophets, and unity among ourselves. Yet free as we now are from everything else in the confidence this love gives us, from this moment on we can do nothing good except "in the way of suffering." We willingly let happen to us what God does; held captive by God himself, we are able to submit in absolute freedom of will and heart to what Christ as the word does in our hearts and in our lives. God's loving-kindness, the truth of his love and justice, the unity of his peace, and the freedom of his life are the foundation of all that the holy scriptures testify. The writings of the Old and New Testaments are of divine origin. Therefore no one can understand them except those enlightened by the divine spirit, because only in such does this same living source well up. Only when our will is moved by God are we in living harmony with Christ's voice, for as the word of God, it lives in our hearts. Then we understand the scriptures.

Divine enlightenment takes place in the depths of the heart, and yet it is recognizable. Every evil and unenlightened heart betrays itself through arrogance and impatience. Every heart filled with God's loving-kindness shows Christ's humility and the patience of his love. If the divine spirit is not at work in us, cooperating with our faith, if he does not help us recognize loving humility and make it a genuine reality in us, the holy scripture – because it remains something apart – proves a shaky foundation for faith. Only those who bear within themselves the living word as the divine source of all the holy scriptures are in living contact with the great stream of all that God reveals: they live in the truth.

The holy scriptures testify that the new covenant can be received only by those who have the law of freedom (again, testified by scripture) inscribed in their hearts by the Holy Spirit. But those who imagine that they will succeed in following the law of righteousness on their own ascribe to

the dead letter what the living spirit does. Those who want
to glorify the scriptures, yet have let divine love grow cold
within them, should take heed lest they make an idol of the
scriptures, which is what all those scholars do who are not
taught by the Holy Spirit and not led to the kingdom of
God. Hans Denck continues:

> I esteem the scriptures above all human treasures; yet I do not
> esteem them as highly as the word of God, which is living,
> strong, and eternal, free from all elements of our world,
> whereas the scriptures are not. God himself is spirit and not let-
> ter, and he writes indelibly, with no pen and paper but in such
> a way that it can never be blotted out. Therefore salvation does
> not depend on the scriptures, however good and beneficial to
> that end they may be. This is the reason: it is not possible for
> scripture alone to make an evil heart good, however well edu-
> cated in the scriptures it may be. A heart is truly believing only
> where a spark of divine zeal is alive. Only a heart burning for
> God is improved by all things, above all by the holy scriptures.
> Christ alone, as the inner light, changes life.
>
> As long as I approach the scriptures out of my own ability, I
> understand nothing. To the extent that I am driven by truth
> itself and its life-giving spirit, however, to that extent do I com-
> prehend the holy scriptures; but then not out of my own ability
> and merit but out of God's grace. First of all, the foundation of
> faith must be laid; then everything built on it can resist wind
> and water...Your life will show whether God's word is living in
> you. Good can never be achieved by anyone without God be-
> ing at work in the heart. It is impossible to do it alone. God
> will do it through Christ.

Yet God forces no one. Long ago he did everything possible
to help us. He gave up his son Jesus Christ to a sacrificial
death. He made him the means. Christ is the means to

liberation and union. We can accept him or we can reject him. He remains the same. He wants nothing but the love, freedom, and unity that he himself is. Christ paved the way that no one could find. Now we can tread it of our own free will to reach the goal of life. The way is love. When selfishness is overcome, our heart is won over by the gospel. We listen to it – and faith is born. Christ has not only proclaimed or written the gospel, but from the beginning of the world, he speaks and writes it in the heart. Those who have it in their hearts are free and act in freedom.

Whoever is a true disciple of Christ has a living word in his heart: the fiery, loving word whose liberating strength loves nothing but God alone. This word leads them; all they do and leave undone is directed according to this burning love. Even without written commands they would have to do what this love commands. All written laws must give way to love; they were given for love's sake, not love for theirs. Laws are made and broken. But true love is the one God, who cannot create himself although he created all things. He cannot break himself. He is love that is unbreakable. In this or that individual – in the one more, in the other less – a living spark of this love can be felt. Unfortunately, in our times this fiery spark seems to be extinguished in almost everyone!

So much is sure: because love is of the Spirit, the smallest spark, however dimly it may glimmer in us, never comes from us. It can come only from the perfect love that is God himself. Love is spiritual, whereas we are all carnal. Often the spark is very dim. Only perfect love can help. The one person in whom love has been proved to be perfect and at its most sublime, Jesus of Nazareth, is the savior, redeemer, and healer of his people, in accordance with the will of eternal love. Through the power of the Holy Spirit, he showed openly by all he did or left undone what befits love. He proved himself as the promised savior in the midst of Israel. As promised by the true God in the holy scriptures, he was brought forth when his time was come. In Christ Jesus, perfect love conquers the human race.

In these loveless times, we can see that what is now scarcely to be felt came to fulfillment long ago in Christ Jesus. In him, the love that we lack came to fulfillment. Through the spirit of God we know for certain that God's love toward us, and our love toward God, can never be more sublimely shown than it was in Jesus. In the living word of the Spirit, we are certain that God in his compassion for the world will cast aside all the judgment his righteousness calls for in the face of our sin if only we do not despise the one thing: what took place in Jesus. In the course of history the essence of perfect love has been thoroughly taught and sufficiently proved – not by us but by God.

All those who have sought and found the way of God have become one with God, but this One, who never stumbled in going this way, was never disunited with him; from the very beginning he was at one with God and remained at one with him. What this one love taught and did in Christ Jesus is truly right and good – nothing else. In the old and the new law, one and the same love is hidden, but in the new covenant through Jesus it is shown at its most sublime. Whoever longs to recognize and find true love must experience it through this Jesus Christ in the most intimate way. There is no other. Love consists in knowing and loving God. That takes place in Christ. His new law of life makes us sons of God, which is beyond our achieving. The merciful God himself as our one true Father must draw us into Christ so that we are born in him in the very depths of our soul. He himself allows his children to know his innermost will through the living word. This is nothing less than love itself, as it came in Jesus Christ and as it shall continue to be proclaimed by the gospel of his glorious grace. The living word of perfect love is nothing less than Jesus Christ himself.

Those who teach anything different from what love, and love alone, has given us do not build on the foundation of Jesus Christ. They will not be able to answer before love for their actions. Moreover, if they happen to have recognized this foundation and source of all that is good, and yet teach otherwise, they will still less be able to defend themselves before love, which is God himself. Children of love neither say nor do, for love's sake, anything that is contrary to love. Everything that means life streams to them from perfect love, which is Jesus Christ himself. By this it is possible to find out who has the spirit of truth; whoever understands this and yet teaches otherwise is an antichrist; whoever does not understand it has not yet recognized Christ, the Lord. Faith is no faith where Christ is not present. Christ is God's love and his living word.

G od alone can kindle the light that is faith. Whoever is not ready to do God's will, whoever will not accept Christ's attitude, whoever does not receive the Spirit, will never be enlightened and instructed by God to understand the scriptures. Bible in hand, such people hold nothing but a manger without the Christ Child, a wooden cross without the crucified one; a scabbard without a sword, a platter without bread! All our own efforts to grasp the dead letter are in

vain. There is no other key to the Bible except the key to the
kingdom of God. This key is Christ and his Holy Spirit.
Whoever does not have this key stands before firmly locked
gates. He is kept out of God's garden by the iron bars of the
letter, blocking the way.

The letter makes people dull, rigid, obstinate, cold, and
cruel. Anyone whose head is stuffed full of the leaden letters
of the Bible, devoid of the Spirit, is as capable of killing the
son of God and his people as the scribes and Pharisees were.
To this day, all apostles and truly living members of the
church of Christ are punished as liars and put to death with
the help of the letter of the Bible. As long as the Bible is understood literally, it continues to be the murderous sword of
the Antichrist and the dead throne on which he sits. The
Antichrist uses the cunning dagger and the blunt, leaden
sheath of the letter against the drawn sword of the Spirit. He
uses the darkened lantern against the light that belongs in it.

The spirit of the Antichrist has the letter on its side
against the spirit of the scriptures. Black printer's ink is its
favorite color, playing off one wooden letter against another.
It splits the Bible, bent on making the witness of the Bible
divided within itself by means of the literal word of scripture.

It tries everywhere to annihilate the most important attributes of the word: judgment, mercy, and faithfulness.
Those who try to represent biblical truth by excelling in
knowledge of the text will become loveless by nature and
godless in knowledge. Becoming more and more learned,
they never become better. They fight against those who worship God. They pay court to the letter, which God appointed as a tool. They render service to externals instead of
accepting them as a help. What was meant as a picture, as a

semblance or a sign, has been made into into an object of
idolatry.

Whoever will not ask God humbly and reverently for the
true spirit of the Bible, whoever will not beg for the light of
the Holy Spirit to show clearly the deepest meaning of the
scriptures, will keep on being misguided and led astray by
the external word. To such the same happens as to the scribes
in the time of Jesus: with all their knowledge of the Bible
they did not understand the scriptures – they grasped neither their power nor their meaning. They understood to perfection all the words of the Bible from cover to cover, yet
always from outside only! They knew everything that could
be found in the holy scriptures according to the letter of human words. But not one in a thousand could grasp the mystery of the one true word hidden behind the words, which is
God's mystery.

The contrast is conclusive. The letter is of service in reading aloud and reciting Biblical passages, to preserve the Bible
in the true Old Testament tradition. But it knows nothing
about the new covenant of the life-giving word. Everything
it repeats is stolen. Nothing it says comes from the source,
nothing comes as God's free gift. Its ungenuineness denies
the power of Jesus Christ and his apostles. Its works are
empty and unprofitable, and all its efforts are superfluous. It
hauls water to the river; it brings more and more letters
where there was already more than enough preaching and
writing. Yet it can never bring fresh water – the life-giving
word – into anyone's heart, no matter how intensely they
thirst for God's flowing spring; if everything depended on
service to the letter, people would die of thirst in a wilderness of dead words.

God's true word works quite differently. It lives in the Holy Spirit, who is the eternal well of life. Only the Spirit gives new life to what was once written under his guidance; he makes it rise from the dead. He is the only teacher of the covenant of resurrection. He shows the way out of the labyrinth of dead letters to the organic tree of life. In the Spirit, Christ brings to our hearts the unanimous agreement of all God's witnesses as the spiritual unity of all living truth.

As soon as the Holy Spirit reveals God's light, God's cause becomes bright and clear. Pure white light is its color. The Holy Spirit brings all the bright colors of the truth together. In the unity of Jesus Christ, the Spirit reveals the complete accord of God's word. Freed from the letter's deadly law, he makes all truth living and united, united with the living Christ, united with all his prophets and apostles, united with the living church. The understanding of the scriptures given by the Spirit leads to the bond of Christ's peace: absolute unity in all living truth. The unifying light becomes visible as soon as it streams in – when light appears, it can be recognized.

Only God has command over light. Only directly from God himself can we receive what God alone can accomplish. Whenever the personal word of Christ, the voice of the Lamb of Bethlehem, the call of the Lion of Judah, begins to speak in people, it is God who wants to consummate his work in us. God alone is able to do this. In Jesus Christ, God himself descended to lost humankind. Through the Holy Spirit, the word of God became flesh of Jewish blood in Bethlehem, but it did not want to remain flesh. It became creative life. In the Spirit the word is heard and recognized, so that it once again becomes flesh: a new people drawn from all nations – the new body of Christ.

Jesus was the immortal word taking on mortality. He was and is the human incarnation of the spiritual word. He gives shape and form to what is eternal. He is the one we must listen to, the one we should grasp. God's eternal and everlasting word was brought to the earth through the Jesus who took on human shape in time and space. In him, the word of God became flesh and voice – the eternal rock on which the church, as the renewed incarnation of the spiritual word, is built – the almighty word, which is of divine nature and created everything.

In the spirit of Jesus Christ, God's word shows itself afresh as God's arm and God's finger. Something new is created time and again and is there, so to speak, in a twinkling. In Christ and in his spirit, the unity of the first or old creation with the new creation is given. There is only that one word of God, which restores all things so they are kept on the path of his creative will. If God did not speak the word of creation or of the new creation anymore, everything would fall back into nothingness. The word that God speaks in the first creation and in the new creation is the *raison d'être* of all existence.

Only in God's immediate presence does his word stay unveiled. For those who have forsaken God, however, it has long been sunk in concealment. Only to a few in each epoch has the word broken through, pierced the heart, and become available. But when the time was fulfilled, it was brought once again out of its deep concealment to the light of day. Jesus, as the word become flesh, disclosed in a new creation the vanished word of the first creation. The seals were broken. At long last God's letter could be read again. Rediscovered, it brought an overwhelming revelation. God's light no longer glimmered in the distance, enveloped in a fog that spread for miles. In Christ Jesus and his spirit, the word as ultimate clarity emerged out of the depths of the worldwide fog into close proximity.

In Christ Jesus, people began to serve the new covenant, near to God. The new covenant is the new revelation. The apostles of the revealed truth of Jesus Christ were sent out. To the far-off, they brought his nearness (Eph. 2:13). Openly and clearly they testified to God's revealed mystery. Where people formerly held writing in their hands (though they decidedly did not have what they thought they had), now the ultimate was unveiled and offered to them. People were from now on doubly convinced: first of all through the testimony of the witnesses sent out, but far above everything else through the direct witness of the all-revealing Spirit in the depths of their own hearts.

With the coming of the Holy Spirit, the new covenant begins. The new word comes down to earth. Its rulership is established in the heart, in its deepest depths. Whoever is in Christ, whoever is a child of truth, hears this voice within his or her innermost heart – and obeys it. So all that had formerly been quite unknown is now spoken audibly in the heart. The night is over. Where Christ – the spoken will of God – is seen and heard, day breaks in.

Now it is a question of understanding Jesus Christ – his whole life and his words. That means receiving the Spirit into the depths of our heart. We have to live according to this Spirit in the strength of Jesus Christ. Christ wants to open up undreamed-of things in the hearts and lives of the

believers. What no one can believe comes to us. With forgiveness and with the suffering of Christ, what was unknown before comes to our hearts as faith, as the eternal
nature of God. What was always present in God's heart – the
kingdom of heaven – is opened up and given to us.

Everything changeable and transient, everything human
and made by us, must give way before him. It must vanish
before the eternal and immutable peace of Jesus Christ, in
which God has opened his heart. God's love was sent to be-
numbed and frightened hearts. The almighty word came to
the weak. God's love became our brother. Jesus brought the
true picture of God into our midst and still recognized us as
brothers and sisters. Everything God's inmost heart ever was
or willed among people from the beginning comes with
Christ to them. In Christ, everything will be accomplished
among them and perfected according to God's will.

When this greatest event of all history took place, it had
to be written down so that we ignorant people should believe that this word of love, born in the land of Israel – this
Christ of Jewish history – can be grasped by people today
for their present lives. The same Jesus Christ has to be given
the same form and life again everywhere through the life-
giving spirit.

Here the one way becomes visible, the one door opened.
Through Jesus – the Jesus of Roman and Jewish history,
who became flesh, was slain, and rose again from the dead –
through this Jesus, everyone can have direct access to God.
In him, all God's mysteries are revealed. Everything God
does and everything we are meant to do with God for others
is given in Christ. He who has gained mastery over human

life, through the Spirit and the word, overcomes death. He brings the Spirit to victorious rule over all flesh. This Christ penetrates hearts as the peace of God's kingdom, in the power of the resurrection, and with the renewal given by the Holy Spirit. From there, he wants to lead all created things into a life of new justice. Christ is the new justice of God's creation. Through the Holy Spirit, his origin, his life, and his suffering – victorious over all evil – are shown again as God's righteousness. The church is the new Christ. The former Christ has risen. He is present as the life-giving energy of the church. In the new Christ, the birth, the life, the suffering and death, and the resurrection of the former Christ are repeated as the all-embracing justice of God's kingdom.

The beginning of Christ's way, its course, and its end cannot be altered for any member of the church. Every member of the church is filled with the unchangeable Christ, as he always was, as he is now, and as he will be eternally. He fills all members with his death and with his life. If we refuse to let Jesus Christ live and die in us, then Jesus was crucified in vain. Even chopping Jesus into a thousand pieces would not help us. Nothing can help, nothing can be called the saving word of God but letting the crucified Christ penetrate our hearts. Then, going out from there, his spirit and life determine everything as they did in the life of Jesus.

Christ alone is the purpose and meaning of the holy scriptures. Christ filled the disciples when they wrote the scriptures. He alone is the golden scale for testing the spirits. On them, he proves all other spirits to be misleading. As the living word, the Son reveals the Father through the

Holy Spirit. He confirms the Christ of the Old and the New
Testaments. He alone gives them meaning. He does so by
entering our hearts with his word and life, through the new
reality of his death and resurrection.

Thus the history of Christ becomes a power in the
present: here and now, Christ enters in, faith receives him,
we live according to his spirit; here and now we experience
in Christ that God is uniting the world with himself completely. God enfolds us in his love. The power of his heart is
shown clearly. By grasping the Father in Christ, we reach the
Father's heart in the Holy Spirit. In Christ, what God's heart
is and what God's heart can do is made clear. In the living
spirit of Jesus Christ, God speaks to our hearts.

The written scripture speaks to our hearts in a way we can
understand. It speaks directly to our hearts. All it says leads
to the revelation in which the Holy Spirit will be poured out
over all flesh. This revelation is needed. Whatever God does
and says is for its sake. The word had to be written and has
to be proclaimed afresh all the time for the sake of this revelation. Christ is the revelation of God. Its perfect and most
living, its first and last picture is and will be to all eternity
the life of Jesus. God in all his fullness dwelt in a body. Jesus
is the Christ. He is what he teaches. He gives what he promises. He is the source of what he reveals.

This revelation of God in Christ Jesus is the inner light of
the Holy Spirit. From within, it illuminates the whole of life
right to its outermost aspects. In the power of this light, the
same deeds done by the historical Jesus will be done again.
There is nothing here but Christ. The revelation of Christ as
the perfect light tolerates no light and no work of humankind.
God carries it out himself. His truth needs no human sup-

port. The truth of Jesus Christ needs no masters – what it needs is pupils. The revelation of God's truth needs simply a gathering of listeners, who, without this light, sit in the dark. The only demand God's truth makes on people is that they shake with hunger and are parched with an agonizing thirst.

As human beings, we can never be masters of the divine. We have lost the source of light that was originally given. Through dark covetousness, through self-will and owner-ship, the will to the light that used to flow freely in everyone dried up. Of their own free will, people deviated from the light of God's will constantly breaking in. Alienated like this, they could not reconcile themselves to their position. They became overbearing and presumptuous. Out of their own dark power they wanted to steal for themselves what belongs to God alone.

But the new man, Christ Jesus, has taken upon himself the guilt of this defection. In Christ it is eliminated. We are reinstated into the supreme freedom of God's will through the degradation and suffering of the son of God. It is for Christ's humble love that we are won. All presumption dies away. Covetous self-will and arrogant ownership are buried with Christ. From now on, everything belongs to God. In unity with Christ, with God's heart and spirit, the new life breaks in – the light of the risen Christ that frees. In this rev-elation, all believers are brought to complete unity. There are no masters, only brothers. Wherever the truth is taught, God's unity exists. God alone is listened to and obeyed; we allow him to speak and work. That is why all true brothers and sisters are united; for God never contradicts himself. The revelation of God's truth leads to the complete unanim-ity that is within God himself.

When supposedly brilliant preachers obviously contradict themselves or each other, it proves that they have risen before they were awakened, they have set out before the sun came up. Without being appointed, they have taken liberties with what they do not understand (Jer. 23:21). They have gone to work at nighttime: they want to thresh without light and have no idea what they are hitting – they thresh nothing but empty straw. They hit out at each other; no light has united them and led them to work together.

The Holy Spirit never brings into being his life (which is creative and unites) by means of an unenlightened and disunited spirit. He uses means that correspond to the end. He does what is good only through good. He awakens life only through the living. He proclaims the kingdom of God only through those who live according to it. Only those servants who are filled by Christ and as God's mouthpieces speak out of the Holy Spirit – only they are able to sow Christ in people's hearts, implant and inscribe Christ in their innermost being and bring Christ in renewal and rebirth. To proclaim the word of God means bringing Christ with it and imparting the Holy Spirit.

Those with this service, therefore, must carry everything they say as coming from the Holy Spirit within their hearts. What they proclaim, they prove in their lives by the visible working of the Spirit. As apostles of Jesus Christ, they must be able to say to others, "You are my handiwork in Christ; it was Christ who called you and re-created you when the word came to you. You are God's handiwork, just as I am." Actual life proves the truth of Christ's saying: "If you do not want to believe words, you must believe works" (John 10:38).

Whoever believes Christ, will do the same works as Jesus and greater works than he. Love is mightier than anything else. Where the unity of Christ's love is not demonstrated in harmony between word and life, there is neither faith nor vocation to the service of his word. Peter was not allowed to approach the flock until he had been asked three times whether he loved; he was not allowed to work until he had received the spirit of perfect love.

We need to wait for the Holy Spirit. It means waiting for love. And it is not only at the beginning of the way that we wait for it: whoever has once been gripped by the spirit of love must become the hand and mouthpiece of God daily; he must learn again and again to say and do everything, not in his own strength, but in God's. Only in the Christ-spirit of love are we given the reverence not to say or do anything earlier or later than God's hour dictates – not even to want to do it. God's word leads to God's Sabbath. When we rest from all our own words and works, we let God alone speak and work.

It is through the serpent, who is God's enemy, that free will was corrupted and turned into self-will. Through his poison, man and woman were weakened and wounded to the quick. The word implanted in them as the breath of God has been swamped and buried by poisonous, muddy tides of the hostile abyss. Yet the word has never been completely lost; God is mightier than the devil. In spite of the serious poisoning of the human heart, the breath that God breathes into us is by nature indestructible. God has never for a moment forsaken his work, the work that has become unfaithful to him.

Christ steps in at this God-ordained point. As the new word of love, Christ raises the old word of the first creation out of the mud of the hostile forces that had buried it. Then new birth from God becomes possible. The deeply hidden image of God comes to light again. Like a spark from stone, it is coaxed out of hearts that have grown cold. The kindling word that is Christ falls from God with its bright new fire into the sparks of the old creation, which were threatening to die out under the smothering ashes, and makes radiant flames flare up again…Through the new, the old is roused to new life insofar as it was truly of God as the first creation: the new word of the final revelation is stronger than the old word of the first creation. The greater deed is that the new Christ sets human nature free from the self-will, self-chosen power, and possessions that have buried it since time immemorial. What had slipped almost completely out of God's hands is brought back through Christ to unclouded community with God!

What matters is God, the beginning of creation, his prophetic word given to people's inmost heart, the word that became flesh in the historical Jesus, the renewing word of the spirit of the indwelling Christ (the end of all human works and interpretations), and the recognition of God's word in Jesus Christ as the sole authority – all this is what matters, and quite especially for a real understanding of the holy scriptures!

In this regard, the case of the radical reformer Thomas Münzer is instructive. At first Münzer was a follower of Luther; later he became a social-religious revolutionary. As a leader in the Thüringian Peasants' War, he was taken prisoner and executed.

A supporter of armed insurrection (though this was only an unfortunate footnote to his activites as a leader), Thomas

Münzer was not only an enemy of the princely authorities of his day; he was an enemy of the gospel they loved so much: the gospel that merely edifies, maintains the status quo and offends no one. Münzer protested this gospel. Not only did he feel it was false – he felt it had become petrified.

Münzer believed that the word of God must sound through every age anew, in a living way. As people become open to it, they hear it as God's voice in their hearts. According to him, faith in Christ is more than a state of mind: it means willingness to become his pupils. As believers, we must be ready to be by taught God himself:

> Each one has to learn the wisdom of God, the powerful word of the Father, from the enlightenment of the Holy Spirit. We have to be filled with the Holy Spirit in the length, breadth, depth, and height of our soul. Through him, we must learn to suffer the works of God. We must be so completely ready for our own nature to be exterminated that our name is made to stink spiritually among the godless, and only then may we preach God's name. Christ must preach in our hearts first; only then can we give a witness to his word. God's hand must first bring us to humility before him; otherwise we are unable to recognize the truth. We must be taught by Christ himself. We must go to the original source so that fire is sent into our hearts and consciences. Then the word of God will enlighten us; the Spirit will explain the truth to us and transfigure it in such a way that we are ready to give our lives for it. We must call to God in prayer until he reveals himself and is ready to show himself to our hearts and reveal his word. Then we must give witness to this innermost revelation of the divine. Only like this can we understand the holy scriptures.

To Thomas Münzer the worst sin of the institutional church was its attempt to monopolize God's word. Where freedom of the word is forbidden, he felt, we must do everything to bring it back; and we should not allow ourselves to be restricted in or diverted from this freedom. The teaching of the Spirit and the word is so universally understandable that its demands can be grasped by the humblest and lowliest. Its uniting sparks leap past the letter, past human erudition, to reach and kindle even the dullest heart.

God wants to speak into our hearts, says Thomas Münzer, though we shall not be able to hear it, until we gain an insight into our own innermost hearts. First of all, after we have conquered our fear, we must be ready to crucify completely all our desires, our urge for ownership, our covetous urge for possession, otherwise the field of life stays full of thorns and thistles. Before the seed of the living word can enter into us, the plowshare must break up the field and root out the weeds. Without this new plowing and turning over from rock bottom up, no one can be a Christian. No one can become sensitive to God's work and God's word without overthrowing all feelings, ways of thinking, and will. The pious want nothing to do with all this because they reject the bitter Christ, they gorge themselves to death on the honey of their sickly-sweet piety.

> They lack the whole Christ because they have lost the bitter cross. The teaching of the bitter Christ, the witness of the completely revolutionary cross of Christ in all its seriousness is in sharp contrast to the imaginary faith held by the general run of the pious. Only when the Holy Spirit speaks into the depths of a purified and freed spirit can the bitter Christ be revealed as the redeemer. The lying fabrications of false Christianity must

be torn up so that the true and authoritative epistle of Christ can take its place.

Addressing the miners of Mansfeld, Thomas Münzer declared:

> It is impossible to say anything to you in God's name as long as these tyrants rule over you. The oppression is so great that the poor are no longer capable of reading things that might move their hearts and make them glad. And then the false prophets come along and preach in the most shameless way from their pulpits that the poor should continue to let themselves be worked to the bone by the tyrants. That, they say, is the right way of Christ, to be made humble. When should the poor read the scriptures, then? When should they come to a recognition of the truth? When will the false prophets tell the rich and the princes to divest themselves of all their power and riches and humble themselves? And when will they tell them that they are not going the way of Christ, because they keep aloof from poverty and degradation?

Thomas Münzer was admittedly a bitter enemy of the economic and political tyrants of his day, yet it should be noted that his enmity sprang from opposition to that metaphysical, meta-political, meta-economic, and superhuman tyrant, the devil.

> The most thorough liberation from the ultimate tyranny is liberation from the power of the devil. People become free from this power only when they wait with eager, expectant hearts for the living word of God, the liberating word of Christ, with which Jesus put Satan to flight. We need outward freedom in order to gain inner freedom; we need stillness for God, room for his liberating inner word.

We must first become quite empty before God in Christ can enter into us through the Holy Spirit. Stripped of all comfort and all pride, we must lie prostrate at God's feet before God can come to lead us, the dead and the slain, to resurrection. An utter agony of despair must knock at the doors of our heart – only then are we allowed to hear about faith. Those who dare to speak about faith in any other circumstances have stolen it; they preach what has never been tested in themselves. In truth, they are completely devoid of faith and love; they even hinder the working of the Holy Spirit with their vain talking. Everything they preach about faith and love is stolen goods, which can go to no heart. Therefore, instead of preaching empty words and dead Christianity to people, our aim must be to bring them first of all to ignorance. They shall no longer know anything, no longer be capable of anything, so that they can now be taught by the Holy Spirit himself, the spirit of truth.

> The false prophets of today want us to burst suddenly into faith; they do not want the experience of fighting their way through disbelief and despair. But anyone who refuses to go through this experience really knows absolutely nothing about faith. He is nothing but a treacherous scribe, who uses the stolen scriptures for his own honor and glory. He knows nothing of what God himself says. He gladly accepts the written word itself, but he will not accept the One who inspired it.

Those who have never had faith without any faith, hoped against all hope, loved against all love, know nothing of God. They have not yet seen the lamb who alone has the power to open the Book. Faith begins only when the word becomes flesh in us, when Christ is born in us, when we are transplanted from Adam into Christ, when we are reborn, and when the love of God is poured into our hearts. The word that is merely heard and read, kills; it never gives life:

> Reading and hearing alone is ape-like mimicry; to accept the outward scripture is to feast and drink at Christ's expense; just as the most cunning thieves manage to steal the best books, faith in the Bible is like the empty faith of rogues and scoundrels…
>
> All popes and tyrants, whether in Rome or Wittenberg, must be overthrown, for it is they who cannot understand Christ because they themselves want to be preachers of the gospel. They are puppet popes, who cannot change for the good because they preach for their own glory with heart and soul, flesh and blood, bone and marrow. Those who are gripped by Christ, however, must follow in Christ's footsteps; and no commentary on the Bible, no man-made glossary of the holy scriptures is a help. All these defenses of human faith can only be a hindrance.

The son of God has said, "The scripture gives witness." The scribes say, "The scripture gives faith." Witness it can give, but never faith. It can be a help or a service – therefore it should be read and proclaimed – but it can never itself be the cause of faith.

In an interpretation of Psalm 19 addressed to one of his best pupils, Thomas Münzer says that the word of God must be taught afresh practically, not according to an outward understanding of the word, but rather from the living voice that comes down to us from heaven.

> We must understand everything with our eyes fixed on the dawn of Christ. After the long night, the sun must rise out of its true origin – God. We must first of all know that we are in the night, and then after this night the true word will be shown

abroad in full daylight, and the beloved Bridegroom will come
from his chamber like a strong man. We have to make a sharp
distinction between this inner word of our beloved Christ and
the outward scripture. The latter is a pointer, an interpretation,
a convenience, or a witness to the innermost treasure – an instrument. But then the Spirit must supervene, for he alone can
give the melody, impart the vital content. Therefore you must
not take one passage from one place in the Bible and another
from another place, out of context. You have to grasp the
whole spirit of the scriptures, zealously comparing passages
with each other, which is possible only with the help and enlightenment of the Holy Spirit.

Therefore in truth no scholar understands the Holy Writ.
The universities are the greatest confusers of the word of the
Bible and always will be to the end of days. They give all kinds
of meanings to outward things, but they do not recognize the
essential meaning. Nothing will be disclosed to them because
they do not yet walk in the Spirit. They cannot come to faith
because they are still rich in their own spirit. They are not yet
shrouded in the deepest darkness, therefore the nightingale of
the Holy Spirit does not sing for them. They lack the inner
word in the depths of their souls because they imagine they already have enough big books. They lack the true word, on
which the Holy Spirit depends, because at the bottom of their
hearts is nothing but scholarship of the letter. They want to
conjure the spirit out of the letter of the scriptures, like magi-
cians telling fortunes with cards. They want to make the true
dawn of the new day arise out of tattered pages. They want to
place the outward testimony above Christ. They are not even as
far as Moses, for Moses was conscious of the strength of God in
the depths of his soul. They think they can teach faith with
human theology, and they have not yet realized that faith can
be given only in the cross of utter poverty of Spirit. For them,
dawn cannot break because they deny the night. The day can-

not dawn in their hearts because in the midst of night they imagine themselves already in the day.

Bible scholars say that the written word is the voice of Christ. They take the birdcage for the bird. The bird is no longer inside though. They put a music box in the birdcage to make sounds like a bird, but with that, the living bird is by no means there. They make a trumpet of the letter, but they cannot blow it because the right sound is not in it. The right sound has to be added to it, otherwise the trumpet must be thrown away.

So the Bible is not to be understood through semantics but through the Holy Spirit, who alone gives us understanding and grants certainty in divine things. Here is a way toward the interpretation of all mysteries; an explanation of ecstasy; the revelation of the innermost word; the unlocking of divine treasures; and the omnipresence of God.

What no one is able to perceive from without or experience from within is given as a revelation – how good God is, how he loves to speak to each one who will truly listen to him.

Only those, then, who have a revelation from God may speak of the word of God. There has always been this revelation. The wise men of the East had heard the word speaking within them and had seen it shining above them; and so they came to the Christ who, although he was still to be born, was already born in their hearts.

Things become known that in the coming kingdom of God are to become reality. When Jesus said, "My words will not pass away," he was not speaking of the print in books, for that is not at all important. He meant that those words spoken by him as Mary's son on the way to the cross, to the resurrection, and to his ascension – that these words of his will be spoken in the hearts of believers everywhere and at all times through the Holy Spirit. Therefore we may not say with the false prophets: Jesus said that, for it is written in the Bible. Rather, we have to say with the true prophets: This is what the Lord says; he says it at the present time; now, in the present, he is doing it. With God, nothing is in the past; everything is present. The revelation that goes on in the church is the revelation of this inner word. God is always ready to speak to us.

Everyone can read the scriptures, the word that is in his or her heart, and yet Münzer says:

> Christ is never born in a greedy heart. God speaks his holy word in our inmost soul. He points the despairing soul to the new birth. Our inmost heart is like the document on which God writes his immovable will and eternal wisdom. The word begins to dawn on the conscience. It is spoken into the soul. It is born there. But what is then born is not just anything general, indefinite, or incomprehensible – but the king of the Jews, who was crucified under Pontius Pilate, Jesus Christ, the son of Mary. He reveals his fullness in the depths of the human soul. In the coming kingdom, it is he who will lead in the rulership of God over all the earth.

The word of Jesus Christ and the truth the prophets and apostles represented from the beginning can only truly come into its rightful authority when it is carried out in a life that has been renewed, a life lived in common with others, filled and guided by the fire of the Holy Spirit and the fiery light of the living word.

This is the way God's truth is revealed. We see it in the unity of the church in the early Christian times. It is always a question of hearing the living word of God directly from the mouth of God through his Holy Spirit. This faith by revelation as a recognition of the truth goes hand in hand with the holy scriptures. This, then, is the unity of the apostolic church: taking hold of the perfect unity of the kingdom of God through the living word and at the same time recognizing this word in the Bible, as it was once given directly to the prophets and to the apostles.

The church of Jesus Christ must be built up new again and again through the word of God. She must be kept from going astray through the word of God; she must recognize error and must receive into her heart the pure wisdom of the living seed, that is to say, the direct word of God given through the Holy Spirit. The church of Jesus Christ expects this revelation daily. What the Spirit says directly to the open and expectant church cannot be said by any man or woman. The divine will is made known to her by God himself. When that really and truly takes place, we are completely at one with the Bible of the prophets and the apostles. Everything the Spirit says to the church now has long ago been put into words by the holy scriptures, only it is hidden and inaccessible until we are taught directly by the Holy Spirit. We must let ourselves be instructed by him in all the things asked of us. But we can do that only when we receive Christ.

God wants to speak again and again, otherwise he would be a dumb god, a dead god. We have to turn to God again and again. Any insight grasped through the Holy Spirit is absolutely one with the holy scriptures. Christ is one with the Spirit. He gives the key to the written and printed word. We have to be ready for the word through letting the Holy Spirit move our hearts. Whoever does not know the Holy Spirit is blind, no matter how often he or she may read the Bible.

When God himself speaks his holy word into the depths of our hearts, the working of the spirit in the depths of the heart will become deeds, so that in everything God's work is done. That can only happen when we have become dwelling places for God and his Holy Spirit. Then in the whole of life God's witness is turned into works and deeds.

The whole of life will represent what God imparts directly to our hearts through his living word. It emerges from the innermost recesses of our hearts and becomes a visible reality in life. If that does not happen, then what arises within us does not come from the Holy Spirit. The picture such a life presents, however, will very clearly and definitely agree in every detail with the whole of the Bible and with all the words of Christ. In this way, everything the Holy Spirit reveals in our hearts will be God's work and not ours. The power of God's word will show itself in God's works.

Those who have been taught by the Holy Spirit accept the living word into their hearts and agree with one another in utmost harmony. In all the words the Spirit has spoken they are united with all those who are likewise called, with the whole clear history of the apostles and the messengers of God and all the prophets.

Just as any work requires suitable tools and materials, the spirit of Christ needs the word of the apostles and prophets as his instrument. He reminds us of all the sayings we find in the gospels. Through our conscience he urges us to deepen our knowledge and acceptance of the word through constant reading and listening. In our heart he turns the inwardly comprehended word of the gospel into a living expression of his nature. Just as the living word testifies to the powerful influence of Christ's presence, the spirit of Christ turns written or printed letters into an expression of his very being, coming directly from Christ himself.

Therefore when our life has been renewed by community with Christ, we will not demand the appearance of Christ's body, as if it were necessary to bring Christ down from heaven or even up from the kingdom of the dead. Instead, we will experience the living presence of Christ's spirit through the word that has directly pierced our hearts. The life-giving word, as the fullest expression of the experience of our hearts, is spoken out and confessed with our mouth. Faith in Jesus Christ and the confessing of his name are alive as soon as the word, like a living seed, is planted directly into our innermost hearts. When the word is near, it means that God is near. For the word is Jesus Christ himself; out of his spirit is born every sentence of the truth. From the beginning, Jesus Christ is the revelation of the Father, which reached its culmination in history when he became flesh and dwelt among us. His life brought the word among us as the will of God put into practice in actual life. And therefore the keeping of the word can be no blind, outward obedience but is unity of life with Jesus Christ, energetically being put into practice here and now.

Life can be given only through the living and abiding word of truth. If his word is not in us, we directly oppose life and truth: we belong to death and lies, we are enemies of life and reality. When we are truly renewed, our strength comes from every word that proceeds from the mouth of God. Our inner life will be strong and victorious to the same degree that we make his triumphant word real. Our life exists and gets its power from every word of God.

The indivisible spirit of God is alive and at work in the whole word. When we suppress parts of his scriptures, push them aside, or refuse to acknowledge them, we withdraw our life from the light of truth. If we are unable to see how to apply some part of the Bible to our life because it has not yet become important to us in an inner way, we should remember in what way God's life came into our hearts. What we have experienced from Christ as an inner word used to be mere letters, cold and alien to us. Out of the unfathomable depths of the word (which are perhaps still remote to us), the Spirit wants to let undreamed-of aspects of the living reality of God and Christ sink into our hearts. If we try to avoid God's working in any area of our life, we avoid the way of truth. We lose the life God gives. "Man lives by every word that proceeds out of the mouth of God." Life from God wants the whole of the written word to become alive in his church.

The word is the seed of life. The state of the soil is decisive for its well being and growth. Whoever receives the word with joy and tries to have faith for a time, only to fall away again and lose everything in a moment of temptation, is left with nothing in the end. The hour of temptation tests whether or not the word has been deeply planted in us and has taken root. Those who after they have heard the word cherish it are like the good soil. They love him, and in them the Father and the Son make their dwelling.

Love and loyalty to the word are determined through the innermost direction of the will. That is why Teresa of Avila describes love as an arrow shot by the will. In his word, God makes known his will, which is love. He lets the truths of this word pierce our hearts as the sharp arrows of his love. In the same way, only a firm and taut-strung will is capable of sending our love toward God's heart and of showing the same love to all by carrying out his word faithfully, using love's weapons. Only such a decisive will can recognize the word of Jesus as the true expression of God's nature: "If someone wants to do the will of him who sent me, he will know whether this teaching is from God." The energy for all acts of obedience is born out of a common inner will with God, in which the heart says to God, "What wilt thou have me do?"

For this reason, the power of our inner life shows whether the word of God is alive in us. Without the inner word alive within us, no prayer will be answered and no evil overcome. Through the sword of the spirit, the Lord has overcome the Tempter. The firm word of God in the hearts of the disciples is the rock foundation on which they feel secure. It fills their hearts with certainty: they have the fulfillment of their prayers before anyone else can see it. Without the living word within us, there is no victory over sin; "I have kept thy word in my heart so that I do not sin against thee!" There is only one way of abiding in the Father and in the Son: letting the word we have heard from the beginning abide in us.

The written word becomes so alive in a believing heart that at every crossroad and in every danger it is ready to be our unerring guide. Through his word, Jesus comes to meet us as our Lord. His authority to lead us and to direct our lives in all things is felt in our innermost hearts to be his holy right, and to obey it is our highest calling.

In today's culture, the ideal of a "born leader" is sometimes glorified as a noble personality, a character of charismatic grace and authority and strength. Above all, it is emphasized that leadership is an avocation, which no one can be given from without; that a true leader is not chosen by his followers but appears among them, and chooses them.

Only Jesus is this real leader. In truth and purity, he fulfills the longing of youth – of all people. Spirit and love are united in him in one person. It was Jesus who came up to his people and called out with unhindered authority, "Follow me!" "Whoever does not leave everything and follow me is not worthy of me." Today his word brings his presence near and sends the same call of discipleship to his chosen. For the word is his personal will, through which he shows his authority, overpowering all those who hear his call and winning them for himself.

Imitation can never replace the Spirit's leading. When one hears of an accident in the mountains, the first question is always whether the victim has been climbing without a guide, trying to imitate as best he could those who, though no more capable, were still safely led. No one is able to manage without a guide in the dangerous regions through which the narrow way leads us. Anyone who ventures into the rugged paths of life without the clear inner leading of the word is traveling toward certain disaster, no matter how much he or she keeps the example of others in view.

In other words, the Holy Spirit must speak anew in every heart. Like an illuminating flood of light, the Spirit pours onto our path, where in spite of our human light we had lost our bearings. When the word comes over us in this way, it is like the sun suddenly breaking through the fog to show the lost traveler the way.

The living word within us wants to lead, master, and rule the whole of our life. It wants to put God's will into action. And in truth, it is only in deed that we can show that we are truly letters of Christ, written with the spirit of the living God.

O ur lives can be transformed only from within. Yet the aim of the word alive within us is that it should be put into practice in deeds and in truth. Only so will it be proved that we are an epistle of Christ, written with the spirit of the living God on the fleshly pages of our heart. The word gives us strength and clarity in all situations and in all the demands of the daily struggle so that we are strong and can overcome evil. We shall be able to carry out the worldwide tasks God has given us only when the word is alive and kept alive in us.

The living word discloses the will of God to us, that world history has to work toward the one goal: the kingdom of God, the sovereign rule of Jesus Christ. Only when humankind is ready to be ruled by the will of God alone, and not by its own nature, will the joy of true peace and genuine righteousness be able to rule among us.

The final and complete rule of God lies still in the future, as the horrors of our age have proved time and again. But there is a clear relationship between the rule of Christ in the hearts of believers and the future rule of their Lord as king.

For the kingdom of God is nothing less than the will and nature of the Highest become practical reality.

Wherever the peace of God that the world yearns for becomes reality, it reveals itself as new life: new joy, new energy, and new love. This happens not only in heaven, but here on earth, wherever men and women become alive to God's will and submit to it. For there is no greater goal worth striving after: God's rule in the coming kingdom of Jesus Christ.